JAGUAR BOYS

JAGUAR BOYS

TRUE TALES FROM OPERATORS OF
THE BIG CAT IN PEACE AND WAR

IAN HALL

GRUB STREET • LONDON

Published by
Grub Street
4 Rainham Close
London
SW11 6SS

A CIP record for this title is available from the British Library

ISBN-13: 978-1-909808-15-7

Printed and bound by Berforts Group, UK

Grub Street Publishing only uses
FSC (Forest Stewardship Council) paper for its books.

CONTENTS

THE FAVOURITE – Ian Hall

It was intended to be a trainer, but became a Cold War strike/attack aircraft of impressive capability. Despite an initial reputation for lack of performance, it sold abroad to 'hot and high' countries. It went to war on several occasions with foreign air forces, and saw active service in the Gulf and the Balkans with the RAF. On operations it surprised everybody with its adaptability. In the Gulf Conflict it flew more missions per airframe than any other British type, moreover without any losses. It played its part in the increasingly unstable world order thereafter, being upgraded in the very model of what became known as the 'smart procurement' process. Then it was cut off in its prime. Can there have been any more unlikely stories in the post-war history of fighter-bombers?

During an RAF career spanning thirty-two years and including front-line tours on five different types, I of course formed an opinion on what makes a good aircraft. Once I moved to civilian aviation the focus tended to be more on the crew meals than on aircraft types. But even so, captain and first officer were usually curious about each other's previous flying experiences. So I often found myself being asked which of the military types I'd flown had been my favourite – to which I invariably answered that the Jaguar was. Usually this would provoke incredulity. "I thought it flew like a brick," my colleagues would venture; "Haven't we heard that it couldn't turn?"

Well, there was some truth in the rumours. As my first Jaguar squadron commander Mike Gibson was reported to have said: "People have tried to design aircraft without lift or without thrust before but the Jaguar was the first to try it without either." So yes, that was always an issue.

It neither turned like a Hunter nor accelerated like a Phantom or a Tornado. But it nevertheless did a magnificent job as a Cold War stalwart. And anyway, the fact was that, when asked the 'favourite' question, I could never simply isolate the airframe. The machine matters, of course, but there's more to life than that. It's where you are based; it's the people you're working with; it's the job you're doing. There's also the small matter of how the aircraft performs in combat, and as later chapters will show the Jaguar scored well there, too.

But it would be hard not to single out 'who you were with' as the factor that transcends all. Jaguar people were, one and all, good guys, and it's a pleasure to turn to many friends and colleagues who will demonstrate in the chapters which follow their affection for – and joy at having flown – the Jaguar. They called themselves, and were known throughout the RAF as, 'Jag Mates'. But the title of this book will do just as well, so for tales of my favourite aircraft let's turn over to the Jaguar Boys.

NB: The reader will find an introductory piece to each chapter, written by myself. Moreover, there is, of necessity, much technical detail and jargon included within these pages, so I have provided an extensive glossary (see pages 187–189) which I hope will be helpful.

CHAPTER 1

THE FIRST ELEVEN (PLUS RESERVES)

In 1968/9 I was a young and humble pilot officer, kicking my heels at 229 OCU at Chivenor in Devon while waiting for my Hunter conversion course. The squadron leader in charge of training called me in one day and gave me a task; I was to collect a van from the transport section, take it to an address on the officers' married quarter patch, and assist with the removal of Flight Lieutenant John Pym's furniture to a rented house in nearby Barnstaple.

No doubt the task was very character building, not to mention good for my physical conditioning, and I expect the squadron leader registered my day's efforts as 'general service training' or something similar. I completed the job, and forgot about John Pym. In due course I got on with my first two tours, on Hunters and Phantoms.

In 1973 John, by than an extremely experienced Hunter pilot, was selected as one of the initial cadre who would see the Jaguar into service, becoming a member of the Jaguar Conversion Team. So by the time I met him again on my arrival in 1977 in Germany, he was also a very experienced Jaguar pilot. There are few better qualified to tell the story of those earliest years.

SQUADRON LEADER JOHN PYM (RETD)

During the late 1960s and early 70s, in the musty garrets of the Ministry of Defence and RAF HQs various experienced 'fast-jet' staff officers toiled, assisting their masters to 'plan, provide, direct and control' the introduction of a sleek new beast, in more or less the form envisaged by its designers. Meanwhile, posting staffs attempted to select the team to introduce it into service.

The 'conversion team' model had proved itself during Harrier introduction, and again, experienced instructors with significant ground-attack/close-air-support exposure were selected from the Hunter, and now the Harrier, forces.

Wing Commander John R Walker (now Air Marshal Sir John) had been earmarked for some years to lead the JCT. Germany and Hunter experienced and a former Central Fighter Establishment trials pilot, he had distinguished himself on exchange with the USAF during the Vietnam War at HQ 12th AF. The 3-star general commanding

TAC was impressed enough by this junior 'Limey' staffer to praise his attributes and achievements during an MoD visit. On return to UK 'JR' was promoted and, in his JCT role, worked with MoD and Command staffs to finalise the Jaguar introduction plan. Formidable as a member of the RAFG gunnery team and in the water polo arena, he prided himself – generally accurately – on being 'a reasonable man'. Rather like his robust namesake in the Dallas series, however, we were to learn he took few prisoners! Squadron Leader Neil Hayward had completed a tour at Warton as the MoD(OR) liaison officer and was a natural choice as OC JCT Squadron.

In replacing the F-4 – to be redeployed in the air-defence role (for which it was designed) – the Jaguar brought numbers, improved avionics and single-seat economies to the NATO front line. It was less an F-4 replacement than a modern Canberra/Hunter – chosen to combine the nuclear and conventional roles in a single-seat aircraft (a first and only for the RAF). It shared with the Hunter a prime asset – economy. Single-seat, properly equipped and automated 'light' strike/attack aircraft (the exceptional F-16 followed) are sustainable, in times when two-seat 'heavy-metal star-ships' are not – outside the US. Remember the UK socio-political and economic climate during 1968-73!

The essential skills required of a low-level, close-support, tactical-reconnaissance, interdicting Jaguar pilot, as defined by those most familiar with them, were generally to be found in a single-seat, 'mud-moving' ground-attack pilot, nurtured in the Hunter/Harrier environment. This thinking was well justified and widely accepted.

229 OCU at Chivenor had, by that time, largely become the RAF's repository of ground-attack expertise, and had seen the majority of the RAF's rapidly expanding fast-jet forces pass through their pre-fab hut portals on the introductory courses that had evolved there over the previous five years or so. All benefited from this grounding, prior to progressing to front-line type conversions on Lightning, Buccaneer, F-4 and Harrier aircraft. With two exceptions from the Harrier force, it was hardly surprising that the majority of the initial batch of JCT instructors, and a fair proportion of initially-converted squadron pilots, came from 229 OCU – where I was finishing a tour.

The 'first eleven' gathered at Lossiemouth in June 1973. The plan was to settle families in as necessary and complete the admin requirements, before heading south to begin the round of manufacturers' courses scheduled for July and August.

After the soft hills and folded valleys of Devon, Morayshire was a real change – a wide-open, big country. The towns we had passed through on our way north were very – well, Scottish – all brown stone, their dun facades relieved by 'chippies' and pubs. Elgin and Forres had life about them, probably the result of many years hosting the Fleet Air Arm and the RAF Kinloss 'kipper fleet'. Inverness was a bustling centre and Findhorn was a most attractive spot, not unlike Hamble with a Gordonstoun accent. Lossiemouth town was quiet, although Moray Golf Club, on the outskirts and carved into the heather and gorse on short finals, was to prove a haven. Relieving one's frustrations on the tee in a force eight, and then searching for the ball in rough like barbed wire must have been good for the soul; we certainly kept at it!

Although recently rebadged 'RAF' Lossiemouth, the station continued to display its RNAS heritage and had a rather basic wardroom. We, the advance guard of the 'crab' invasion, were viewed with a mixture of mild indifference and slight suspicion. However, the general air was one of a relaxed acceptance and enjoyment of life – the RN there did not seem to take anything too seriously.

Some aspects of the 'naval way' were quite admirable. Because of the whole resupply-at-sea thing, nothing was ever thrown away, since at sea – and perhaps also in the north of Scotland – if something broke there was often little chance of it being replaced quickly. Over the centuries a 'gash store' system evolved, alive and well on HM warships today, if any remain. At Lossie this Aladdin's cave shared an old hangar with the station cinema. Every imaginable bit of surplus and obsolescent kit was stashed away there, including probably much which 'providence had misplaced'. Time and again ingenuity mothered invention, and a jury rig could often be cobbled together from the 'gash' of the past!

The recently-arrived RAF CO was old-school V Force and, if a little stuffy, a thorough gentleman; as Jaguars and their ilk were somewhat alien, he sensibly left us to get on with it. There are hazy memories of filling in forms, inspecting (and naturally accepting – no choice) houses or flats (most of which were pretty damn grim. Navy husbands of course spend their life at sea and the wives apparently make do!) and attempting to complete the arrival process, before setting off for BAC Warton and our date with 'Le Jaguar'.

I have recollections of a stand-out and voluble passenger group as we boarded the BEA Trident at Inverness. The cabin crew seemed puzzled when quizzed on the ages of the pilots, and the passengers were clearly intrigued by JR's general admonition not to retract the flaps too soon after take-off (memories fresh of 'Papa India' at Heathrow).

Warton started noisily at a 4-star (?) hotel on the front at Blackpool, booked by Lossie's 'bean counters'. After northern Scotland we had warmed to the prospect of 'The Front' and a little nightlife. Although all rooms were en-suite and boasted colour TV, practicality intruded on discovering it was necessary, before getting into bed, to place the TV and stand in the bath. Reality remained through the night as we slept fitfully to the beat from the disco below. With BAC's help, next day we moved downmarket into the boarding houses of Lytham St Anne's, close to Warton and what we had come for. However, there were certainly compensations. Lytham had – still has, probably – the best fish and chips in the UK, there were great pubs close to decent accommodation, and Blackpool's distant diversions were less likely to disrupt our nightly studies ...

Boarding house life in the genteel, but nevertheless staunchly Lancastrian, surroundings of the Fylde coast had its surprises. At breakfast one morning JR asked for a further helping of toast. The landlady, an imposing figure and fully his match, replied: "No, you can't have any more toast – you've had quite enough already!" A couple of splutters and then – silence!

Then, at last, 'Day One': arrival at Warton. Initial, tedious, unavoidable admin, followed by a quick, familiarising tour of the main features of the place. The first impression of 'our' aircraft up close was visceral! It exuded menace, purpose and speed. The slab-sided box intake, the high-wing, the empennage – its resemblance to TSR2 was remarkable.

Turning to the ground-school course we had come for, the facilities were frankly disgraceful and prompted a graphic introduction to JR in 'displeased' mode. It did not require many of his pointed observations (including on the importance of the RAF contract for 200 aircraft in the BAC 'future scheme of things') before changes were made, very quickly.

Our first meeting with the BAC test pilots was quite an event. It would have been difficult to cast them more authentically from Hollywood. It was all there – steely-blue eyes, grey temples, lantern jaws – even blonde locks. Possibly the waistlines were more Dad's Army than Magnificent Seven but they were an impressive, personable group. Led by 'Gentleman' Paul Millet, they included Dave Eagles – ex RN, who smiled when he called us 'Crabs' – and John Cockburn, a kilted (on occasions) full-blown Scottish Laird. Their relaxed, professional involvement helped make our stay pleasant and valuable.

The 'village' at Warton in 1973 might equally have been plucked from a Pinewood Dambusters' set and given a makeover. Passing through the main gate and security, 'Main Street' meandered away through a maze of semi-derelict Nissen huts and pre-war brick buildings, abutting prefabricated glass and chrome office blocks thrown up in anticipation of projects such as ours; vistas opening with each turn, threading its way generally westwards, towards the production-line hangars bordering the north side of the airfield. An incessant stream of people and vehicles bustled past throughout the day; the noise, with jet engines under test, aircraft departing or arriving and the throb of an industry's incessant heartbeat, was constant and palpable.

The production-line hangars were impressive. Huge spaces, brilliantly lit by hundreds of neon tubes, were filled with lines of Jaguars in progressively different guises, increasingly recognisable for what they would become, surrounded by platforms and gantries, their upper surface skins unfinished or peeled back to reveal their skeletons or covered with equipment and components and crawling with workmen. The almost frenetic activity on the production lines was also unexpected – until one realised deliveries were to commence in a matter of weeks.

The weeks passed as we got our heads around this 'winged cat' amalgam of British brass and Gallic flair. As far as we could tell, then, it promised to do the job. The main focus for us at Warton was on the airframe and the aircraft systems; in the coming weeks and months, at Lossie and elsewhere, we would familiarise ourselves with the avionics and weapons system.

The Lemon Tree was a little gem set into the Fylde crown, on occasions adding a modicum of grace to our social life. There were bars and gambling facilities, pleasant music and convivial company from various backgrounds, with whom one could pass an hour or two after a long day and an evening's study – discussing sport or politics or the stock market. Fortunately, 'black tie' was not required and one did not have to impersonate Sean Connery to be able to have a little flutter on the tables – Black Russian cigarettes, however, were available at the bar for those so inclined.

At the other end of the spectrum was the 'Cordon-Bleu Chippy', at which we regularly dined. One evening's repast was somewhat disrupted by the distressed waitress, a pretty lass, apologising for the delay, explaining that she had 'aemorrhaged' (had a nose-bleed) over the chips and they were being replaced! However, the food there really was so good that it was suggested we 'dine-in' one night with our ladies during their brief 'behaviour audit' visit – and we duly did, to much amusement. Though alcohol-fuelled, the idea was inspired, and we survived the inspection.

To quote Ian Ord: "We endured the tedium of a five-day course designed for engineers, crammed into four weeks – learning of the electrical importance of, inter alia, 'the now-dormant contacts of relay X' (for which Mr Roy Stoop will never be forgotten!). If it hadn't been for The Lemon Tree and the Cordon-Bleu Chippy, life could have been grim. But we fortunately had a great bunch of characters and the days were full of mirth."

We departed from Warton after nearly five weeks, somewhat weary. The

The first team squad at RAF Warton: From the left, Barry Horton, Jeff Morgan, John Pym, Sam Goddard, Ian Ord, Bob Fowler, Neil Hayward, 'JR' Walker, Terry Lloyd, Chris Shorrock, Martin Molloy, Bill Langworthy, John Quarterman, and John Lumsden. The aircraft, one of the early 'S' models, lacks the GR1's trademark 'chisel' laser nose. On the wing is a telemetry pod, related to early testing.

classroom, living in boarding houses, summer on the Fylde coast and studying late all took their toll and Lossie, and our families, beckoned. But we had not finished; more courses were on the menu.

After a week of R&R with the families (during which we began drafting ground-school lectures) we set off again for another two weeks (and 1,500-road miles) with Rolls-Royce, Marconi and Smiths Industries. Suffice to say the courses were useful and mercifully short. We were all too well looked after and set off north again, aware of how light our wallets were in comparison with our persons.

Back at Lossie and into the ground-school subjects each had been allocated, the necessary OHP slides (the forefront of technology in 1973) were cobbled together before we delivered a dry-run ground-school course for a dozen or so moderately interested staff officers. No such thing as a free lunch! The dry run was received 'with reservations', so it was back to the drawing board, slides and coloured Letraset (how that stuff ruled our lives) for a while.

Before starting our conversions, some of us returned to Chivenor in October for a few days refresher flying on the Hunter. This was magic. I managed eight sorties in three days: T7 transit/check; cine; combat; strafe; aeros; low level; and simulated attacks – and finished in a perfect 63 Squadron F6 with an air-to-air gunnery detail and 74%. After ten years, a last ride in the mighty Hunter.

Meantime, the Jaguars had begun to arrive and our necessarily incestuous conversion began – c'était magnifique! The precise syllabus, put together by management while we were subduing the OHP slides, was never really precise, as we gave ourselves – with authority's absolution and as serviceability, weather and range availability demanded – a degree of flexibility. One of Lossie's greatest strengths as a weapons training venue was Tain Range, twelve minutes away at 420 knots, with rarely any weather or, in those days, capacity problems. So we looked forward keenly to throwing ourselves, and some weapons, at the ground.

However, there was just one small problem. The Handling Squadron at Boscombe Down, rather than focussing on clearing the aircraft for the 'normal' lay-down, shallow and medium-angle dive delivery profiles in time for our work-up, had been busying themselves, as part of a 'test programme', staggering up to 35,000 feet to do 'wind-up' turns with asymmetric stores. So we were not yet cleared for weapons delivery and training. On hearing this, JR's collar immediately shrunk and a rosy flush appeared, as he did his 'reasonable man' impersonation while speaking to some unfortunate squadron leader at MoD.

Soon after, two worthies from Boscombe managed to really wind up and then spin a T2, from which they then smartly exited. The first needless airframe loss, fortunately with no loss of life, and the test schedule priorities were altered soon after. Why whoever devised that trial – having due regard for in-service 'flight envelope'/release to service implications – had imagined at that stage that a Jaguar might be delivering stores at 30,000 feet plus, quite beggars belief.

The origin of the 'wind-up turns' trial was the discovery at Boscombe that during a 5-6 g recovery from an attack pass (near sea level, where the wings did develop some lift), the aircraft rolled right. It happened that the TP concerned had 'well-developed' (well – fat!) thighs and had difficulty in correcting the roll with a fully inflated g-suit. As a result, Boscombe determined that the Jaguar stick was too short.

One can imagine the subsequent telephone conversation between Lossiemouth and Boscombe Down:

"Excuse me, have you discovered why it is rolling right under g in the first place? The Hunter did not do that."

"Yes. The spine is bending, this is sensed in the rudder controls, causing a rudder deflection."

"What are you going to do about it?"

"We are putting a rheostat in the spine to detect how much bending, and feeding a compensating signal to the rudder autostab mechanism to correct it."

"What will be the long-term effects of all this?"

"Don't know really – it should be OK. Meanwhile we'll get BAC to make the stick longer. But stay away from wind-up turns with asymmetric stores."

At about that time a flight safety poster appeared featuring 'Fred the Wheel-Tapper's Hammer'. Fred's hammer indicated that a large number of railway carriage wheels were defective, and these were scrapped, before someone thought to check the hammer. Shades of 200 Jaguars with long sticks!

The spine-bending compensation worked well, but one memory of the 'short/long stick' saga is a vision of the JCT assembled in a Warton hangar at lunchtime, stripped to their y-fronts and wearing g-suits, waiting in turn to get into a cockpit to see how much spoiler deflection they could get under a simulated 4g. A large crowd of BAC workers were watching this performance with great amusement. Would have made a great scene for Mr Bean!

Sam Goddard collected the first 'long stick' modified GR1 from Warton at around this time and the assembled throng meeting him was keen to know what difference it made. His reply? "It made me crank my seat up higher." Hey ho!

One important issue emerged from all this. Over the coming months and years as the squadrons formed, deployed and started operating, several deficiencies concerning 'cockpit ergonomics' became evident. A major one was the need to look down and reach forward to make selections on the NAVWASS (nav/attack system) control panel on the centre pedestal – significant for those 'vertically challenged' ones among us. This need could and did arise at any time while at low level. The longer stick possibly encouraged a higher sitting position, useful for some of us, but the pilot then had to stretch further to reach the panel. I am not alone in having experienced an adrenaline rush following such a selection at a busy moment, then seeing 150 feet radalt and reducing rapidly. It was not until the introduction of an upgraded avionics system, when all controls were placed in the forward field of view, that this problem was removed. Sadly, it may have cost us a pilot or two before that came to pass.

We learned later that this problem had been clearly identified during development, but due to budgetary/commonality issues (the FAF had a very different inertial system and uniquely UK costs were an absolute no-no) MoD(PE) would not agree to funding the relocation of the control panel, despite MoD(OR) pressure.

In fact as other latent design and build aspects surfaced, the real irony of the military procurement process sank home; 'the system' will always try to meet a requirement as cheaply as possible. Politicians, manufacturers, system sub-contractors and civil servants all have an interest in spending as little as possible. With budgets that are continuously under microscopic scrutiny, what barely passes muster operationally must at times be reluctantly accepted. Clearly the need to get equipment into service in a world of conflict has priority, although economics often demand that operational preferences be met and funded *mañana*. But it certainly made for frustrations in the early years.

Fully laden, a Jaguar more than doubles its empty weight, and the need to refer to angle of attack ('alpha'), rather than air speed (a largely meaningless reference when manoeuvring with 10,500lbs of external stores) was well provisioned, with HUD indications and a gauge beside the HUD. F-4 and Harrier pilots were familiar with the concept. As for the rest of us, we soon realised this transition was vital, and it seemed to be absorbed without difficulty by all pilots early in their conversion.

The first RAF production Jaguar (S4) had been delivered to Lossie well before our arrival, and immediately ripped to pieces for the training of our growing band of engineers. And then put together again – several times. JR threatened that any of us stepping out of line would be 'selected' to air-test S4! At the appointed hour, no one had sinned odiously enough to qualify, so Sam 'volunteered' (again). There were allegedly no snags, but no-one believed him so he was programmed to fly it again the following day.

An early formation work-up sortie was briefed to conclude with a tail-chase at 3-500 yards separation. As number four I was 'spat out' by turbulence, following which it took a second or two – and lots of red lights – to realise the vibration was still continuing and I gently closed the throttles. At idle power, some lights went out and the vibration stopped. Slowly opening the throttles in turn established that one of the engines was still functioning relatively normally and I gingerly returned for a precautionary landing. I learned about 'boat-tail drag' from that and still have several chewed-up Adour turbine blades mounted in perspex – courtesy of Mr Brian Guilder, the resident Rolls-Royce rep – to remind me of our 'Number One Burn-Out'.

Aircraft deliveries accelerated during the autumn and early winter. We continued our conversion/familiarisation flying flat-out during January and were more or less on top of things by the time the first operational squadron, No 54, arrived to begin their flying in February 1974.

Led by Wing Commander Terry Carlton, 54's ten pilots who assembled at Lossie for the conversion were a highly-experienced bunch, from most of the RAF fast-jet fleets. Their arrival in the mess, as a detachment of unleashed pilots *de chasse*, made things look up socially. Bar profits were boosted more than somewhat, as the mess had previously been a rather staid home for a few administrators, Shackleton drivers and the 'gals' from air traffic. The Bothy Bar (a Bothy being a Highland mountain refuge) had been readied in time for their arrival and it saw consistent and heavy action throughout their stay.

Apart from minor delays with serviceability in the growing fleet, the course progressed well. All of them took to the Jaguar enthusiastically and the results they produced were consistently good. Formations ranged far afield to exercise the aircraft's long legs and utilise the distant ranges in the Wash and Wales, while attacking and 'recce-ing' simulated targets in Wales, Northumberland, and up and down the length and breadth of Scotland, often culminating in practice bomb FRAs on Tain and Rosehearty Ranges. That winter the weather was fairly kind to us and the first course ran pretty much to schedule.

There had been an amount of loose talk around the RAF about the Jaguar's thrust, and the cold weather enabled the exaggerated guff about the 'lack of poke' to be put into perspective. 'Underpowered' is a relative term; yes, the initial Jaguar was underpowered when compared to an F-16. 'Overpowered', on the other hand, might describe a Lightning that could do Mach 2 – and not much else before it must go home. While, relatively speaking, a Jaguar could reach targets in Poland at low level. Until the Jaguar was operated at MTOW in the German and Mediterranean/ Balkan summers, its lack of thrust was relative, and by the time of Bosnia it had received the first of two power-plant upgrades.

This largely jealous drivel soon stopped when the aircraft started operating, and its overall performance was measured against that of other types, where it regularly out-performed most of the opposition in every relevant facet of operations.

54 Squadron were also highly active socially; actually, they were a mob of party animals – in the nicest sense, of course! While they were at Lossie Prince Philip visited the station. Squadron Leader Phil Dacre happened to be wearing the BAC 'solo' tie (black with a red, white and blue 'vic' of Jaguars – previously banned with uniform by JR), which caught the duke's attention. On being told what it was, his response was, "excellent choice". Thus 54, on the basis of this 'Royal Appointment', continued to sport it – and in due course the tie became standard uniform throughout the Jaguar Force.

At the party that evening, 54 were banned (again!) from smashing and burning an old piano (a 54 'rite of passage' with pre-WW2 origins). However, Air Chief Marshal Sir Fred Rosier (then a BAC director who had retired as C-in-C Fighter Command) asked after dinner "Where's the piano? 54 always smashed a piano in my day!" One was produced, duly smashed, set alight and – not normally scripted – Flight Lieutenant 'Ducky' Drake 'streaked' through the flames! He was later seen disporting himself, somewhat singed but now right into the part, around the married quarter patch.

Some of us were also present at a 54 visit to the Glen Grant distillery. By the time we'd worked our way into the eighteen-year-old malts, most present were incipiently legless. On the way back the coach followed Fred Trowern, then OC Simulator Squadron, in his car, with great difficulty. JR duly stopped the bus and ordered Fred to get aboard. Subsequent distillery visits were somewhat more subdued.

54 Squadron were finishing their conversion as 6 Squadron were starting, although 54 remained at Lossie and continued to work up. 'Shiny 6' were, on balance, possibly a slightly quieter bunch than 54, at which JR would have heaved a sigh of relief.

We had begun to see F-4 pilots making up the numbers on 54 and 6; they were quick to throw away the 'Linus blanket' and trust the map between their knees (rather than the voice from behind). Particularly, they knew the NATO 'flank' and RAFG environments. In fact the progressive impact of F-4, Harrier, Buccaneer and Lightning pilots on the force was most noticeable as it expanded; they brought, variously, strike/attack deployment and close air support experience with them. In particular the Taceval world and how to 'play to win' were areas in which they helped their Jaguar squadrons to come of age.

At about this time, as total Jaguar in-service hours flown mounted, a problem began to emerge concerning the reliability of the aircraft's avionic performance. Marconi, so the story went, had had a barrel or so of spare gyroscopes after a cancelled missile programme when the invitation from BAC to bid for Jaguar's digital/inertial nav/attack system popped through their letterbox. Well, one thing led to another, the off-the-shelf gyros were incorporated into the inertial platform and, to ensure the system performed to spec, 'Herr Schuler's Loop' was recruited. With the assistance of some complex maths, and by rotating the inertial platform every forty-two minutes, gyro drift was kept within reasonable limits.

The 'kit' worked as advertised at first, but as the sortie rate increased, performance and reliability fell away. This was initially put down to teething troubles and bedding-in issues. However, the incidence of platform/gyro failures increased steadily: "The kit's dumped" was the regular cry. Our aircraft possibly had less feather-bedding than those operated at BAC and Boscombe Down, and this probably informed their initial response to our concerns: "Ensure alignment procedures are fully complied with, data entries are as accurate – blah blah, etc." However, the fact was that the kit was neither as reliable nor accurate as it should have been.

JR was an ardent supporter of the capabilities of the Jaguar, and its success owes much to him; the phrase 'Bomb in a Bucket' came to exemplify the goals he set. And when it was good it certainly was very, very good. At its best, the system commonly delivered a 'dumb' bomb from a conventional delivery profile to within 20 feet of the target. However, it was also true that 'when it was bad it was horrid'. When the inertial system was not on song, rather than putting the bomb in the bucket it was a different story. Especially when, as we were to learn a year or so later when introducing toss-bombing, it was all we could do to plonk it on the range – or even, in the confines of Europe, on the right country!

This turned out to be a more complex issue than just the effects of a rumoured slack handful of cheap gyros, although its origins were that you get what you pay for. Initially, 'black-box replacement' servicing had seemed to work, but it was soon realised that a holistic approach was necessary to improve consistency and accuracy. Each aircraft ideally required NAVWASS components to be synchronised/harmonised in situ to produce the best results; this had not been anticipated, specified, funded, nor found possible since the introduction to service. However, although this certainly improved overall system performance where it could be justified and was undertaken – during trials and competitions for example – component reliability did not improve noticeably. Eventually, as we shall see, NAVWASS was replaced with FIN1064 and the problem disappeared.

A minor event occurred during 6's conversion that had repercussions and which clearly marked JR's modus operandi. Mike Gray and an instructor were returning to Lossie in a T2 and had not long coasted out north of Tain when Mike spotted a Jaguar at 2 o'clock, opposite direction – the normal track into the low-flying area. The instructor took control and turned right to make a '180 sighting bounce'. At 1,500m they realised the closing speed was excessive, and as Mike turned away they saw the gear drop! "Golly," said the IP (or words to that effect) – "what's Kinloss GCA traffic doing out here?" On landing the instructor was invited to report to Officer Commanding OCU's office. "Mike, I Sense Huge Immediate Trouble ahead," he mused prophetically. Indeed there was, JR had escaped the office to get some 'stick time', courtesy of Kinloss's Nimrod-sized GCA patterns.

Deemed guilty of unauthorised activities, he was relieved of instructing duties and sent to Tain Range as a relief RSO. While there and not on duty he played golf, went fishing and most nights drank in the pub with the locals. Returning after three weeks, he learnt he'd been posted (thanks to Terry Carlton) to hold on 54 Squadron at RAF Coltishall and would join 14 Squadron the following year at Brüggen. However, the message JR wanted to transmit, as the Jaguar Conversion Team matured, was now loud and clear to all.

The JCT was wound up and the unit received its badge as 226 Operational Conversion Unit was re-born. Following a number of changes at the top, Acting Group Captain J R Walker took over the station – prior to moving to Germany to oversee the introduction of the Jaguar to RAF Brüggen – and Acting Wing Commander Fred Trowern stepped up to become OC 226 OCU.

In the forty years since we formed the JCT I have often thanked the fates for allowing me to participate in the genesis and early successes of the Jaguar. For ten years between 1973 and 1986 I was very much part of its world – seven years with the RAF on the JCT/OCU, 54, 14 and 6 Squadrons, and three years in Oman on 8 Squadron SOAF. Yet I value most the chance to have met and known and befriended, flown and 'fought' beside, and lived with, so many generous, honest, decent, salt-of-the-earth, 'Jaguar mate', brothers-in-arms.

CHAPTER 2

EARLY COLTISHALL OPERATIONS

With the Jaguar replacing the Phantom in the strike/attack role and the latter moving to air-defence duties, the changeover produced a manning problem. This was soon adopted by the RAF Staff College as an exercise in logical thinking and argument, one which was presented to students for years afterwards. It went something like this. We've got a bunch of pilots trained to operate the single-seat Lightning in the air-defence role, and a similar team who know all about ground attack through flying the Phantom – albeit with navigators to help them. Now we need ground-attack pilots who can operate the single-seat Jaguar, as well as air-defence pilots who will share their Phantom cockpits with navigators. So how best to maximise capability while minimising re-training time and costs?

There was no staff answer, and students normally came up with a kind of mix-and-match solution, with any pilots left over going to the Red Arrows. Which is more or less what the RAF posting staffs had concluded, too – although not, perhaps, the bit about the Red Arrows! One result was that the Jaguar Force soon included a strange group of people known as 'WIWOLs', so called because, regardless of which squadron they were on, they always stood together in the bar and started every conversation with the words: "When I was on Lightnings…"

So at Coltishall a mix of pilots came together to operate an aircraft with exciting new equipment. Although it is generally imagined that the latest avionics will ease the pilot's task, all sorts of factors seem sometimes to conspire against that being the case. The availability of new capabilities often results in stiffer – perhaps even over-ambitious – targets being set. New tactics and procedures pose challenges to minds set in old ways. Those new equipments also often bring with them teething problems. So how did that new mixture settle down? For the answer we turn to one of the early squadron commanders, George Robertson.

WING COMMANDER GEORGE ROBERTSON (RETD)

I came to the Jaguar having previously spent five years on the Phantom FGR2, so was well-used to the ground-attack role. I found the Jaguar to be a delightful aircraft which handled well in the low-level high-speed role for which it was designed. It had a small wing and didn't turn very well, but neither did the Phantom. I missed the Phantom's radar and the air-to-air capability, also the very capable navigator

in the back to make it all work. The Jaguar though, was easier and safer to fly at very low level, and I had to stop myself from sliding down to 180ft or lower, instead of the minimum of 250ft, because it felt like the Jaguar was in its natural element at a lower height.

The first generation NAVWASS was great when it worked, but was not very reliable and had to be backed up by traditional map-reading skills. The navigation computer had a massive (for its day) 8k of magnetic core store memory – that is 8 kilobytes, not megabytes or gigabytes! It is amazing that the designers managed to pack so much into so little. But after all the initial enthusiasm and unjustified hype, the truth during my time was that you would be lucky to achieve a bombing average of 50ft on first-run attacks. And of course we learned to live with jibes from other operators that the Jaguar only got airborne due to the curvature of the earth. All in all, when the aircraft first entered service it was really still a work in progress, and many modifications throughout its life would improve it hugely.

I took over 6 Squadron from Wing Commander Neil Hayward in December 1977. Neil had a well-deserved reputation as 'Mr Jaguar', having worked on the development project at MoD, followed by the introduction to service at Lossiemouth. So 6 Squadron was already well set by my time, and many of the initial teething problems had been overcome.

The first few years of squadron service had certainly not been without their problems. Coltishall had experienced a couple of fatal accidents in 1976. Military aircraft were not then fitted with flight data recorders, so boards of inquiry had to depend on post-crash analysis, witness reports and the like. This meant that definitive conclusions as to causes were often difficult or impossible to determine. Certainly, in those early accidents disorientation seemed to figure prominently, and cockpit ergonomics and especially the HUD were implicated. Jaguar was one of the first RAF fighter aircraft to be fitted with a HUD, which displayed flight information on a reflector glass in front of the pilot. This was meant to be the primary instrument reference, so the head-down instruments had a secondary or standby role. The HUD was supplied with attitude information from the inertial platform, but both the HUD and the inertial platform had reliability issues in the early days. If the inertial platform 'dumped', then the HUD would occult, and the pilot had to revert rapidly to a head-down instrument scan. Also, difficult and potentially disorienting switch selections at a late stage of an attack were well-recognised. All of these issues would be addressed in later upgrades.

The mid to late 1970s saw the peak of the Cold War, and our training was directed towards the low-level attack role where our only tactic was high-speed, low-level penetration, flying below SAM engagement heights and evading enemy interception. We became highly adept from constant practice, often in quite marginal weather conditions. Fortunately, in those days we didn't have any 'hot' wars to worry about – these came later. Instead we had competitions both national and international, which were taken incredibly seriously. The RAF was expected to take on all comers and to win, nothing less would do. The Americans in particular became thoroughly fed up with always being trounced by the Brits in NATO tactical weapons meetings.

1978 Tactical Bombing Competition winners: 6 Squadron.
Rear: Malcolm Bartle, George Robertson, John Pym. Front:
Rick Lea, Bernie Mills, John Hodgson, and Russ Peart.

Just before I arrived at Coltishall, the wing had been told to field a team for the 1978 Tactical Bombing Competition. The other squadron commanders had had a head start in figuring out pressing reasons why they couldn't do it. I ducked too late, and was given what might have been a poisoned chalice. The C-in-C Strike Command of the day had declared a personal grudge match with his US equivalent in Tactical Air Command.

In fairness, we were given extra resources for the work-up, including our own Marconi Elliot rep to help with tweaking the NAVWASS. The work-up period was run as a trial, and results were quantified in an attempt to identify the specific strengths and weaknesses of the Jaguar with a view to future modification programmes. The project officer for this was Squadron Leader John Pym, my OC B Flight. John is a charismatic Australian and a gifted fighter pilot. He was also a QWI, and he ran the work-up and the competition with great flair.

Back then the culture within a typical fighter squadron embraced natural rivalry and sometimes intense competition between young men who wanted to be the best they could be, fuelled by testosterone and adrenaline. Status in the hierarchy was determined as much by rank as by weapons scores and combat ability. Rivalry and lively banter continued in the debrief and later in the bar. Translate that culture into an international competition, where not only personal reputation is at stake, but also that of your squadron and the RAF itself, and you will see that the pressure to succeed is immense.

Selection of the team for the competition was by a series of fly-offs, but the final six were selected for both ability and experience. We needed team members with big-match temperament. We were required to field a four and a pair. The four-ship was led by John Pym, with Flight Lieutenants John Hodgson, Rick Lea, and Flying Officer Bernie Mills. The pair comprised Squadron Leaders Russ Peart and Malcolm Bartle. Rick Lea and Russ Peart were, incidentally, both Lightning pilots who had successfully transitioned to ground attack.

The competition took place at Lossiemouth in July 1978. The teams were: 6 Squadron, 31 Squadron Jaguars from Brüggen, and 15, 16 and 208 Buccaneer squadrons. The Americans had formed a special unit to take us on, from the 23rd Tactical Fighter Wing at England AFB, Louisiana, flying Vought A-7s. They were formidable rivals with a very capable aircraft, indeed with similar avionics.

The Americans, we later discovered, had a 'B' Team whose main objective was to waylay the Brits into late-night drinking sessions and nobble them for the next day's flying! The start of the competition was delayed by weather, and with poor conditions forecast for the following day we all retired to the bar where the beer and banter flowed freely. Later on I went out for some fresh air to discover that the sky had cleared. On ringing the met office I found that the forecast had improved and flying would be 'on' the next morning, so it was back to the bar to shepherd my team off to bed – quite a challenge with the party in full swing.

In the end 6 Squadron won five of the seven available trophies. The team trophy went to the Americans, who achieved a brilliant score on day two of the competition (although 6 had a better aggregate score over the three days). We also won the Marconi Elliot trophy for best RAF team, and the Adour trophy for best Jaguar team. The BAC trophy for best leadership in bombing and navigation went to our Russ Peart, and the gunnery trophy went to John Hodgson, who achieved a remarkable strafe score of 75%. John was and is the complete gentleman, and the antithesis of the braggadocio and swagger of the Tom Cruise character of Top Gun fame. The poor old Buccaneer squadrons went home empty-handed. It was no longer possible to compete internationally without a modern avionics suite – but of course for them the Tornado was on the horizon.

The work-up and the competition itself produced a host of data which helped define later improvements to the aircraft. Despite our successful results, it highlighted the limitations of the original NAVWASS in terms of accuracy and reliability, and it resulted in a new method for harmonising the Aden guns for better accuracy on strafe.

In the early years there was a great deal of interest in the Jaguar from the media, senior officers and other notables. One such was the well-known motoring journalist L.J.K.Setright who wrote for *Car* magazine for many years. He was a Latin scholar and a man of great erudition and wit, although physically rather frail. He had spent his national service as an air traffic controller in the RAF, so he knew a bit about aircraft. LJK had been commissioned by *Penthouse* magazine to write a gee-whiz article on what it was like to be a fighter pilot in the RAF's latest jet.

Gordon Hannam was given the job of briefing and flying him. Gordon was one of our senior flight lieutenants and a qualified flying instructor of some experience. LJK describes his first impressions.[1]

'Within a couple of minutes of reporting at the guardroom I was met by the man who will fly me, Flight Lieutenant Hannam, obviously fairly young, but not very (he has had too much to learn) and very fit but not athletically hard, a man who talks and moves quietly, economically, smoothly, quickly.'

LJK would fly in the rear seat of the two-seater, flying as a pair with a single-seater flown by one of our first tourists.

'We are joined by a wiry young flight lieutenant whose badge declares him to be Steve Morgan. He will fly the single-seater and bubbles with enthusiasm for its performance.'

The flight profile involved a transit at medium level to Northumberland, followed by a descent and return at low level. The outbound leg went well, with the single-seater positioning to provide LJK with plenty of photo opportunities. After descent, the Jaguar was in its element, barrelling around the Cheviots and down through the Yorkshire Dales.

'We are down, racing parallel with the ground, skating in on a thin ice of air between our ventral fins and the green earth, and SLAM, we go into a steep turn heading for a gap in the hills. SQUASH – that ham hand of a g suit squeezes my guts and my stomach flies up to my throat ... wherever we are, there is Mr Morgan alongside us lifting and falling with us ... lining up for our practice attack precise and prepared.'

After a while it all went quiet in the back of Gordon's aircraft as the physical demands took their toll on the slight frame of LJK.

'The hi-lo-hi trilogy played itself out unnoticed. I must have escaped in some way from my consciousness of that awful physical inadequacy for a war that men like these pilots would have to face on my behalf.'

After a night's recuperation in sick quarters, LJK was well enough to continue his journey home in a different type of Jaguar, an XJ12 that he was testing at the time. Gordon Hannam went on to fly for the Red Arrows and later for Cathay Pacific, retiring as a senior training captain. Steve Morgan also flew as an airline captain after leaving the service. I assume they gave their paying passengers a smoother ride than they did LJK!

---

[1] Extracts reproduced by permission of Helen Setright, Leonard's widow.

The middle ranks of the squadron's pilots, coming from Lightnings, Phantoms, and Hunters, provided the solid core of experience essential in developing the skills of those more junior. Our first tourists, though, were an exceptional bunch. They were the pick of the crop from the RAF training machine, highly motivated, keen to learn and generally a delight to work with.

These 'youngsters' were mostly in their mid-twenties, as delays and bottlenecks in the training system had postponed their arrival on the front line. In a typical RAF squadron, we worked and socialised hard, and the first tourists were always at the forefront of organising parties and beer calls.

Two particularly handsome young men, Bernie Mills and Chris Daymon, were in constant demand to star in RAF recruitment advertisements, a role that resulted in a great deal of good-natured teasing and banter from their contemporaries. Chris Daymon, a young, fair-haired Adonis at the time, was also selected to appear as a sponsor on the Hughie Green talent show, which he did reluctantly but with a good grace.

We were extremely fortunate in our engineering team. Squadron engineering was largely autonomous, a necessary requirement for our mobile role with many overseas detachments. The squadron engineers dealt with both first and second-line engineering and rectification up to minor servicing. Major servicing was conducted at RAF Abingdon, where one of our aircraft would generally be in deep servicing.

From an establishment of twelve aircraft we therefore would have eleven at Coltishall, from which we invariably had nine or more serviceable on the line every morning. Having come from the Phantom, which was difficult to maintain and a nightmare for the engineers, this was a revelation to me. The Jaguar had been designed from the outset with maintainability in mind. Access was straightforward, and line-replaceable units could easily be swapped and returned to the bays for servicing. Even the Adour engine was modular in construction and could largely be serviced at Coltishall. This meant that running a flying programme was more straightforward than I had ever experienced, with fewer cancellations due to aircraft unserviceabilities.

The close ties, both professional and social, between the pilots and engineers were partly due to our frequent overseas deployments where we worked and played together. We had two engineering officers, a flight sergeant in overall charge of the troops, and chief technician trade managers for each specialisation. Flight Sergeant Hugh Brown ran a tight ship, and in charge of the line was a little Yorkshire ball of fire, Chief Technician Pip Curzon. The trade managers were all chief techs who took immense pride in their work. Out on the line in all weathers were the flightline mechanics, refuelling, re-arming, and turning round the aircraft.

The integration of engineers and aircrew in the Jaguar Force was closer than I had experienced in any other squadron, and explained in many ways the high morale that was typical in Jaguar units of the time.

RAF Coltishall had a great atmosphere, enjoying the nickname 'Happy Valley'.

Unlike our Jaguar compatriots in Germany, we were free from the nuclear role with all its attendant intensity, QRA duties, and life in HASs. We were assigned to NATO's northern region, and our war base was at Tirstrup in Denmark, where we would deploy for exercises and for real. There, the aircraft were housed in HASs, but the personnel had to live under canvas, at least in the early stages of alert – an anomaly I found very strange at the time. Food was provided by an excellent RAF field kitchen, and we lived, ate, worked and played together with all ranks.

Warsaw Pact forces outnumbered us three to one but lacked sophistication, so our low-level high-speed tactics worked well at the time. We preferred to fly operationally under a low cloud base with limited visibility so that defences had few opportunities to find and follow us. As one commentator said at the time, "in typical northern European weather, just try and stop a well-flown Jaguar".

But times were beginning to change. My tour coincided with the first of the 'Flag' exercises, Red Flag at Nellis AFB Nevada, and Maple Flag at Cold Lake Alberta. Unlike the Germany squadrons, we were qualified in AAR, so it fell to us to ferry the aircraft to and from the USA and Canada. Watching the mountains of Greenland drift past from a Jaguar cockpit was always a unique and delightful experience.

These exercises were designed to simulate as closely as possible the conditions of a real war. For the first time we were up against AWACS, the all-seeing eye in the sky from which there was no hiding place, no matter how low or fast we flew. In addition, the new generation of fighters like the F-15, with a sophisticated look-down-shoot-down capability, could take us out before we even saw them coming. The Warsaw Pact had not yet caught up with this capability, but it was only a matter of time.

So tactics and training had to change to reflect a post-Cold War situation where we would only go to war as part of a coalition, with local air superiority, defence suppression, and smart weapons delivered from medium level well away from AAA and small-arms fire. All credit to Jaguar that, through a series of upgrades, it could be adapted to these new scenarios.

As well as Denmark and 'Flags', our routine was frequently punctuated by other overseas deployments. We had our annual weapons practice camps at Decimomannu in Sardinia. Squadron exchanges with our NATO allies were always popular, and during my time our guests were a Danish F-100 Squadron and a Canadian F-104 Squadron. They were still flying the previous generation of aircraft, and by comparison, our Jaguars were the height of sophistication. They were soon to leapfrog us, the Danes with the F-16 and the Canadians with the F-18. The theme of NATO integration continued at squadron level where each Jaguar squadron had two NATO exchange officers. We had Captain Jean-Marie Allier, a French Jaguar pilot, and Captain Gys Schoor, a Dutch F-104 pilot. I was always amazed at how well they integrated, not just operationally, but with RAF culture, especially the robust and sometimes very non-PC sense of humour.

The Jaguar served me well and never let me down. On one occasion at high speed over the North Sea, my right engine swallowed a large seagull and came to an abrupt stop. The left engine kept going though, and brought me safely home. If I had been in an F-16, I would undoubtedly have ended up with wet feet. In my time at Coltishall there were no hull losses and no fatal accidents. The Jaguar continued well past its original sell-by date and was still an effective fighting machine right to the end. After half a lifetime and many more thousands of flying hours, I still look back on it with great affection.

Over its service, the aircraft underwent many modifications and upgrades, not least from its participation in Gulf War One. When I later visited Coltishall for 6 Squadron's ninetieth birthday celebrations in 2004, I had the opportunity to fly the simulator and was amazed at the transformation. The uprated engines and completely new avionics suite meant that it was a world apart from the Jaguar of the mid-seventies. It had finally realised its full potential. If only we had had that capability back then!

Fancy flying. 6 Squadron celebrates its seventieth anniversary, 12 May 1984.

CHAPTER 3

THE SHARP END

There was another place. Not far (only 200 miles as the crow flies) from East Anglia, but nevertheless an area of mystery to those who didn't serve there. Its buildings painted a dull green to match the forest within which it crouched, it was a place of menace. Surrounded by high fences topped with barbed wire, its scant, (just over 100 miles) distance from the East-German border contributed to the mystique.

But that other place also had an additional role, and its 'strike' business was another matter entirely.

One who came to know both places and both roles well was Andrew Griffin who, before flying Jaguars, was a Lightning pilot. Later he went on to command the Flying Training School at RAF Valley. Back in 1977 he and I were amongst the first to join the new 20 Squadron, and I also later enjoyed working for him in the MoD. Here is his Brüggen story.

AIR COMMODORE ANDREW GRIFFIN (RETD)

 It is 1976. I am serving on 54 Squadron at Coltishall, and a pair of us land at RAF Brüggen. This is my first visit there, and we are looked after by 17 Squadron. They are on exercise, and it soon becomes apparent that they take things very seriously indeed. We are met at the entrance to the PBF by a sergeant pointing a gun straight at us. Everyone is wearing NBC kit, and the aircraft are all hidden away in HASs. In the UK we never go further than carrying our NBC kit on exercise, while the nearest we ever get to protected accommodation is a piece of masking tape saying 'this window is sandbagged'. Indeed, a suggestion to Coltishall's station commander that we should start sandbagging during exercises was met with the response that there would be plenty of time for that sort of thing if war came!

After a while we are thrown out of 17's PBF. The RAF applies the 'need to know' principle, and although we hold secret clearances, we clearly don't 'need to know' all that's going on here. We refuel and go on our way.

That was my first brush with Brüggen, but I was soon to find out just how different it really was. For, shortly afterwards, I was posted there as a flight commander on 20 Squadron, which would be the station's fourth squadron and would complete the wing. The first sight greeting me at the gate was a large sign saying 'THE ROLE OF THIS STATION IN PEACE IS TO PREPARE FOR WAR. DON'T YOU FORGET

IT' – all of which was something of a culture shock. The station commander was the man who had commanded the OCU when I was on the course, and his arrival interview with my new squadron commander had reputedly started with the words 'I am a vindictive man'.

Brüggen was already operational in the nuclear strike and conventional attack roles with three squadrons – 14, 17 and 31. There were four dispersed sites, one in each corner of the airfield, each with nine HASs and a hardened PBF. Alongside each was 'soft' accommodation intended for normal day-to-day use. However, the pace of life was such that we all operated entirely from the 'hard', which could supposedly survive anything except a direct hit.

We were immediately plunged into our operational work-up. The evaluated categories were readiness, operations, support and ability to survive, with the scores 1-4 denoting exceptional, good, marginal or fail. 'Ones' were rare in NATO and 'fours' not unknown. The wing had recently had a NATO Taceval and scored the unusually high rating of three 'ones' and a 'two'. It rapidly became apparent to us that Taceval was more important than anything else, and the station's prevailing view was that, having just done so well, the only thing that could spoil things was the arrival of 20 Squadron.

Nuclear strike qualification was our initial hurdle. Here, we were well served by my fellow flight commander Martin Molloy, who had been on the original JCT. He had come from a short spell on 31 Squadron and, although it's hard to believe, the strike experience he gained there was shared by only one other of 20's pilots. One's natural initial impression could easily have been that anyone could fly around on their own and attack a huge target – which was the essence of a strike mission – but it was all the surrounding procedural stuff which was going to make it difficult. It would be a steep learning curve, and we started by trooping out to a HAS to look at a WE177, the British air-dropped nuclear weapon.

Actually, this one was a blue-painted training round, but had to be treated as if it were real, so we went through the procedures for 'accepting' the weapon. At the nuclear stage of proceedings (exercise or real), two pilots would go to the loaded aircraft and follow a checklist to set up the weapon. The reason for two pilots was simply that the HAS was what was known as a 'No-Lone-Zone', the idea being that one person would never be allowed to get near the bomb on his own.

The checklist and procedures all came from an organisation called WST – weapon system training. Pedantry ruled, and a couple of problems immediately became apparent to us. On a Vulcan it was probably necessary to use a step ladder to set the panel on the weapon. But on the Jag the bomb was low down and the panel difficult to see. If you were to lie down to get a clear view of the settings, WST would say that you were in danger if the weapon fell off and crushed your legs. Second, the checklist had probably been designed for the V Force with its several crewmembers. In the single-seat Jag you didn't have enough fingers to mark different parts of the checklist, since it failed to follow a simple sequence.

I like to think that 20 Squadron changed all this. Our strike training officer (this volume's author) wound a wet towel round his head and disappeared from view for a while. When he emerged he thought he understood what we were trying to do, and attempted to make it logical. Eventually, he redesigned the checklist to work as a simple sequence that could be read right through. Much to our surprise, WST accepted the revisions.

We rapidly found that the same was true of running any exercise. There was no simple sequential guide of what to do when starting up the squadron after an alert. We rewrote the guide for running the ops desk in a similar fashion, and it was adopted by the wing.

And so, after an intense work-up, we qualified as a strike squadron. We settled into the Brüggen routine, which revolved around monthly Minevals and a yearly Maxeval and Taceval. Taceval was an evaluation by NATO and there were a range of different nationalities on the team. Maxeval was the final dress rehearsal which preceded it, and was run by HQ RAFG with help from the other strike base at Laarbruch, which operated Buccaneers and recce Jaguars. There was a definite 'not invented here' tendency with Maxeval, which made it the hardest exercise of the year.

The Salmond Trophy was a major annual event. It involved all the strike/attack and recce squadrons in Germany, flying navigation and bombing sorties to competition rules. We flew as singletons, with each pilot having to hit an entry gate and overfly a field target on time before dropping a timed bomb on Nordhorn Range. The competition was intense and the four Brüggen squadrons were very different in their approach. One, 14 Squadron, in our perception allotted a large proportion of its annual routine training to winning, which, to their credit, they did three times in a row.

However, we were all quite good at it as the sortie was not over-demanding – although the standard was high. The field target was simply a grid reference with no lead-in features for about a minute and no decent IP for two or three minutes. Two bored staff officers stood on some lonely road about 50 yards apart and we had to go between them wings level, on a specified heading and exactly on time. The run to Nordhorn Range was simpler but the IP to target run was five minutes long and, again, timing was everything. This was before the days of cheap quartz watches, and the cost of the station phone bill as each pilot called up the German speaking clock must have been enormous.

As on much of the flying over the North German Plain, poor weather was always a factor. There were many apocryphal stories about low flying in truly appalling weather, but a mile-and-a-half visibility was not uncommon. This was apparently accepted by higher authority, and I well remember on our first Salmond competition missing the IP for the field target half a mile to the right and seeing my life flash before my eyes; amazingly I hit the target on time and even saw one of the unfortunate staff officers. But I failed to see the bombing target until about three seconds to release, which led to a poor score.

Following several years of Brüggen Jaguar victories, our station commander moved on to a staff job at HQ RAFG. There, he lost no time in changing the rules, and the uncharitable might say he was trying to make it harder for his successor to

A good reason for keeping the clear visor down when low flying.
The Jaguar side screen regularly proved itself no match for a 450kt seagull.
Andrew Griffin models the result.

win. The new rules included a line search, which was tailor-made for Laarbruch's Jaguar recce pilots and two-seat Buccaneers. The Nordhorn target was also changed to that routinely used by the Buccaneer force. My own experience in the next competition was rather more successful, except for the line search. I flew down the specified road but saw nothing. The recce rules stated that you had to submit the result within ten minutes of engine shut down, so I took advantage of this rather odd rule. I sat there after landing, burning valuable fuel while peering at the map looking for inspiration. Eventually I found a track off the road which I knew I had not seen and submitted a report of one Land Rover at a grid reference on that track. For this piece of inspired guesswork I got a score of 60%.

Ours was by then an experienced and capable squadron and we were actually favourites to win; senior staff officers at Rheindahlen even had money on us. But despite similar efforts by all my fellow Brüggen pilots, we were all defeated by the revised competition set up. 16 Squadron Buccaneers won, and the following day OC 16 flew his aeroplane right over the Brüggen QRA compound at about 100ft, thus breaking two rules at once. He ended up as an air chief marshal, so no one seemed to worry.

The wing strove for standardisation, but there were many ways of doing things. 31 Squadron had a strong Harrier influence, and that led them to favour phased training – whereby they would concentrate on one aspect of operations for a month and then move to something else. The result was, as far as we could see, that they were always very good at something but never up to speed on everything. From time to time they also flew four waves a day with empty drop tanks, which improved pilots' rapid-planning abilities and ground crews' turn-round expertise. But to my mind, one of the pleasures of the Jaguar was that it went a long way and one could explore distant regions of Germany. We agreed to differ, but one had to sympathise with the station commander, who rightly wanted to weld the wing together so that we could fly formations with one pilot from each squadron if we had to. Which indeed we did.

The exercise sequence dominated our lives. Every month at some ghastly hour in the morning, the hooter would go and we would stagger into work. For presentational reasons, the pilots had to be in early. But in reality the armourers were far and away the most important people as we had to generate half the aircraft loaded with cluster bombs in six hours and 70% in twelve hours. This was always achieved but, in the meantime, we would sit around regretting that, again for presentational reasons, we had not shaved before starting for work. Then of course the poor armourers had to take the bombs off again and load practice weapons.

On one occasion a film unit was present, making what turned out to be quite a good documentary called Watchdogs. It started with a call out and our SEngO having to stick his head through the hatch and ask the boss "Is it exercise or real?" This was not a question we worried about; suffice to say that, if it had been real, things would have been so much simpler.

A day-and-a-half of conventional tasking would follow, most of which was bread and butter to us. A task came in to the station, the combat operations centre wasted a bit of time and then sent it to the appropriate squadron. Sometimes the weapon load, which had been sent separately to the engineers, was ill-matched to the target and you could request a change. The evaluators, who watched our every move, might be looking to see if we had noticed the mismatch. A change of weapon load could cause delays and make us miss the take-off time – so we were very careful not to let this happen. Generally we had an hour-and-a-half from receipt of task on station to getting four aircraft airborne, which was not very long; effectively under an hour to plan and brief and thirty minutes to get airborne. There was no question of being able to walk to the aircraft as they were dispersed in HASs and some distance away, so we were driven in a minibus, all of which took time. Especially in NBC kit and sometimes in simulated chemical contamination. We got to loathe gas masks in a visceral way.

Wars need luck, planning and determination to win; exercises the same, plus a little gamesmanship. BAC, as they then were, gave each pilot a lavish (!) goody pack on first going solo, all contained in a black plastic zip briefcase. The great majority of pilots used the latter to carry maps to the cockpit as the aircraft had little or no map stowage. The problem was that all the bags looked the same. On one occasion, after the usual rush of planning and briefing, I grabbed what I thought was my bag as we dashed for the door. As I was strapping in I went to enter waypoints into the NAVWASS. I reached for the bag and found it contained a paperback copy of *The Dogs of War* and a bottle of ink, neither of which was going to help me lead the four-ship. I confess to declaring the aircraft unserviceable, which was not entirely true, and handing over to the deputy leader. I also gave up using the BAC briefcase.

We had a pre-planned conventional option to attack a Warsaw Pact airfield with four 1,000lb bombs on each aircraft. Fairly early on in 20 Squadron's time I discovered that no-one at Brüggen had ever flown with a full weapon load. I set about organising this and we planned two pairs. The Jaguar's take-off performance was such that a large proportion of the station turned out to watch us, but careful study of the manual predicted a good margin for error. One thing that was not available was an accurate check on the rate of acceleration, and I did note as I went over the first arrestor cable that I was doing 83kts, so I took that as a good guide for the future. We subsequently flew carrying inert bombs quite often on exercises and brought them back successfully for (slightly) heavyweight landings.

However in the summer of 1979, 14 Squadron was tasked with dropping a large number of inert retard 1,000 pounders to prove a new tail design, and I was loaned to them as they were temporarily short of experienced pilots. Following my leader onto the runway, I noted that he did not line up quite as near the start as I would have done but I obediently lined up alongside him. The temperature was 26°C. He said in view of the heat we would stream rather than go as a pair, and off he went. There was no wind, and he left all his hot air all over the runway. My calculated rotate speed was 174kts. As I crossed the first cable I was doing 82kts, one knot short of my personal safety speed. The aircraft continued to trundle along but as I saw the upwind cable supports go out of my peripheral vision I was still only doing 165kts and only had 1,300 feet of runway left. With a hefty heave to 17° incidence, which was the correct technique, we lifted off and I reached for the gear handle. We were flying, but only just, and it crossed my mind that I might have to dump the bombs to help. According to the aircraft clearance, if you needed to jettison external stores, you could not do so with the undercarriage travelling; it was OK with it down or up, but not in between. My hand moved from the gear handle to the jettison button and back a couple of times before I decided that it was probably going to climb, which it eventually did.

No one expected that we would ever have won a conventional war against the Warsaw Pact. Although 'flexible response' had long ago replaced the Eisenhower doctrine of 'massive retaliation', NATO planning always assumed that we would have to escalate to the use of nuclear weapons. (Some wag had said that we practised flexible response from Monday to Friday and massive retaliation at the weekend.) Anyway, flexible response happened in a graduated way; as the 'war' situation deteriorated, selected pilots would be earmarked for nuclear sorties and taken to the COC for briefing and planning.

Occasionally the evaluators would inject an incident which caused unintended mirth. One pilot, on a nuclear mission, was told to simulate mutiny and say, after the planning and briefing process when being given his final pep talk by the station commander, that he was not going to fly. The Taceval team clearly expected this to generate a substantial incident. Indeed we had heard on the grapevine that a similar scenario had been tried at a German air force base, where the commander had genuinely swallowed the inject, which had brought their 'war' to a temporary halt while he dealt with it. But Brüggen, in particular its station commander, who continued to drive the wing forward by the force of his personality, was miles ahead of them. He merely said to the guard, 'take the pilot outside, shoot him, and bring me another'. The Taceval team loved it!

It was always assumed that a few nuclear explosions would probably not stop the Soviets in their tracks, and that the full works would eventually have to be employed. So inevitably we would progress to general nuclear loading. We only had a small number of training WE177s, so for the exercise full nuclear option we had to load real weapons. Each squadron site became what was known as a follow-on area, which meant line-of-sight guards at the front and rear of each HAS, their weapons loaded with live ammunition. Now, throughout all these exercises we were regularly subjected to ground intruder attacks by simulated Soviet special forces. Because of this, no real ammunition was issued during the earlier stages. This was clearly incompatible with the later situation, and the solution was that all intruder play had to stop during nuclear loading. A broadcast would go out that live ammunition was being issued, meaning that real nuclear weapons were being trundled around the airfield.

It all felt quite serious, as indeed it was. Each HAS had an RAF policeman as the front guard, who controlled access. As the loading progressed we allocated pilots to missions and sent two out to go through each acceptance procedure. In due course the number of aircraft we had declared to SACEUR would all be loaded. We then went through the reverse process where the real and training rounds were removed and practice bombs substituted.

Eventually the code for the general release of nuclear weapons would be given. Even one of the QRA aircraft (those permanently armed and manned ready for very-short-notice launch in the event of sudden attack) had, by this stage of the exercise, had its real WE177 removed and replaced by a practice weapon, and was the first off for the mass launch; a high-profile sortie for the Taceval team to watch.

Keeping the two-man principle going in a single-seat aircraft was tricky. When you manned the aircraft, the ground crew were in the HAS, which covered the requirement. The hooter was sounded for the launch, and at that stage one of the HAS doors was opened so you could start engines. A broadcast from the COC eventually gave you a release code which you wrote down and showed to the policeman on guard. If it agreed with his code, the other door was opened and at that point two-man control ceased. There were contingency plans if this system failed, leading eventually to a personal visit from the station commander. In this scenario I think we must all at one time or another have been put in mind of Doctor Strangelove.

We were required to demonstrate the launch of about three quarters of the wing, and each aircraft was given a ground speed to fly, one of two routes, and a time on target for Nordhorn Range. The first off got 480kts and a short route and gradually the speed reduced – then someone got high speed on the longer route, with subsequent aircraft on that route flying at slower speeds. The end result was that the whole wing arrived at the Nordhorn IP at one-minute intervals. It was very clever and we ended up with an average timing error (I remember it being three seconds) and an average bomb score for the wing. Even the recovery was an interesting exercise. We had a track to navigate back from the range, still at one-minute intervals. The route into Brüggen was tortuous and flown quite slowly, so one minute didn't take us many miles. With inevitable slight variations in decelerating, things were not always as orderly as they might have been.

But it was all a lovely party trick, and not entirely exercise-focussed, for of course the real operation was also extraordinarily closely planned and timed. Great emphasis was, naturally, placed on the avoidance of other NATO nuclear bursts.

In the majority of exercises that was the end and we went to the bar. ('endex' beer-calls were always the best.) However, it was never enough, and eventually on one Maxeval some bright spark decided to add some 'post-Armageddon play'. The scenario had a number of aircraft returning having failed to drop their weapons, and it was decided by the force commander to send them all to 20 Squadron. The resulting chaos had to be seen to be believed as we struggled to re-establish No-Lone-Zones and guarding – which seemed somewhat futile when all of Europe had supposedly been reduced to radioactive rubble. Fortunately the Taceval team never played this particularly sadistic trick, and in the following Taceval Brüggen got an unheard-of four 'ones'. So 20 Squadron had made a difference!

It was an unbelievable time and place to serve. The wing was extraordinarily professional in its approach, but some of the younger and less experienced pilots were under enormous pressure. In the ten years of Jaguars at Brüggen, we lost twenty aircraft. My own, possibly harsh, assessment is that sixteen of those were largely due to pilot error. In the same period, the recce squadron at Laarbruch lost five aircraft – none of them owing to mechanical failure.

But the bald term 'pilot error' fails to acknowledge the factors which induced the errors. There can be no doubt that the Jaguar was a demanding aircraft. An article in *Flight International* by test pilot John Cockburn entitled 'Jaguar – One Man Band' and published before it entered service, drew attention to the high cockpit workload. We must add to this the truly appalling cockpit design of the original model. The main control panel for the NAVWASS was low down behind the stick and not easy to reach or master. The weapons control panel was easy to

17 Jaguar Squadron hands over to 17 Tornado Squadron.

see and reach on the left coaming. However the meaning of the buttons changed depending on whether the computer programme installed was for conventional or nuclear weapons. Add to that a poor reputation for handling characteristics and there was a tendency for some pilots to be almost frightened of the aircraft. In reality it was perfectly safe if flown correctly and if you understood the limitations.

So it wasn't always the aircraft. Nor was it just the junior pilots; the overall pressures of the job were palpable, so let me close with a couple of examples of how these affected quite senior people.

First, on a November exercise during my 20 Squadron tour, the station commander wanted a mass launch on one of the pre-planned options. The boss said the weather wasn't good enough and that he would not authorise our pilots to fly. He was instructed to do what he was told and get on with it. The result was that twenty or so Jaguars diverted to a Luftwaffe base, Jever, which was the only station in north Germany with weather anything like we could fly in. They were there for three days, to the consternation of HQ RAFG with so many of its strike assets out of reach, before Brüggen's weather cleared.

Second, I returned to Brüggen in 1983 to command 17 Squadron for its last eighteen months as a Jaguar unit. We were selected to go to Exercise Red Flag in

1984 and tasked to drop fourteen laser-guided bombs. For a variety of reasons, none of which turned out to be our fault, the first seven missed. It's worth pointing out that, for this type of delivery, there were no fewer than seventeen switch selections or checks to be made between the IP and target, all the while flying at 100ft at 480kts. These checks and switches were scattered around the cockpit, and some required changing hands on the stick. Anyway, we dropped two in an academic profile to prove it could work and I led the second pair in our next 'operational' four-ship. All of this would have been fine if the SASO HQ RAFG had not arrived and stated publicly that he expected at least a 50% success rate! As the CO, I simply could not afford to make a mistake, especially as I had removed one pilot from the sortie for earlier making a switchery error.

Finally, on one occasion I also chose to fly the aircraft out of QRA on the mass launch at the end of an exercise, a mission normally given to one of the junior pilots. It had to be airborne in fifteen minutes and was of course the highest-profile sortie; again the pressure not to make a mistake was enormous. I think the junior pilots put up with a great deal and probably did not get the credit they deserved; nor perhaps did the rest of us.

So that was Brüggen in the Jaguar days, but I wouldn't want to leave you with an impression that life was entirely composed of serious matters. I've had no time to touch on the marvellous social life, the opportunities for travel, the extraordinary job satisfaction and the camaraderie, all found in abundance. And all of which made sure that Brüggen was a place none of us who served there on Jaguars will ever forget.

CHAPTER 4

SO WHO NEEDS AN OCU?

Following one of the RAF's periodic crises in manning the front line, I was given four days notice to leave my job as a Hunter instructor at the tactical weapons unit and report to Lossiemouth for the start of No 15 course. In fact not only was I rushed to make this date but I was also to do an abbreviated course so that I could be on my new squadron within three months. I made it, and the whole process seemed pretty quick. But others converted to the aircraft in even more expeditious fashion, and Nigel Day now recounts his unique experience.

Nigel's and my paths crossed several times during our careers, most unusually when we both served in Scandinavia. He flew on exchange in northern Denmark at the same time as I was enjoying a similar tour in southern Norway. So at that point we were able to visit each other occasionally as nearest RAF neighbours, albeit separated by the Skagerrak! Nigel later went on to command the Dambusters and RAF Lossiemouth, but he'll never forget his Jaguar conversion story...

_____

AIR VICE-MARSHAL NIGEL DAY (RETD)

 It was February 1976 at RAF Brüggen and I was idly reading another back copy of *Air Clues* over a cup of coffee. The crew room of 17(F) Squadron was in the offices at the back of the hangar. The airfield was a building site, with HAS sites under construction in all four corners. It was also hidden in a blanket of dense fog and covered with a layer of snow and ice. In fact most of Europe was in the grip of frost and fog. Apart from Lossiemouth and Kinloss, both gloriously 'blue' as usual, every other airfield in Europe was seriously 'red' and stayed that way for most of February. Not a wheel had turned at Brüggen for several weeks.

Air Clues used to be an exciting read in those days, full of hair-raising incidents and accidents, with the best saved for 'Accident of the Month'. And there certainly never seemed to be a shortage of events for the editor to choose from. Indeed, I had barely 1,000 hours total flying and had already featured in two of them; the first was a catastrophic engine fire swiftly followed by ejection on my pre-solo check in the Gnat, and the second a partial and then total engine failure in a Hunter FGA9. This culminated, after twenty minutes stuttering across an angry, cold North Sea, in a glide (as in 'brick') landing at RAF Leconfield. They don't make engines quite the same these days – thankfully. Nor does one fly high-performance jets around the skies in all weather conditions trusting on compass, stopwatch, steam-driven instruments, a fablon-covered map and dead reckoning. Those were the days – or were they?!

Anyway, I was now at the end of a tour flying Phantom FGR2s in the strike/attack role and awaiting my next posting. The squadron was folding as a Phantom unit at the end of the month before re-appearing equipped with some new Anglo-French trainer called the Cheetah, or Jaguar, or something like that. 14 Squadron already had this new machine, although its introduction seemed less than impressive to us hardened F-4 drivers. The Phantom was a real man's aircraft; mean, muscular and with an ugly sort of beauty. It could carry thousands of pounds of ordnance while toting an array of long-range Sparrow missiles, with pulse-doppler radar to match and a pair of 20,000lb-thrust Spey engines to give the whole package a certain frisson of performance. And in-flight entertainment, of course, through a repeat radar scope in the front cockpit and friendly banter (" ... just where do you think we are ...!?") with your ever-helpful back-seater. All in all an aircraft for men. But as for this new-fangled toy with a couple of sewing machines for engines, a black box for a navigator, and instructions in French, well, that was for the birds. And I suspect that, of the two, the birds would better survive a collision. No, definitely for the more feline members of the flying fraternity – not for 'real' men.

My reverie was disturbed by the boss popping his head into the crew room: "Couldn't just see you for a moment Nigel? I've got a posting for you." Gulp – perhaps it'll be Buccaneers – that's another 'real' aircraft. Fingers crossed.

"You're going to Jaguars."

Jaguars? OK, be positive; fantastic! Brand new single-seat aircraft with inertial nav, head-up display, and a pair of throaty Adours. Unbelievable, I can't wait.

"You're going to hold with 31 Squadron until the autumn before joining a Jaguar conversion course at Lossiemouth and returning to form the nucleus of 20 Squadron here at Brüggen in about fifteen months time."

My initial euphoria was somewhat dented; a long sabbatical from the front line was bad enough, but holding as a 'gopher' with that funny lot in the hangar at the end of the airfield, well I wasn't so sure about that. Anyway I duly took my 17 Squadron badges off and made my way down to 31 (Phantom) to be told that I'd be of more use to 31 (Jaguar) who were in the process of setting up in the new HAS site in the north-west corner of the airfield. I wandered on to find an embryonic unit emerging from a clutter of packing cases amidst the wet paint and pristine concrete of brand-new HASs and PBF, a rather strange environment after the windowed offices and open flightline I was used to.

At this early stage, 31 Jaguar was a unique unit: nine pilots; a quorum of engineers; fifteen brand-new aircraft and a boss who was determined to keep them in the air. Wing Commander Terry Nash had flown Harriers previously. His other pilots were relatively inexperienced, if not in overall flying hours then certainly in role. Both flight commanders were ex air-defence Lightnings; there were four junior pilots straight out of training; the QFI and QWI were direct from the OCU staff but neither had Germany strike/attack role experience. With limited time available for the squadron to achieve combat-ready status, Terry's solution was short, sharp, Harrier-length sorties, extracting the maximum training value from every minute airborne. The aircraft were flown clean (no drop tanks) with four sorties per pilot per day quite routine. As an interested and very envious observer, I could only hope that I'd be lucky enough to get the odd back-seat ride and, soon enough, the opportunity arose – with the new station commander, Group Captain Johnnie (Whisky) Walker. So, best behaviour, then.

It was a still, warm, sunny March day and we were in a fully-laden two-seater. We strapped in and started up; the IN aligned, the moving map lit up. The HUD came into focus – all new toys to me and absolute marvels of modern technology. I was already seriously impressed and couldn't wait to get my hands on the aircraft myself, but that would have to wait several months yet. We taxied out and lined up on the runway. Rotate speed was calculated as 165kts with lift-off at 180. I awaited the Phantom-style surge. The brakes came off and we started to trundle down the runway. We passed 70kts. Clearly the station commander had forgotten to select afterburner – but I was sure he'd remember soon. 100kts – still no afterburner and the runway ahead was disappearing rapidly. I summoned every nerve to prompt him: "Afterburner, Sir?" I squeaked. "Of course. We light them prior to brake release in the Jaguar."

Arrghhh ...! My hands moved promptly to the comforting Martin Baker ejector seat handle in anticipation as the piano keys at the far end of the runway rushed to fill the windscreen. But no, at the last minute the nose raised sharply skywards and we staggered off the end and into the air. My first, of many, Jaguar take-offs.

Once airborne, the aircraft proved a delight. The combination of the ride and the suite of modern nav and weapon-aiming equipment was brilliant. The station commander even let me pole the aircraft around a bit, and talked me through some of the nav/attack system routines, a far cry from stopwatch and compass. He even let me have a couple of goes at landing from the back seat – all a piece of cake it seemed, and leaving me more eager than ever to get my hands on the aircraft properly. Disappointed, though, that it would be more than a year before I would get back to front-line business.

That evening my wife commiserated with me over the long delay before I would start, let alone complete my conversion to type. "Wouldn't it be sensible for you to do the Jaguar conversion here at Brüggen?" she ventured; "it would save so much time and we wouldn't have to be separated for over six months while you do the course at Lossiemouth." (1976 was well before the easyJet era, and travelling to northern Scotland by any means was a considerable trek.) "Absolutely no chance," I replied; "things like that just never happen in the RAF – far too much red tape to allow anything as out of the ordinary as that, however sensible it might appear."

31 Squadron continued its break-neck flying rate. On his last sortie in March, having completed fifty hours of forty-five to fifty-minute sorties during the month, one of the junior pilots flamed out an engine breaking into the circuit, hurriedly relighting it before landing a bit 'shaken and stirred'. The Adour engine had recently been modified to reduce smoke emissions, thus eliminating red-hot carbon in the jet pipe which had, unbeknown, hitherto been acting as an auto-relight. With this carbon eliminated, a problem with 'fuel dipping' was exposed, giving the engine a penchant for flaming out if throttled back too quickly below about 80% RPM. JR's comments on the incident report were in his usual direct style: "If one must handle the Adour like a coal miner, then one shouldn't be surprised ..."

A few days later, Terry Nash called me in. "Nigel, the station commander and I have had an idea which we'd like you to think about. The squadron is seriously short of role-experienced pilots like you and it seems a total waste that you're going to be out of the system for another twelve months. However, we think we have a window of opportunity to convert you here on 31; we've more aircraft than we need at present, and both the QFI and QWI have come straight from the OCU staff. Would you be happy to have a go if we can swing it?"

Happy? Delirious more like! I went away pinching myself. Over the next few weeks the telephone lines between Brüggen, HQ RAFG, the MoD and Lossiemouth buzzed. Germany thought it a good idea but the hierarchy at Lossiemouth were firmly opposed. Typical comments included: "Dangerous precedent"; "flight safety would be compromised"; and "undermines the credibility of the OCU".

Every argument you can think of to stop my in-theatre conversion was trotted out, but eventually, and to my great delight, it was agreed that I, uniquely, could convert to the Jaguar on 31 Squadron at Brüggen. The only provisos were that I should attend the full ground school and initial simulator sorties on the OCU at Lossiemouth; then I should complete the entire OCU flying syllabus at Brüggen. No worries there, then. A few days later I found myself making the long journey by train to the frozen north (it was only May) to complete the ground school and simulator training with a regular course – albeit I was excluded from the course photograph.

With this under my belt I returned to find that the squadron had detached to RAF Laarbruch while the Brüggen runway was resurfaced, but we immediately set to work with my conversion. My memories of the course are of an intense but enjoyable flying phase flown with 'colleagues' rather than 'staff'. It was a hot and humid summer and I can distinctly remember noticing that the approach lights at Laarbruch had a very slight but significant upward slope to them as we staggered off the end of the runway in heavyweight fits. I flew my first sortie with Martin Molloy on 19 May and finished the 'op' phase on 28 July. In just over two months I had completed the full seventy-hour Jaguar conversion course that usually took the best part of five months. More importantly, I was returning to the front line some twelve months before the original plan.

My work-up to combat-ready status was also very short, having mostly been completed during the conversion course, two for the price of one, and I soon became a useful member of the squadron. Within a few months I had a couple of hundred hours flying the Jaguar and, despite any misgivings in some quarters about my in-theatre conversion to type, I seemed to be getting on quite well. I certainly hadn't made any major errors and soon found myself an authorising officer, four-ship leader and deputy flight commander – and yet only eight months earlier I had been a very junior pilot and general dogsbody on an F-4 squadron.

This was just in time for an influx of new pilots in late summer and the squadron's first visit to Decimomannu in Sardinia for APC, an intense three weeks of short sorties on Capo Frasca Range to hone the squadron's weapon delivery skills.

And then to cap it all I was selected to attend No 3 Jaguar QWI course at Lossiemouth in March 1977, less than twelve months after I first flew the aircraft. It was a professionally demanding and rigorous course at the best of times, so I knew I'd be under the spotlight given my unusual introduction to the aircraft.

The syllabus was certainly challenging, but my abiding memory was of reading the necessary books in the 'drying rooms' of the vast, chilly ex-RN officers' mess to stay warm. We all managed to stave off the cold for three months and graduate successfully – and my photograph appeared on the hallowed walls of the Jaguar OCU. Socially acceptable at last!

My tour on 31 Squadron was a marvellous experience, but eventually came to an end. I didn't particularly want to move on; I was enjoying myself too much. But in 1978 my appointer rang up and asked if I'd fancy being the first RAF exchange officer with the Royal Danish Air Force flying Drakens at Karup. Needless to say I wasted no time in packing my bags, and my experiences over the next three years in that lovely country were wonderful. But must presumably be reserved for Draken Boys, should that ever be published!

On my return, I flew Jaguars again, accumulating a further host of stories and memories. But I can't close without returning to the subject of the infamous length of the Jag's take-off roll. Like many contributors to this volume I've made comments about it, but in truth that aspect did become a bit of a tired old cliché around the RAF. Those in search of a cheap joke certainly managed to relate it to the most unlikely factors, as in the observation by an un-named Harrier mate on the extraordinary number of future 'starred' officers and chiefs of air staff (three) the Jaguar Force produced. He asserted that it was not a reflection of the quality of officer on Jaguars, but because: "Jag pilots have plenty of time to study for promotion exams during the take-off roll!"

To put the record straight I have to say that the Jaguar performed much better in the sprightliness stakes than its reputation gave it merit for and, certainly in my experience, better than some other, similar-generation types. And in this I speak not just from Phantom and Draken experience, but also as a Buccaneer pilot. My assertion stems from the following.

My final flying tour was as station commander at RAF Lossiemouth in the mid-1990s. I had in the interim commanded 617 Squadron flying Tornado GR1s, and the focus of attention at Lossiemouth during my time was the phasing out of the Buccaneer, to be replaced by the Tornado. The Jaguar OCU, then commanded by John White, was still on the north side of the airfield, and for eight months there was concurrently the rump of the Buccaneer force (with a handful of Hunters for training) and two Tornado units. I was therefore in the enviable position of being able to keep

It would have been hard to shine on the front row of this QWI course! Back row, left to right: future Air Marshal Sir Dusty Miller; future Air Chief Marshal Lord Jock Stirrup, chief of the defence staff; and future Air Vice-Marshal Nigel Day. In the front, Chris Daymon, Scotty McClean and Martin Selves.

current on all four aircraft types and being able to compare them directly. Without doubt the winner of my slowest and longest-ever take-off roll was not the Jaguar.

I was most likely the last RAF pilot to convert to the Buccaneer and probably, with a total of just over seventy hours, remain the least experienced on type. The aircraft was well loved by its crews but, compared to the more modern aircraft, had a few idiosyncrasies. Cockpit ergonomics in particular were a problem – even by Jaguar standards. On my first high-level transit from Lossiemouth to Decimomannu we were almost entering French airspace before I eventually found the TACAN control box, cunningly located somewhere below and behind my left buttock in the deeper recesses of the ejection-seat well. However, it was the take-off from Deci en route to Gibraltar that remains etched in my memory.

I was encouraged to complete a 'blown' take-off in which some 20% of engine power is diverted over the wings to reduce stall speed. This is highly desirable for steam-catapult carrier operations, but the consequent reduction in forward thrust makes it more than somewhat sluggish down a normal runway. On this occasion, the aircraft was heavyweight, the temperature high and the wind calm. The calculated take-off speed was only 151kts, but it took more than 8,000ft of the 9,000ft runway to reach it. Had my heart not been firmly in my mouth for much of this time, I would not only have had time to study for a promotion exam, but to pass it as well!

Needless to say I turned down the offer of another 'blown' take-off from Gibraltar's 6,000ft runway the next day and, instead, completed a standard, partial-fuel take-off, then refuelled at RAF St Mawgan before pushing on to Lossiemouth.

With my tour at Lossiemouth at an end, my days of flying operational fast jets were over. I had been very fortunate in having flown six types during my operational career: Hunter; Phantom; Jaguar; Draken; Tornado and Buccaneer. Of these the only aircraft on which I had, uniquely, not trained at the recognised OCU was the Jaguar. And yet it was the one on which I completed the most hours and the most tours – and the one on which I elected to fly my last solo sortie as 'pilot-in-command'.

CHAPTER 5

RECCE ROOKIES

The qualifications to be a tactical reconnaissance pilot have altered over the years. When I was a young Hunter pilot it was not normal to be posted to recce until one had a couple of tours under one's belt. Recce aircraft were specialist variants, while the role was a skilled art. One needed to be both experienced and of well-above-average ability to be selected. At least that's what the recce pilots told us.

Nowadays it seems quite different. Podded equipment, capable of digitally down-linking its material to ground stations for immediate exploitation, may currently be mounted on any Tornado GR4, and the need for specialist recce versions of tactical aircraft has receded. Owing to the regularity of operational deployments over the past couple of decades, it has become impractical always to deploy specialist recce crews. So today, every tactical pilot has effectively become a recce pilot.

The Jaguar sat somewhere in the middle of this evolution. Its equipment was podded, so there was no separate recce model. But specialised recce squadrons were still formed, albeit with an important difference: first tourists were posted to the role virtually from the beginning. One of those was 'Ozzie' Osborne, whom I first met and flew with as he came through Brawdy on his Hunter course. Before moving on to a career with the airlines, he spent his entire RAF time flying reconnaissance, largely on Jaguars.

SQUADRON LEADER NOEL OSBORNE (RETD)

The sun was shining high above the clouds just south of the tip of Greenland on that day in May 1990. The flight engineer and I were having our lunch, while in the background the constant drone of the four Rolls-Royce engines continued as the old 747 Jumbo headed towards Vancouver on the first leg of my final line check. Soon I would be qualified and on the first rung of my new career as a junior pilot in British Airways.

Several thousand feet below, coming in the opposite direction, was a formation of Jaguars from a 41(F) Squadron detachment returning from Goose Bay with a VC10 tanker. Little did their leader, Squadron Leader Andy Morris, know that I had been in touch with the squadron and knew their flight times and en-route frequency. I had made a rough calculation of the expected relative positions based on the plan, and it was time to dial up the frequency.

"Andy, how's it going? It's Ozzie here," I said with a big grin on my face.

"My dear chap," was the startled reply; "what on earth are you doing on this frequency?"

There followed much banter about sitting in a white, short-sleeved shirt and having salmon for lunch on a tray, contrasting with the boys in their 'goon suits', pee bags strapped to their legs and a snack box for lunch. The miles stretched out between us, and soon it was time to leave them to continue their journey home and their next refuelling bracket. My captain had indulged me so far but, as the airwaves went quiet, he could contain his curiosity no longer.

"Well, what was all that about Ozzie?" We still had several hours to go, and he seemed genuinely interested.

"How long have we got, Skipper?" And this is the story I told him…

It had been a long hard slog along the way, and I had suffered from air sickness on the Chipmunk and Jet Provost. How bad was that? Well, I once threw up after a briefing on spinning before we even left the building! There were times when I would go to bed and pray for rain in the morning so that I would not have to suffer the next day. However, despite several attempts to chop me, and with a lot of support and encouragement from my instructors, I finally passed the advanced flying course at RAF Valley. I was never the ace of the base, and the posting I got when I left was to the Hunter holding squadron at RAF Wittering where I would, hopefully, hone my skills waiting for a front-line posting.

Before that would be a course at RAF Brawdy's wind-swept tactical weapons unit. While a couple of our number were chopped there, the course went well for me, and one Friday afternoon the boss called several of us into his office. Based on our performance to that date, he told us, there were going to be some changes to our provisional postings. Both I and my new-found wingman, Wyn Evans, were to go to the Jaguar, with our course starting later that year.

And so it was that, in the summer of 1976, Wyn and I took that long road through the Highlands to RAF Lossiemouth, blissfully unaware that we were to be amongst the 'chosen ones'. That first Saturday night the course ahead of us had planned a beach party, and we were duly invited to the barbeque and to witness the 'all-night daylight' at Lossie. It was here that we met many pilots for the first time who were to become our new squadron mates, and we were also let in on the secret that we were destined for one of the two recce squadrons, namely 2(AC) and 41(F). Surprising, for at that time first tourists could not even spell reconnaissance, let alone think about becoming recce pilots. Also present were our potential new bosses Sandy Wilson and John Thomson (both later to become air chief marshals).

One morning early in the course as we sat waiting in the crew room for the bad weather to clear, the OCU boss walked in. Fred Trowern was a man with much presence, and one of the students leapt into action with an offer of "Coffee sir?" "Oh yes please," he replied, "I'll have a black bugger." I leapt to attention and shouted "Yes sir, will I do?" He turned and saw the first black Jaguar pilot. A great smile lit up his face: "So I guess you'll be Osborne?"

Over the next few months we were taught the nuances of flying the Jag on a specially-tailored recce course where we also learnt some of the specialities of our new trade. One such aspect was the line-search, where you follow a route along a road, looking for military equipment. Or, in our case, trucks over a certain size; we would hang on for dear life at the road junctions, with the throttles open wide and reheat more often in than out, just trying not to fall out of the sky. We mastered the techniques of flying angle of attack for landing and manoeuvring, often taught to us by ex-Harrier mates who would never be happy unless you landed with the 'alpha' indication off the scale.

It was November by the time Wyn and I arrived on 41(F) Squadron to join the third first tourist, Bryan Collins (our new partner in crime) who had arrived a couple of months before. The squadron spent the next few months working up and getting ready to take over from the Phantoms at Coningsby in April 1977. We had a wealth of experience on the squadron, including father figures like Ken Rae, who became a great friend and mentor, and our German exchange officer Jack Nebel. Jack always seemed to be the aristocrat, driving his red Porsche; I remember that he had a selection of different cigarette brands with distinctive colours, and whenever he changed brand he would always have a matching cigarette lighter bristling with gold or silver. And of course there was our 'Baggers', the infamous and respected Dave Bagshaw, who was older and wiser than everyone, and who would later become, and remain for a long while, the most experienced Jaguar pilot around.

Whilst the attack boys on 6 and 54 Squadrons were out every day in their formations, we spent much of our time flying as singletons with our huge recce pods strapped on the centre-line station. 'Alone, unarmed and unafraid' was our motto, and one of our rituals was known as 'trip of the day'. This was a daily competition for which a selection of four targets would be chosen; there would be the inevitable plank over a stream (always advertised as a bridge), a difficult line search, often along minor roads on the map with a few junctions or corners to sort the men out from the boys, and two other targets such as power sub-stations or perhaps a storage facility (most likely a shed in the corner of a farmer's field). Everyone available would fly the trip, and after each target we would have to record enough information to be able to write our report. This would often mean a quick sketch and a few notes on your kneepad, or you might choose the high-tech option and switch on your tape recorder to record your thoughts as the world flashed by at 250 feet. Either way you would need to be able to recall the details of the target later, as the reports would be marked.

On landing we would make for the RIC and be shown into the room with the film table, and meet our allocated PI. They could always tell by the look of glee or sheer pain on your face just how well or badly the mission had gone. Soon we were sat at the table with that exam feeling as we delved back into our memories with our chinagraph sketches and smudged notes, trying desperately to describe what we had seen. The film would arrive and we would go through the four oblique cameras and the nose camera with the PI, looking for the 'event marker' which we hoped we had remembered to press as we'd screamed past the target. If we had forgotten, all would not be lost, but it was another point scorer. The main object was of course the photo itself, which had to meet certain aesthetic criteria such as size and position in the frame. For example, bridges had to be parallel to allow you to see the parapets and detail, other targets were not so critical about the direction of the pass, but heaven help you if the target was not perfectly placed one third of the way up the frame on the outer camera which gave the best scale. Anything less and the debrief would not go well.

The line search was the hard one. We needed the start, end and mid points on film, and a picture of any target on the route. These were not always vehicles, but sometimes a target such as a small mast on the roadside, often difficult to see amongst trees. The last part of the route would, more often than not, head down a dirt track hardly visible on the map under the yellow highlighter used during planning. Whilst throwing the aircraft about trying to stay close to the line, in and out of reheat, map in one hand, pen in the other, thumb on the camera switch, and perhaps talking into the tape recorder, there would be no excuses for not coming home with the goods.

At the end of the day all the pilots' efforts would be paraded on the wall in the briefing room. Names were at the top, with pilot reports and photos in rows below. Just like an art exhibition the pilots would examine the exhibits quietly, making mental notes of who had done well or badly that day. It would then be time for the formal debrief by the duty flight commander, who would publicly humiliate anyone who had missed a target or committed the heinous crime of 'falling off' the line search. The best would be rewarded with the 'shining light', and the worst offender would get the 'pig of the day'. It was not your day if 'Tiger Tim' Thorn was debriefing, and on more than one occasion he hurled the pig in my direction suggesting that if I could not navigate properly I should go and fly for one of the attack squadrons. It was of course an unwritten rule that, if you missed a target, you never went around again to get that photo for the debrief; in any case if you had run the cameras on the first pass, it would not be wise.

One Friday we were all sent on our trip-of-the-day mission. It was to Wales at medium level, let down to low level, get the targets and fly low level home. The NAVWASS initially seemed to be working well as I hit Wales and the first target went fine and on time. But the weather was not great and I was dodging rain showers and mist on the hills. I was now needing to update the navigation system every couple of minutes to keep the moving map display with me, but if the system was not having a good day it was not unusual. The next two targets went as planned, although I reckoned they were not the best photos, but hopefully they would be good enough to avoid the 'pig'. Suddenly, coming down a valley, the weather closed in and it was time to climb above cloud. After several minutes on top I found a break to get back down; fuel was just about OK and I still needed to get the last target.

Now my map did not seem to match the countryside around me, and I realised that the PMD had drifted badly. Luckily a prominent feature turned up and I regained my bearings, updated kit, and headed for the last target. It was down a valley and I could see the escape route was in weather, but I resolved to go for it. I got the target, pulled up above the weather, and headed for base. But when I got down to low level again, my moving map appeared to have taken me to the end of the world and thrown me off the edge. I was lost. The route home was congested and I couldn't risk violating any of the restricted areas, or waste any fuel. Discretion being the better part of valour, I dialled up the emergency frequency; announcing myself with a fake call sign I asked for a range and bearing to Wittering. The aim was for them to think I was a Harrier and spare my shame. The rest of the sortie was uneventful and soon I was back in the RIC. Luckily the debrief went OK and I was neither the winner nor the loser that day. So I was happy.

The late Wyn Evans.

But later, in the bar, the boys were letting their hair down after another busy week and recounting their exploits during trip of the day. Wyn sidled up to me: "Come with me Boyo". He took me to one side and told me that he'd been monitoring the emergency frequency and had recognised my voice; I would need to buy him beer for an unspecified time for him to keep my secret. So my deception remained hidden for months until, on another Friday night in the bar, Wyn could contain himself no longer. Out he came with the story of my misdemeanour. Tiger Tim was not happy!

It was ingrained into us that recce pilots could navigate by hand-held maps better than other pilots and that use of the NAVWASS was optional. Indeed 41's combat-ready check trip, which had a chase aircraft assessing you from behind, included navigation 'Hunter' style with a map and stopwatch. To ensure this happened the engineers would remove the bulbs from the PMD so that there wasn't even room to cheat a little. Privately, I thought the whole idea of the latest technology was to help us navigate in an increasingly complex operational environment, but then as a JP, I guess I did not have the 'big picture'! This was recce and, for the time being at least, ours was not to reason why.

There was a fair amount of inbreeding between the two recce squadrons, with many pilots being posted to the sister squadron for their next tour. And there lay my future; after four years on 41(F), including a lengthy extension due to a broken ankle, I was posted to 2(AC) at RAF Laarbruch in Germany.

My wife and I moved into the military quarters at Goch, and it was the day before my planned start date when the phone rang. The squadron adjutant informed me that my presence was required for a beer call in the mess that evening. A new first tourist, John Warnock, had arrived that day and they wanted to get the arrival drinking session over in one go! I had met many of the boys before, but there were still a few new faces; I was happy to be there. Over the years, I thought I had become a seasoned drinker, and that there was nothing they could do to hurt me. But suddenly, out of the blue, came 2(AC) Squadron's speciality, Ratziputz. The barman dutifully concocted the potion behind the bar, and there were many rumours about its contents; some say that it contained lighter fluid. Whatever it was, John and I were 'history' within thirty minutes, and the rest of the evening was a blur. I was later deposited at home in Goch much the worse for wear, with my wife wondering just what she had let herself in for.

Later that night there was a deafening, but familiar noise in the street. The sirens were going off, signalling a station exercise; the phone rang a few minutes later. But I was too far gone to attend or even care, and in any event it was the day before my official start. The next morning I struggled into my uniform and made it to the squadron on time, only to find the doors locked and no one at home. Not to be outdone, I drove to the boss's house and reported for duty on time, only to be told that he was still sleeping – he of course had been up 'til late on exercise. His wife offered me some coffee and toast, and suggested that I slept on the sofa until he awoke later. A good start, I thought, for my second tour, and I knew that not arriving on time would not go have gone down well with my new boss – Tiger Tim.

But I settled in and the time at Laarbruch flew by. On one occasion we took our Jags out to Goose Bay in Canada for ultra-low-level training at 100 feet. Unusually, we staged out via Kinloss, Keflavik, and Sondrestrom, which was a great experience. The first leg was fairly straightforward, then onwards to Reykjavik for a night stop. That evening most of us tried the reindeer steaks as recommended by the natives, which turned out to be the most expensive meal I think I have ever eaten.

The next day found us flying over the mountainous terrain of Greenland, then down the fjord into Sondrestrom for a non-precision approach in cloud. Our boss was by now Frank Hoare, an ex-Red Arrows leader whom we trusted to lead our formation down the correct radial until we were visual. But then what a sight as we ran in for the break into the circuit at 1,500ft: turning onto the downwind leg, the radar altimeter rushed down to around 500ft as we flew over the hard grey rock that surrounds the airfield. Lunch in the USAF canteen was not quite as exciting as the night before (but, thankfully, much more affordable) and then we were off on the last leg to Goose Bay. It was a memorable detachment, not least because we left two of the Jags either in or close to the river after a mid-air collision over the base. Both pilots ejected safely, but it would take a separate chapter to cover that story.

By the time the end of the tour approached I was a QWI, which wasn't bad for a 'recce puke'. So it was time to try to negotiate my next posting. I loved Germany and knew that there was an exchange position coming up with the Luftwaffe, flying the RF-4E recce Phantom at Bremgarten in the Black Forest. After some wrangling with my posting officer (a recce mate, hopefully looking after his own!) and of course the duty warning from the station commander that a move like this would be bad for my career, I finally got the job. After three months' language training, and a fourteen-hour basic conversion onto the Phantom, I left the Jag boys for a spell, but my heart would never be far away.

In late 1986 I found myself back at Lossie on my second Jaguar conversion course. Compared to the RF-4E the Jag was very modern, and in my time away the 'kit' had improved, so it was great to be back. Whilst I did miss the sheer power and brute force of the Phantom, that was now a thing of the past.

Back on 41(F) Squadron as a flight commander, things were very different after six years on the front line in Germany. Pilots were hiding away in rooms working on their commercial licence exams, and life was pretty relaxed. Trip of the day was still in fashion, and the combat-ready check was still a singleton Jag being chased by the supervising aircraft, although we did not have to navigate any longer like a Hunter; at last the new technology was being embraced and used to the full.

Having been a pioneer first-tourist recce pilot I now found myself surrounded by them, and the new generation were a great bunch of guys. During those next few years recce was moving forward, and I would like to think that it was my idea to change the combat-ready check to a two-ship recce sortie, with interceptions by a Jag 'bounce' and a Phantom en route. Often, we would throw in a bomb drop on Holbeach Range as a starter. Trip of the day became less of the norm, with two and four-ship flying appearing regularly on the programme. A new innovation called Recce Attack Interface was formalised, the idea being that, in a fluid environment, it was not always possible for the lonely recce pilot to go in ahead of the attack formations and bring film home for intelligence interpretation. There was a need to develop a system of communicating with an attack force that was only minutes behind, but needing an update for the target position. Passing a new grid reference for the attack pilots to plot at low level was not ideal, so we developed a simple system using a pre-determined target grid reference or 'bullseye', and updated the position quickly using a clock code based on the bullseye, which was overlaid on the target map before departure.

I was an experienced chap on 41, but there was still something to learn. AAR was routine and, having only been introduced briefly to it before heading to Laarbruch, and 2 Squadron not having had the role, my first real experience of this had been with the Luftwaffe. But they had used the American system, with an operator in the tanker tail steering his boom into the fighter's receptacle. All the receiver pilot had to do was maintain formation, so it was relatively easy.

Now I had to master the probe and drogue. One day I was planned to lead a two-ship low-level sortie down to the west country, pick up fuel from a tanker, and then drop back down to low level for the return home. All was going well, and as our fuel got down to 'Bingo' it was time to head for the tanker. As usual, my first-tourist wingman had his probe in the basket within seconds and was soon topped up. Now, getting short of fuel for the return to Coltishall, it was my turn and the pressure was on. On the first attempt the probe hit the basket edge; "Rim, no damage", was my call. I backed off and steadied. Next time, the probe hit the basket at an angle, bits flew off, there was a loud bang, and a huge plume of flame from the back as my right engine blew up. This was not looking good, and the tanker driver was far from pleased. My wingman escorted me to the naval base at Yeovilton with one engine shut down, and said goodbye to me on finals as I got my crippled jet onto terra firma.

Another fine mess, I thought, as I parked the jet and prepared to call the squadron. Very quickly Wyn Evans, now on 54 Squadron, was dispatched in a T-bird to come and get me, and late in the afternoon I arrived back in the squadron. The crew room was almost empty as most pilots had gone home. But I hadn't got away with it totally. I was met by young Andy Cubin, who had taken the trouble to find an old squadron trophy and to dust it down ready for a presentation. It was a wooden phallic with a bronze plaque on the stand which said 'Prick of the Month Award'. He strode boldly over, thrust it towards me and said: "I think this is yours, Sir!" A fair cop, I guess.

It was becoming something of a demon, and for our next Atlantic crossing I offered to lead the advance party to Goose Bay in the transport aircraft. But the boss, Dave Milne-Smith (better known as DMS), was not having any of it; I was to lead a two-ship across the pond. On the appointed day we met the VC10 tanker over the Wash, but unfortunately it had one of its three baskets unserviceable. To make all the maths work for the diversion options, one of the two Jags would need to refuel twice as often to ensure that we always had enough fuel. I invited my wingman Bob Neilson to do the extra tanking, but he respectfully suggested that I needed the practice more than he did. After a few scary moments north of Lossie, and a stiff talking to by the captain of the VC10, I finally got my act together, and am proud to say that I never missed again.

During my years in the recce world, several of the pilots were destined for high places. Sir John Thomson was tipped for the top but unfortunately died in his early fifties. Jock Stirrup always stood out from the rest as someone who was only going in one direction, and he made it to chief of the defence staff. Both Glenn Torpy and Steve Dalton made chief of the air staff. I mentored Steve in his early days, and I used to tell everyone that, in preparing him, I wrote everything that I knew about anything, put it on a postage stamp, and sent it to the wrong address. So I guess I can't take the credit for his success!

As for me, well I was happy just to enjoy life, and take whatever came my way. I was a QWI, managed to escape ever doing a ground tour, and as a squadron leader spent the last year or so as the executive officer on 41(F) Squadron.

In 1989 at the age of thirty-eight, with my civil licence complete and with a loving family, it felt right to move on and take my option to retire. My final trip was leading a four-ship to France for a night stop and, on my return I was expecting a quiet reception. It was not to be; a crane and a fire truck awaited. Soon I found myself dangling six feet in the air, covered in flour in an attempt to turn me white, and being hosed down by the enthusiastic fire crew. Family and friends were there and, guess who: Tiger Tim. And so it was that I went into my new life having been 'alone, unarmed and unafraid' for four consecutive recce tours.

It had been a great life, making many friends, but sadly we lost a few 'mates' along the way. And of those I count the greatest loss as my fellow recce rookie and great buddy, Wyn Evans. He made it to group captain, being awarded an OBE on the way. But sadly, he succumbed to cancer at a horribly early age. To his marvellous wife and family I dedicate this story. A sad note on which to finish.

The 747 droned on. "I hope that gives you an idea of what life was like Skipper, and good to see that I haven't bored you to sleep," I said jokingly, as I reselected a new frequency on the second radio box. "I'll get the latest weather for Vancouver."

CHAPTER 6

TESTING... TESTING...

Test pilots as a breed are usually viewed with suspicion by the front line. As an example, I remember an occasion at Coltishall when a mode of the then-new FIN 1064 nav and weapon-aiming system needed to receive its formal release to service – it was a toss-bombing delivery. Boscombe Down (I think it was) sent their USAF exchange test pilot to do the work. He only had about fifty minutes flying time on the Jaguar but that, to the testing world, was by no means a handicap. It would enable him to be completely objective; test pilots were more or less superhuman anyway, and certainly didn't need the sort of currency that we mortals needed to carry out their work.

Anyway, the chap launched off to the Wash Ranges. An hour-and-a-half later he returned with reams of notes to the effect that the Jag was hopeless as a weapon-aiming platform; 1064 and, in particular its toss-bombing function, was next to unusable.

Well! As 1064 had begun to come into service we at Colt had instantly learned to love it. Compared with the old NAVWASS it was marvellously user-friendly, accurate and reliable, with the new cockpit layout being something we had hitherto only dreamed about. Indeed a few of us had already had a surreptitious preview of the mode in question, dropping a couple of bombs in the proverbial Jaguar bucket. So you can imagine how the TP's verdict was received.

One way and another the mode eventually did get cleared for use, so I've likely been over-exaggerating the incompetence of the gentleman in question. It's a cultural thing; all front-line pilots view the testing world's modus operandi in the same, jaundiced light. So to put the record straight we need to hear from a real test pilot about how it actually was.

It is summer 2010. 'Tagg' Taggart and I are sitting, sipping cool beers, at the poolside bar of an Athens hotel. We are both captains with a regional UK airline which, having been hit by the recession, has wet-leased four of its aircraft to Olympic Air for a year. Both of us have volunteered for this very pleasant secondment, and are thoroughly enjoying spending our flying dotage pottering around the Aegean. We had met only briefly during our respective times in the RAF when Tagg had visited Coltishall from Farnborough. But I now learn a lot more about his testing career, as well as his time on Canberras and, post-RAF, corporate jets. It turns out that we have many mutual friends, and I'm sure we bore the rest of our Athens gang silly with our 'there I was' reminiscences.

But the most interesting of our conversations (at least we think so) concern Jaguars. So we order a couple more glasses of Mythos beer, and Tagg continues…

SQUADRON LEADER ALASTAIR 'TAGG' TAGGART (RETD)

One Friday afternoon on my second Canberra tour I got the message to go to the boss's office right away. The usual fright set in: what the hell had I done? However, the boss was cheery and told me that my posting had come in. Since leaving Germany I had been promised Buccaneers, and the low-level role was appropriate, so my initial fear was replaced by a warm fuzzy feeling. "Jaguars," he said. Hang on; the Jaguar hadn't yet entered service. Fuzzy was replaced by confusion, and then disappointment as he added "… As a ground school and simulator instructor." Hell, castration! The next stop had to be the bar.

I joined the Jaguar project at RAF Lossiemouth in autumn 1973 as a late entry to the JCT, the flight instructors having completed their ground training earlier at the manufacturer's factory at Warton. There was no ground school and no simulator, and the building for these vital training tools had yet to be finished. However, the flight instructors were similarly handicapped because there were no aircraft. So the excitement of the new project was akin to arriving at the ball to find no orchestra, no food and no women!

That the training and simulator complex at Lossie was not complete for the first few Jaguar courses was strongly rumoured not to have been because of tardy construction management, but because the original structural steelwork for the large buildings had been assembled upside-down. Therefore, it had had to be dismantled and then reassembled correctly. But Jaguar simulator training was deemed essential for all training. Therefore for the initial courses students and simulator instructors were dispatched to RAF Wildenrath, where RAF Germany's Jaguar simulator had been completed long before the arrival of the aircraft over there. Incidentally, like pretty well all of Germany's simulators, it was located at the 'wrong' base for the aircraft type. For the next fifteen years, Brüggen and Laarbruch-based Jaguar pilots would travel to Wildenrath for their periodic training, while Phantom crews would make the reverse journey for theirs.

Dispatching Lossie courses to Wildenrath may seem simple but it was a logistical nightmare. Trains between Aberdeen and Inverness did not operate at all over the weekend. So about two dozen pilots had to get to Aberdeen on a Monday to catch the overnight sleeper to London, transfer to another train to Luton and then, finally, catch the Britannia Trooping flight to Wildenrath. Those two days of travelling were followed by an intensive, two-week, 24/7 training regime, before everyone returned to Lossie via the same tortuous route.

The Jaguar was a brand-new aircraft; the folks at Wildenrath were very hospitable and German beer was as good as ever. So this recipe made up for the long and tiring training. Actually, those detachments were very successful, because everyone was able to work and play hard without distraction.

Eventually Lossie's facilities were ready, and from the outset the six-axis full-motion simulator was an essential part of the support for training and operating the Jaguar. Each simulator had three terrain 'models' with computer-controlled cameras traversing them according to the tracks flown by the pilots; their pictures were transmitted to screens in front of the trainee pilots, providing a realistic low-level environment.

When transiting between terrain models the cameras briefly 'flew into cloud' between areas. Intense illumination of these models was essential, which required about 250 one-kilowatt light bulbs to accomplish; this, in turn, also meant that extensive cooling of the models and cameras was required. All in all this probably accounted for a massive part of the station's energy bill.

Everything in the simulator focussed on one objective: pilot training. The whole complex (and expensive) machine had no other purpose. The fidelity of the simulation was excellent. Pilots could criticise various features; for example, while their 'g-pants' did inflate just like the aircraft, there was obviously no 'g'. However, all aspects of flying the Jaguar could be practised; if the pilot ejected the simulator would 'freeze' and survivability discussed with all parameters printed out for debriefing. Furthermore, the simulator session could be videoed and reviewed during debrief. The ability to record reinforced debriefing and avoided pilots making false claims. NAVWASS management in the low-level environment became second nature because of the training provided by the simulator. Some pilots, even experienced ones, were uncomfortable with the HUD, and the simulator was excellent for providing confidence and support in its use. All in all, the simulator was a very powerful tool for initial and recurrent training.

No tale of the ground training set up would be complete without making appreciative mention of the fact that the OCU boss regarded his ground-school staff as just as important as his flight instructors. To give us credibility, he made it policy that ground staff qualified to fly the real aircraft, and that their 'solo' certificates were displayed prominently in the ground school.

That was fine, but not quite the real thing. Before long, though, I got what I wanted, a posting to an operational unit. This was 6 Squadron at Coltishall; a great tour, and I particularly recall an incident from our first Exercise Red Flag. Immediately after our arrival, four Jaguars were scheduled to get airborne for a training and familiarisation sortie. They lined up on the runway and, at the 'nod', all aircraft engaged reheat – situation normal. Almost immediately there were a number of muffled bangs and large amounts of black smoke – situation not normal! It turned out that the USAF was using a slightly different kind of aviation kerosene which the Adour engine did not like. Clearly we could not change the fuel, so on return to the ramp our Rolls-Royce representative got to work and tweaked the engines; all was fine for the time being.

Back at home a longer-term solution was being sought. Meanwhile we got on with the important stuff, which naturally included 'flying the flag'. To assist with this we had planned to entertain our hosts with a party some days later and, to this end, a C-130 Hercules was due to arrive with a consignment of authentic cheese and wine. But when the tailgate was lowered, horror! No cheese or wine but a lot of modified engines for our Jaguars. The supply system had worked magnificently but not in a way that our aggressive combat pilots had wanted. The party reverted to plan B, which featured local cheese and wine.

The engine episode, together with a number of other foibles of the aircraft, intrigued me greatly, to the extent that I developed a wish to enter the world of development and test flying – and at the end of my 6 Squadron tour I was lucky enough to be selected for test pilot training. Before going on to tell about that, though, it's worth describing in detail some of the Jaguar's peculiarities.

It was a fascinating aircraft because of its provenance and characteristics. In the mid 1960s the UK had identified a requirement for a Folland Gnat replacement. This new trainer, like the Gnat, was to be tandem-seat and transonic. Meanwhile France had identified a similar training need, and the French company, Breguet had completed an early design for its Breguet 121. Both countries were also looking for a limited number of light attack aircraft. Political imperatives now intervened, and the UK and France agreed on a joint venture. For this project a UK-French company, SEPECAT, was formed.

Now the mechanism was in place to agree and design the final article. The nice fat wing of the Breguet 121 was super for students practising circuits and landings but useless for the transonic regime. So the wing had to be much thinner – but this would result in unacceptably high approach and landing speeds. To mitigate this the final design incorporated full-span double-slotted flaps together with full-span leading edge slats. Full-span flaps meant no room for ailerons, so lateral control would have to be accomplished with spoilers. However at increasing angles of attack, such as during landing approaches, spoilers became increasingly ineffective, so roll control would have to be supplemented by a novel, differential, all-moving tailplane.

The initial simple design was becoming a mite more complicated. But there was more. At high speed the differential tailplane would produce unacceptable loads on the empennage and, worse, a similar problem arose with the rudder. So the design incorporated a gradual phasing out of the differential tailplane as speed increased such that there was zero differential above about 400 knots IAS. The rudder problem was simpler; a high authority rudder was available with the gear down and lower authority with the gear retracted.

Then there were the avionics. Here there was no entente cordiale and the UK proceeded to fit an inertial navigation system. The good news was that it included a HUD. The bad news – it was cheap and unreliable.

So the new Anglo-French 'trainer' now had two engines, an empty weight of about 7.5 tonnes, and fairly sophisticated and complicated avionics. Meanwhile, economics and politics were affecting other projects. The UK's TSR2 development had come and gone, closely followed by the RAF's F-111 order. The Phantom was coming as an interim strike/attack aircraft, but with a plan to be moved to air defence duties after five or so years. The Anglo-French Variable Geometry project had been still-born, while the collaborative Tornado was at an early stage. And the Jaguar was now recognised as being too expensive and complex for its intended use as an advanced trainer; the new Hawk would fill that role. So eventually the RAF's Jaguar requirement was altered from 150 two-seaters to a full-blown attack fleet of 165 single-seat aircraft and thirty-five two-seaters.

With most combat single-seaters, the two-seat trainer variant follows later as a compromise design. With the Jaguar, though, the reverse had happened; the two-seat version was the primary design and the single-seater the derivative. That was fine, but to be a bomber it would have to carry its own weight in fuel and stores. Clearly, though, loading it up made its original, sprightly performance (take-off and climb to 30,000ft in about three minutes) much more laboured. One could also say that its supersonic capability was now completely superfluous in the bomber role. On the other hand the Adour engine, also a joint project, was much lighter than an unreheated Avon but with similar maximum thrust. It provided excellent low-level flight cruise SFC.

Much of these seemingly ad-hoc revisions of operational requirements go to explain why the Jag was viewed, at least initially, with such a jaundiced eye by those who didn't know it.

With any large project employing new and refined technology, it would be near impossible to introduce it to service without encountering unforeseen problems. Furthermore, due to development and flight test schedules where problems are identified with insufficient time and resources to provide the necessary fix, it becomes necessary to bring the aircraft in with deficiencies. This sometimes places temporary limitations on the use of the product, and such was the case with the Jaguar. Most were forgotten once modification action was taken, but here are a few.

Some time into the flight test phase it was determined that if the pilot applied simultaneous full aft and lateral stick – possibly needed for a cross-wind take-off or landing – his thigh or groin could interfere with the applied controls, as written earlier. Naturally, this was influenced by the size of the pilot's thighs (or groin!); however, it was decided to modify the fleet with a control column lengthened by about 5cm. For a while there was a mixed fleet of long and short sticks. At the time, apart from ribald comments, there were pilots who had strong preferences both for and against a long stick.

The first Jaguars delivered did not have the guns fitted, and indeed, it would be some years and extensive modifications before guns could be fired. When eventually approved for use, it was found that, during the 5g pullout required for air-to-ground strafing, the aircraft rolled without pilot input. Eventually, after extensive measuring and testing, it was found that during the pullout the fuselage was bending and effectively becoming 'banana' shaped. However, the flight control rods positioned along the upper spine of the aircraft did not bend. This was possibly a consequence of the mixture of innovative materials which went into the various sections of the Jaguar – some of the skin sections were constructed of an aluminium sandwich. Anyway, the overall effect was to produce a rudder input without rudder pedal movement. The fix was to apply sensors to the aircraft to measure the bending of the fuselage and, through the rudder auto-stabiliser, provide an equal and opposite input to the rudder. It worked.

The original Adour was a small, rugged engine with a dated mechanical fuel metering system. An undesirable feature was that fuel was not burnt efficiently, and this resulted in carbon deposits building up in the combustion chamber. After a few seconds the carbon build-up was blasted out through the turbines to atmosphere producing puffs of black smoke. Whilst the black smoke was bad news tactically, it had the even worse effect of causing premature turbine ablation. The fix was to re-design the combustion liner to provide more air for more efficient combustion. The result was to produce more black smoke but, even worse, during rapid throttle retardation the engine flamed-out. It turned out that the engine had always flamed-out with rapid throttle retardation – but this had previously been masked because of the afore-mentioned globs of white-hot carbon relighting it almost immediately. The further fix was to modify the somewhat dated fuel metering system.

Something for which there was no fix was the aircraft's propensity to depart from controlled flight when the angle-of-attack limits were exceeded; it was simply a characteristic of the design. Spinning the Jaguar was prohibited, largely because it was unlikely to recover. Incidentally, I had investigated this area in the simulator, which would spin if provoked. True to predictions, it rarely recovered.

So here was I, keen to find out more about what makes an aircraft fly and a system work – and I was off to test pilot school. Not just any test pilot school mind you, but as an exchange student to the USN school at Patuxent River, USA. A year later, after flying all sorts of exotic and exciting birds, I graduated and was posted to RAE Farnborough as an experimental test pilot. Once there I also qualified on rotary wing.

There was much going on in the test and development world. Avoiding enemy attack while on the ground was a hot topic at the time, with the Swedish developing the concept of road operations and the RAF Harrier Force going the whole hog and taking to the woods. Jaguars had, on occasions, exercised on sections of German autobahns, and it had always been recognised that the aircraft's big, squashy undercarriage and low tyre pressures could possibly permit grass operations. Indeed during my time on 6 Squadron we had occasionally taxied on the grass at Coltishall. One of my TP colleagues, Chris Yeo, actually trialled grass take-offs and landings from Brüggen (avoiding the flock of sheep which routinely grazed the airfield to keep the grass under control!). But, even though the concept of operating the Jag from rough fields seemed feasible, for one reason or another it was not pursued.

But by far the most active testing area for me was that related to night and poor weather ops. After all, a Soviet attack was hardly likely to be limited to nice days. Thus far I had spent most of my flying time at low level, indeed sometimes employing ultra-low flying techniques, to use the terrain to reduce chances of detection and engagement. However, low flying was a visual activity, and therefore limited to day, clear-weather ops. While terrain-following radar did allow automatic low flying at night, such flight was essentially 'over' rather than 'through' the terrain. Terrain-following radar was very expensive, radar emissions forewarned the opposition of the bomber's approach, and TFR would never facilitate landings in poor conditions.

When I arrived at Farnborough, solutions were being sought. Helicopters were by then routinely using night-vision goggles for low flying. Another exciting development was experimentation into the use of low-light television in flight. LLTV uses the visual spectrum and is therefore an 'image intensifier', so some ambient light must be available. The size and shape of these bulky devices initially favoured use in helicopters, but re-packaging technology and miniaturisation resulted in podded devices, making use in fast-jet aircraft technically feasible.

Soon I flew an experimental Jaguar fitted with a LLTV camera mounted in a pod on the centre-line pylon, which provided an image to a wide-angle raster-scan HUD. However, because the nose gear obstructed the camera with the gear down, using LLTV during landing and taxiing was a problem. Also, when turning in flight, the camera 'swung out' in the direction opposite to the bank, so it was impossible to see 'into' the turn. Additionally, because an aircraft effectively 'pitches' while turning, the fuselage also obscured the required 'upward' view into the turn. Flying down a wiggly valley in the dark could be very exciting! Nonetheless, at least the possibility of using EO sensors to fly low at night was proven to be viable.

The next stage was to investigate the use of forward-looking infra red in place of LLTV. Rather than using the visual spectrum, FLIR produces an image entirely due to thermal variations in the terrain; no light is required. The first FLIR was fitted to a two-seat Hunter fitted with an IN and raster-scan HUD. The detector was fitted in the aircraft nose, giving an unobstructed view of the scene while taxiing and during approach and landing.

For technical and budget reasons, that Hunter was only fitted with one HUD. So the 'safety pilot' seated beside the evaluation pilot flying at night and at low level had no view of the scene; this was not only terrifying, but also meant he couldn't do his job. Some test pilots at RAE were both fixed and rotary-wing qualified, so the local solution was for the safety pilot to use his rotary wing helmet and NVGs so that the level of terror could be managed. And pretty soon it became clear that the safety pilot, using night-vision goggles, could obtain more data from the terrain than the evaluation pilot simply by moving his head left and right – something the FLIR could not do. Most importantly, using goggles the pilot could look and see into a turn.

There was a potential problem. The forces on the pilot's body during ejection are extreme and, by design, just tolerable. What would happen if a pilot ejected with NVGs attached to his head? The 'binoculars' would probably have generated considerable lift when suddenly ejected into a high-speed airflow, with the possibility of neck injury. Moreover, when released during ejection the 'lightweight' NVGs would probably break up, becoming two missiles about the size of 30mm shells. The solution initially was to accept the risk because, with an immediate ejection during take-off or landing, the forces would be low with minimal risk of injury, while at high speed there would likely be time to tear the NVGs off before going for the ejection handle. The Institute of Aviation Medicine devoted much effort to addressing and eventually solving this issue.

On finals to land on the autobahn, occasionally practised in Germany.

Because NVGs were image intensifiers, they unfortunately also did a brilliant job of amplifying every source of light in the cockpit. But by use of simple but elegant filters the 'boffins' began to create a cockpit environment where the NVGs worked well. By now we were low flying in the deep valleys in Wales at night using visual techniques. With FLIR and NVGs, both images were available to the pilots, and the way forward was becoming clear – both literally and figuratively. Moreover, we had discovered that it was possible for the FLIR to 'see' through mist and fog which the NVGs could not. We were increasingly referring to the complementary nature of the EO sensors we were using. Using two separate and distinct devices, pilots were able to fuse the data and use it to maximum effect. By now it was also becoming evident that we, the British, were the only people undertaking this work. We were making excellent progress, and interest was developing at home and abroad.

So what of the Jaguar? At the time it was not found technically possible to fit FLIR – even a podded version – and no affordable capability argument could be made for such a sophisticated upgrade. At that stage there was no clearance or 'release to service' to allow extensive and coordinated squadron use of NVGs. However, the use of NVGs was actively promoted and coordinated with the RAF through its own Central Trials and Tactics Organisation.

As experimental test pilots we did not require an RAF release to service because the RAE provided its own clearances. Also, there were no rules or, for that matter, advice of any sort from any quarter because we were the only people on the planet doing this kind of activity, so, in the true spirit of flight testing, we had to 'make it up as we went along'. Which we did – very carefully.

Although most of our experimental flying using EO sensors was done using the Hunter T7, we did need to ensure we were pursuing the right operational application and therefore, whenever possible, we used Jaguar as well. We were able to demonstrate that NVGs alone provided an astonishing tactical capability to fly low level at night. This would mean that the protection afforded by low flying during daytime could now be extended into night-time.

So the wheel was coming full circle. In WWII the RAF resorted to night bombing to minimise bomber losses. The Dambusters bombed from 60ft, while Lysanders flew into enemy territory, landing and taking off at night without any special equipment (albeit requiring some ambient light). In the 1950s low flying was introduced to the RAF to mitigate possible losses due to the development of sophisticated enemy radar and air defence systems. But fast-forward to the early 1980s and we were returning to night ops, this time using EO sensors. We had demonstrated the possibility of flying 'through' the terrain and around obstructions in high performance air systems. It would now be up to the RAF to fully exploit this development. Eventually the Jaguar would gain a significant NVG capability, while our FLIR-NVG combination would form the basis for the Tornado GR4 upgrade.

To pull together neatly my simulator and testing experience, I note that in the current F-35 Lightning II project, every aspect of even the test programme is preceded by high-fidelity simulation. We've come a long way.

And of course the old Jaguar was extensively modified with other, improved avionics and engines. I have become unfamiliar with these new and excellent systems, and while the aircraft is an old friend it is now also a stranger. But when I review my association with this magnificent aircraft I am still amazed at how the two-seat Gnat trainer replacement morphed into an exceptional front-line nuclear strike and attack aircraft.

Many things have been said to the Jaguar's detriment. Invariably those who gainsay it haven't flown the aircraft. Some of the things said were true, but the certainty is that its pilots fully exploited its capabilities and made up for any and all of its shortcomings. It is this combination of aircraft and pilot that should be judged and not the aircraft alone. Naturally, the Jaguar Boys were the best!

'Ready for another Mythos, Ian?'

CHAPTER 7

THE FROZEN NORTH

The Coltishall squadrons were originally assigned to NATO with plans for their deployment to the northern flank in time of crisis. The two attack squadrons, 6 and 54, would move to Denmark, with operations in the Baltic area in mind, as well as over adjacent land masses. The assigned base Tirstrup, which was situated on the north-eastern edge of the Jutland peninsula, was generally kept empty in peacetime, but was fully-equipped operationally.

The two squadrons would deploy there a couple of times a year on exercise – camping. As well as overland attack sorties, the tasked flying commonly involved practice anti-shipping missions over the Baltic and its approaches. The real enemy would often be encountered – in the shape of combat vessels of the Soviet fleet. In fact a memory of those sorties which remains with me is the prickly feeling on the back of the neck when the RWR lit up – the radar characteristics indicating a potentially hostile ship which was not, as yet, visible in the prevailing hazy conditions.

Those deployments were, on occasions, expanded into full-scale deployed Tacevals. Then, with tented living overlayed by air raids, airfield attacks, intruders and gas masks, the task became considerably more demanding. Another abiding memory of Tirstrup also sticks in the mind – the seemingly constant, raw wind off the Kattegat. But the dominant recollection is that we would always return home with the feeling that we'd had a good time and that it had been a job well done. The Coltishall attack squadrons were undoubtedly, in those days, extremely professional outfits.

The recce squadron, 41, was slated to deploy much further north, with its assigned base lying not far from Tromsø. David Milne-Smith (universally known as DMS), with whom I share the memories of having had a Norwegian exchange tour, now tells his Arctic Jaguar tale.

GROUP CAPTAIN DAVID MILNE-SMITH (RETD)

In late 1986, with three months to go to the end of my year at the Royal Australian Staff College in Canberra, I was contacted by the air attaché and informed that I was to be posted to command 617 Tornado Squadron. My first reaction was: "why not a Jaguar squadron?" But he really did not understand and anyway, the posting was not for negotiation. I finally managed to get a suitable window to speak to my posting officer who asked me to confirm that I would accept a command tour in my new rank of wing commander, before running through the outline that he had prepared for me: leave Australia in early December after graduation; commence Hawk refresher training at RAF Brawdy and, some seven or eight months later, take up my command. In order to minimise family disruption during training I was told that I would be given a quarter at RAF Marham as soon as we were back in the UK. I tried to wriggle out of the Hawk refresher but that was not an option – after only just over eighteen months on the ground, it was apparently deemed essential.

With a posting in the bag and surrounded by Aussies and other internationals who thought it was just the greatest, we began to plan our return to the UK. I chose the 'privately arranged passage' route via Hawaii, Vancouver, Toronto and Montreal, spending Christmas with good Jaguar friends serving on exchange at Myrtle Beach, South Carolina. The deal was that we had to pay our way for the entire trip, being later reimbursed up to the cost of the MoD routing home via Hong Kong.

A few days after Christmas I called the families officer at Marham to see how my MQ application was going, and he informed me that my posting had been cancelled; he knew no more. I managed to raise the air attaché in Washington over the Christmas holiday, another Jaguar man, to be told that I was now planned to command 41(F) Squadron, with a takeover date of 22 March 1987. This basically meant that I had to get back to the UK immediately for a Jag course – and where had I been anyway? "What about my Hawk refresher, which was so essential only a few months before?" I asked. "No time for that, your short Jaguar course started yesterday at RAF Lossiemouth, you simply have to get there asap!"

Suffice it to say that a military flight from Washington did not materialise due to VC10 unserviceabilities, and the family of five of us flew commercial to the UK, arriving somewhat out of pocket. The change was caused by an early posting of OC 2 Squadron at RAF Laarbruch, and the previous OC 41(F) designate being moved to fill the gap in Germany. At any rate it left me with the Jaguar command at Coltishall that I had dreamed of.

Needless to say the short Jaguar refresher was just that, and I spent most of the time trying to get information on this incestuous recce world that I was now about to join. Great attention followed to recce slides, 1:50,000 map-work and line searches, but Lossiemouth had no recce pods for its Jaguars, so flying with the 600kg monster on the centre line would have to wait.

The Jaguar always had a problem with its B over A ratio – big body, little wings – which imposed significant restrictions when carrying centre-line stores. It also had massive control authority in the tailerons, so was easy to over-pitch. With any centre-line store fitted, the alpha limit was low, but straight line and at low level the aircraft was as much fun as ever it had been. Certainly the FIN 1064 inertial navigator was a great improvement on the NAVWASS I had previously known, the former having the computing power of today's child's battery-operated toy under the Christmas tree.

Before I could blink I was at Coltishall and in the chair. My first task was to understand recce, which had always been portrayed as a job one could not do if one had not done it before – like overseas tours and instructing! I well remember the recce flight on my first Hunter squadron in Bahrain. They oft pretended to be in some black world, only fit for super heroes. We always suspected that, in reality, they simply had great fun capturing images of oil drums in the desert and competing for images of the largest drum – equalling, of course, the lowest pass.

Once in control of the primary role I began to think about other aspects. Currency in all the conventional weapons events, night and instrument flying, and AAR kept us busy at home, and what a home it was. Seen from RAF Germany, where strike and attack came together, the Coltishall squadrons were always considered not really to be at the sharp end. In reality, Coltishall had to have been one of the most rewarding stations ever to have served on – three very competitive fighter squadrons flying one of the most enjoyable aircraft in the RAF inventory, in roles that were simply exhilarating. Moreover, with no QRA commitment. Located close to the Wash Ranges and the North Sea tanker tow lines, with the only three AAR-qualified Jaguar squadrons and declared to NATO's Allied Command Europe Mobile Force (Air) – what could be better?

The Cold War task of those remaining after we deployed was to prepare for and receive trans-Atlantic reinforcements. The entire station community was hugely supportive of both roles, and acted as one professional organisation with a common cause. Station social life was superb because of it.

Never a week went by without the Jaguars being detached somewhere in Europe or beyond. AAR to the USA and the eastern Mediterranean, blundering through French airspace having chosen one of the two options of operational air traffic or general air traffic – and usually regretting the decision on the first call to a French radar station. Games of deliberate confusion were played by French ATC; I well remember filing a flight plan to Bordeaux, including all the detail of equipment carried on RAF Jaguars, only to be directed to the VOR beacon – a capability which we did not have. On a gin-clear day, and having requested a visual approach, one simply found the beacon on the inertial driven cockpit map or from a TACAN offset and reported when there.

AAR with the Jaguar was something of a black art, about which tomes could be written. The tanker community had significant footage of Jaguars getting into difficulties during their aerial jousting matches – baskets destroyed, hoses ripped out of their drums and all manner of extremely unsteady approaches to receive fuel. There is little doubt that flight refuelling with the Jaguar was challenging at times. The probe extended into the airflow upwind of the starboard intake, so that the engine had to be set at 90% RPM and left there to prevent it stalling due to ingestion of turbulent air. Controlling fore and aft aircraft movement was accomplished with the left engine only.

The stage was then set for a great contest, and we loved the challenge. The

Top: The Jag's spiritual home. 54 Squadron GR1 over northern Scotland.
Above: Jeff Morgan and Wing Commander Terry Carlton take delivery at
RAF Warton of the fiftieth production Jaguar.

Top: View from the Penthouse suite. Jaguar ops as reported for the top-shelf readers. (Reproduced with permission of Helen Setright.)
Below: Brüggen on a misty night. (Helen Setright)

Opposite top: High over the North Sea. (Helen Setright)
Opposite below: Still a long way to go. Eastbound with a Victor tanker over Greenland on an Atlantic crossing.

Top: 20 Squadron over Neuschwanstein castle, Bavaria.
Below: A relatively rare shot of Jaguars refuelling from a Vulcan. In fact this was the last Vulcan operational sortie, 21 March 1984, and the air officer commanding No 1 Group was at the tanker's controls.

Opposite top: Queuing up for the Victor Tanker. The nearer GR1 is in 41 Squadron's 'winter' camouflage scheme, applied temporarily for exercises in North Norway. The more distant Jag is either wearing a variation or it's only half painted.
Opposite below: A Jag over the Wash Ranges.

Opposite top: Bardufoss in the summer, with the mountains guarding the approach to the easterly runway.

Opposite below: A GR1 in hybrid markings – 'desert pink' but with the badge of training unit 226 OCU on the intake and fin.

Left: 16 Squadron's 'Saints' paint job.

Below: T2 of 16 Squadron on final approach to land. The excellent field of view enjoyed by the instructor is clearly apparent. The Lumsden tartan on the fin complements 16's 'Saint'.

Top left & middle left:
Aircraft of 3 Squadron of the
11th Wing at Toul. Aircraft
A160, 11-RT, bears a red
patch on the fin denoting
SPA 69 'The Cat' 1992-96.
The green patch on the fin
of aircraft A153, 11-RA is of
SPA 88 'The Snake'. French
air force single-seat Jaguars
were readily distinguishable
from their British
counterparts. Different
laser ranging and RWR
equipments meant that they
lacked the characteristic
chisel nose and RWR fairing
on the fin. FAF Jaguars
were, as a rule, painted in
dark green/grey camouflage
although these ones are in
Gulf War 1 colour scheme.
Below: 54 Squadron's
'Foxtrot Charlie' taxies past
6 Squadron's hangar at
Coltishall.

greater the need for fuel, the greater the tension. Taking a few kilograms over the North Sea and almost in sight of land was entirely different from a refuelling bracket over the Atlantic, equidistant from Iceland and Greenland.

41's primary war assignment was to RNoAF Bardufoss, some ninety miles inside the Arctic Circle, to provide recce and attack support in defence of Norway against an anticipated push from the Kola Peninsula. This was the home of the feared Soviet Northern Fleet, and also the base for the expected overland thrust across the frozen lands of Norway or one of her neighbours. Bardufoss was one of those magical places that I was lucky enough to have operated from during a three-year exchange with the Norwegians in the late 1970s. The east-west runway is an 8,000ft sheet of packed ice from November to April – the Norwegians have more words to describe winter weather than we have for weather, full-stop, and they all imply treacherous conditions!

The airfield is situated in a valley with a steeper-than-normal approach from the west, requiring a high downwind leg. Steep-sided valleys surrounded it, and the Swedish border lay but a few miles to the east of the airfield. For instrument approaches, the TACAN inbound turn was also very close to the international boundary and flown on atmospheric pressure (QNH), introducing a 250ft difference between altimeter reading and height above the airfield. Bardufoss also lies close to longitude 18 degrees east, and non-Norwegians (when not on exchange tours) were restricted to 24 degrees east.

When not on exercise, low-level tours to places such as Kautokeino and Hammerfest took one very close to the permitted boundaries, and I am sure they were inadvertently crossed on many occasions. Luckily for us, Norwegian radar coverage in that part of the world was pretty patchy. As far as I know the Swedes never seemed to complain either; perhaps they couldn't see us in the mountainous terrain, or maybe they were concentrating on looking east.

On annual winter deployments we would take our full complement of aircraft, officers and ground crew, as well as the RIC. This unit had all the specialist equipment in fixed and deployable wagons as well as the experts who could make sense of the images that we attempted to capture both on film and the IR linescan system. The PIs were very skilful and painstaking in their work, but if you missed they told you so – as I found out.

Landing at Bardufoss for the first time could be something of a challenge; even in fine weather, the snow-covered landscape around the airfield and the ice-encrusted runway concentrated the mind somewhat. With alternate fuel in hand, external tanks and the recce pod, touching down this ten-ton beast had to be in just the right spot. There was the chute to be streamed and, if necessary, jettisoned with any hint of sideways movement. Then it was eyes on the distance-to-go markers, and left hand ready for the hook. Luckily, the Jaguar was always a pretty steady beast on its feet, thanks to the 'designed-for-carriers' undercarriage. But even a moment's relaxation in jettisoning the chute after vacating the runway could easily cause an inadvertent 180° spin or departure from the taxiway into a snow drift.

Before being permitted to operate in Norway, there was a ritualistic 'special hazards' briefing which pointed out the proximity to Sweden, the many poorly-marked power lines strung across fjords, numerous mink farms sensitive to the sound of freedom (jet noise!), and the dangers of white-out and flying over an Arctic landscape. All too often I remember coasting into one of the numerous fjords and hoping that drift of the inertial system, erroneous position updates, Schuler's Loop or map stretch had not lured me into the valley with the cables. There are numerous tales of aircraft strung up in Norwegian power lines, one of those being an RAF Buccaneer that had a lucky escape. I believe that even this book's author has inadvertently flown under a Norwegian span.

Bardufoss was a POW camp during WWII, and the Norwegian prisoners were put to work on greatly expanding the airfield and in digging out a massive hangar into a mountain adjacent to the pan – the rock hangar. This made it the perfect choice for a military airfield and an RAF deployment base – very remote, pretty basic in terms of infrastructure, and unlikely to annoy the locals with noise. We used the rock hangar to store all ground equipment, and the RIC cabins operated within. Aircraft ops inside the rock hangar would have been a serious health hazard due to CO_2 poisoning, and we therefore used the HAS complex for turn-rounds and overnight storage. These were built courtesy of NATO infrastructure funding, something Norway was very skilful at obtaining.

Socialising with the RN helicopter detachment, there to support Royal Marine Arctic training throughout the year, was about the only option on base, but trading duty-free for almost anything was also a pastime. It was something we were used to from Deci detachments, where cartons of cigarettes had to be offered to get the bowsers to come to your squadron line between waves, or you would be at the back of the queue and risk missing your range slot. A form of prohibition in Norway leads to all manner of problems, particularly over the long northern winter months, when alcohol is the antidote to seasonal affective disorder (or winter blues).

That said north Norway was the most wonderful environment for flying, and low flying in particular. The weather was often excellent late in the springtime for the smaller detachments, with stunning visibility never seen in Britain, not even north of the Moray Firth. Mountains over thirty miles away appeared to be only a few miles distant, and the very dry cold was always invigorating. One of the few recreational activities available to us was cross-country skiing, but more often than not we tried downhill on Norwegian white, military, cross-country skis. I will never forget the sight of our troops dressed in working overalls trying to manage these 'NATO planks' strapped loosely to RAF boots.

The major deployments for NATO exercises and Tacevals were something else. To remain in sympathy with our camping colleagues from 6 and 54 Squadrons, we took over a large campsite – for some inexplicable reason free from holidaymakers in the winter. Its wooden cabins were much more comfortable than the Danish mud encampment, and other facilities for social life were also much better. But it was still a twenty-five-minute drive on icy roads from the airfield. Accidents on the road to and from Bardufoss were common, as most squadron members were simply not used to driving military vehicles in those conditions. For complex logistical and practical reasons, the camp was deemed to be 'out of exercise', but as was always the case, days on base were long and time at the camp-site short; it was simply somewhere to get one's head down for a few hours.

Local fish, goat's cheese and the like were considered a diet too bizarre for the British digestion, so all food was prepared by our UK deployable field kitchen team, the mobile catering support unit. They performed wonders in extremely arduous conditions, with rows of Hydra Burner-like devices – less of a stove, more of a flame thrower!

Days were arduous, and the winter weather took its toll on men and machines. From within the warmth of the protected briefing facility (PBF), all the pre and post-flight business took place in the usual cramped surroundings, but the weather outside was always worth keeping a keen eye on as, in the PBF, one could become somewhat isolated from the outside world. For work-up and Taceval, keeping the real world and the exercise world in the correct balance was certainly made more challenging when deployed to Bardufoss.

NBC and extra Arctic clothing, immersion suits, and all the other creature comforts were *de rigueur*, and all added to the general exhaustion felt by everyone. Once missions walked out of the PBF to be driven to the HAS, life suddenly became very difficult indeed. With the extremely dry cold and slippery conditions, the flying boot was like an ice skate with no directional stability. From the HAS (essentially a large, concrete deep freeze), nudging out into the winter world strapped to one's thirteen-ton sled did focus the mind more than somewhat, and taxiing was undertaken very carefully indeed all the way to the threshold – very often in blowing snow, which was quite different from when it just snowed.

Once pointing down the runway, all became relatively calm again, but formation take-offs were the exception rather than the rule due to the chunks of ice flying off the runway, not to mention the fine surge limits on the Jaguar engines in extremely cold conditions. One did become used to the occasional loud bang as the reheat was engaged, but the engines soon settled down with a bit of forward speed.

Jaguar operators will all remember the cockpit conditioning system, a major weakness as it had to be 'off' for take-off because of its thrust-sapping qualities. And yet demisting was required on icy windshields. So immediately after take-off, we turned the conditioning system to maximum heat, and much scraping of the inside of the windscreen and rubbing of the HUD glass in an attempt to see out was quite normal. Only when the inside temperature was really cooking could the temperature of the cockpit be adjusted downwards.

Missions in that part of the world were very special indeed as one attempted to find camouflaged targets in the winter landscape – snow camouflage was much more effective than anywhere else in the world, as the colours really were only white and dark.

All too soon it was time to return to Bardufoss, recce or attack mission complete. Into the parking bay in front of the designated HAS for engine shutdown, where the recce pod was raided by the ground crew and wires attached to the main gear for the pull back into the sanctuary of the HAS. There was little point in asking returning pilots what the weather was like since, on many occasions, it really wasn't relevant for more than a few minutes. One simply had to trust the aircrew that the conditions were within their capability when they taxied out for take-off.

Outside the major exercises, all manner of exciting aerial pursuits were undertaken from Bardufoss including live weapons training on a range close to the Swedish border, work with special forces, FAC training and work with and against other NATO forces deployed elsewhere in the north. Also spot landing competitions on the easterly runway with the steep approach – the touchdown zone being just opposite the peacetime crew-room window.

There were many opportunities to seek out Soviet naval units in the Norwegian Sea, if only to prove that NATO knew where they were. These vessels, with class names such as Kashin, Kara, Sovremenny and Kresta were oft photographed on training flights. With their distinctive dark grey colour and red decks, they often served as simulated targets for us as they monitored traffic in the Norwegian Sea and on all NATO exercises. These vessels often 'stood to' their crews and tracked passing aircraft with their defensive weapons and radars.

They were regularly accompanied by Soviet fighters, who showed various levels of aggression. We had very vivid memories of this as, in 1987, an Su-27 flew so close to a RNoAF P-3 Orion aircraft that he struck an outer engine, damaging both aircraft significantly. I bet the Soviet pilot had an interesting return journey to his Kola Peninsula Air Base – he certainly would have had time to sort out his story!

Small detachments to Norway were given great freedom and responsibility, but that was not unusual within the Jaguar Force. Jag pilots who have experienced operations in these northern climes will all have their own special memories from their experiences and, I have no doubt, many 'I learnt about flying from that' moments to treasure.

CHAPTER 8

TRAINING THE JAG PILOTS

John White and I joined our first front-line squadron, flying Hunters with 208, within a couple of months of each other. Later we served together on 234 Squadron, again on Hunters, and followed that by moving together to 20 Jaguar Squadron. We even flew our respective mahogany bombers in the Ministry of Defence at the same time, as well as retiring with the same rank. The big difference between us was that John spent a good proportion of his career instructing, so he's certainly the right chap to enlarge on that side of the Jaguar story.

GROUP CAPTAIN JOHN WHITE (RETD)

Along with my three tours on front-line squadrons, for one reason or another I seemed to become somewhat type-cast in the RAF as a trainer. There was a tour instructing on Hunters at 229 OCU (later the TWU). After converting to Jaguars and completing an operational tour, I returned to 226 OCU as 3 Squadron commander. This unit, which later became C Flight of the OCU, was responsible for Jaguar ground school and simulator training. Following another tour on the front line I was posted back to Lossiemouth as the CO of 226 OCU. So all in all I saw training from pretty well all aspects.

Back in 1976 my first encounter with the aircraft was as a member of No 15 course. The first innovation new to most of us was the 'full mission simulator'. This moved in all three planes, tilted, and had an inflating seat cushion to give the impression of acceleration in the vertical and horizontal planes. But the real eye opener was the visual display; this showed a view forward displayed on TV screens around the cockpit. Its cameras 'flew' around highly-detailed 3D models, which seemed to have been built by a very talented, but perhaps lunatic, model railway fanatic. These huge models (there were two at Lossiemouth, one of part of the UK and the other simulating target areas in Germany) covered areas equal to about the size of Gloucestershire and could be used for visual approaches, low flying, and for training in the weapon system.

Spiders and various insects would sometimes roam across the models, becoming unwitting targets. Because of scaling, these bugs would become amplified, providing monsters for pilots to 'attack'. The favourite monsters were ladybirds!

In fact the simulator staff and the engineers developed all sorts of wheezes to surprise the students. Many Jag pilots will recall the naval frigate hidden in a forest. And the naturally-occurring wildlife would frequently be augmented by those soft rubber monsters one could buy for youngsters to stick on top of their pencils. These would be placed in strategic positions around the model, often in the deeper valleys, causing no little consternation as a pilot came across them having rounded a bend at low level – especially as the monster would be mobile to some extent, being agitated by the airflow from the cooling system installed for the lighting in the simulator model.

The simulator cockpit was in its own separate large room, and while it was in motion no one was allowed in. This is because the whole simulator was powered by large hydraulic actuators which provided roll, pitch and heave. When the pilot performed high energy manoeuvres with the 'aircraft', the rolling, pitching and heaving produced startling physical movements of the cockpit when viewed from the outside. Within the simulator cockpit, vision of the terrain (from the models) was provided by cunningly positioned video screens in front of the pilot. For example, when performing a loop the pilot would pull back on the control column; the simulator would pitch and simultaneously heave vertically; the visual cameras would also pitch up and continue to pitch over the top of the loop. The visual scene would disappear in the vertical and re-appear inverted once over the top. The motion and visual would together produce the appropriate body sensations.

Interestingly, when the simulator was updated many years later, the motion feature which had originally been considered so essential was removed. Such was the fidelity of visual systems by the turn of the century that the new wrap-around picture could provide all the motion cues the pilot required. All the 'flying' sensations came to him via his eyes – just as the paying public nowadays 'feels' the action on one of Disneyland's virtual rides.

I shall return to the simulator later, but this and the ground school was my introduction to the aircraft. Thereafter there was initial conversion, instrument flying, formation, low-level navigation, weapon training, and then all put together in the attack profile phase at the end of the course – the whole thing being about four months and sixty-odd hours.

An innovation to most of us was flying angle of attack (alpha) for best performance – particularly in the circuit. Those who were around at that time will recall the mantra continually preached on finals by the renowned OCU QFI Squadron Leader Jim Froud: "... Ooh, careful now, watch the alpha, china!" A phrase never to be forgotten by most who've been on the receiving end of his wisdom. (Although often misquoted as "... watch the china, alpha ...!") Years later, the man himself had his own high-alpha moment during a tailchase on a sortie out of Coltishall and had rapidly to leave his spinning aircraft via Martin Baker. Reaction to this event amongst the Jaguar Boys tended, naturally, towards amusement. But dear old Jim was of quite advanced years by that time and there was affection for him around the force – and therefore relief that he'd safely finished up in his dinghy with no major harm done.

Tactics for the new aircraft developed quickly to suit both its capability and the perceived threat from the Soviet Union. Weapon training focussed mostly on low-level bomb delivery, simulating attacking Warsaw Pact targets with 'sticks' of cluster bombs or retarded GP bombs – or single nuclear weapons. An alternative option was to 'toss' or 'loft' slick conventional or nuclear bombs from some distance out. Most of these practice details were carried out at Tain Range, just fifteen miles from our base at RAF Lossiemouth, using small training munitions. The run-in to the target from the initial point at Tarbat Ness lighthouse was about five miles and was the normal way of joining the range. A couple of miles beyond the target array was the town of Tain, and between these two was Tain's golf course.

An aspect of the weapon system which repeatedly caused trouble was the automatic release facility. Previous weapon systems in RAF service had generally relied on the pilot pressing the 'pickle' button when it was judged from the bomb sight that the weapon would hit the target. But the Jaguar was really designed for an automatic release. You would enter the target co-ordinates into the NAVWASS, or those of a prominent IP plus the target offset from that point. Then, as you approached the target area, and after updating the NAVWASS for maximum accuracy, you armed the weapon system and pressed and held in the release button. The weapon or weapons would be released at the appropriate moment as calculated by the NAVWASS, which had cunningly taken into account height above ground, wind, aircraft speed, acceleration and attitude – plus many other factors. All in all, a marvellous way of eliminating many of the errors inherent in earlier generations of bomb sights. But to inform the NAVWASS that one wished to use this piece of magic, one had to make one essential cockpit selection: place the manual/auto switch to the 'auto' position – which turned the 'pickle' button into a 'commit' button.

Now, this mode was pretty well essential in 'toss' or 'loft' deliveries if one was to stand a chance of any sort of accuracy. But in lay-down attacks there were many who preferred to pickle manually rather than turn it all over to the kit. So yes, you've guessed it; a not uncommon error amongst students (and not always students) was to leave the selection at manual rather than automatic, so that on 'committing' the weapon system the training munition released instantaneously. To compound the confusion, on weapon release the picture in the head-up display would revert from weapon aiming to the navigation mode. Given the kit's unreliability, pilots would tend to assume when this happened that there had been a minor NAVWASS malfunction. The natural remedy would be to reselect weapon aiming and re-commit – which would immediately do the same thing again. Thus it was not unknown for a student to leave a trail of practice bombs between Tarbat Ness and the beach at Tain Range, releasing the full sortie-load before ever reaching the target!

It was just as well that the error caused by this problem was invariably a short bomb, with the impacts in the sea. The toss delivery, which also occasionally suffered from 'auto/manual' errors, involved pulling up at 4g from very low level at 550 knots, so bombs released in that mode had the potential to miss by miles. But considering the nature of our first-generation NAVWASS, the accuracies generally achieved were remarkable. Also pleasing was the fact that, to my knowledge, both Tain and its golf course (both lying beyond the target) remained unscathed.

Although in its maturity the Jaguar had a commendable safety record, in the early days there were a number of accidents. Throughout its life the OCU provided the Jaguar flying display for the RAF. In April 1975, the man filling the role had an extraordinary escape when his survival/dinghy pack in the empty back seat of the two-seater he was using for his display practice became dislodged and jammed the controls during a low-level roll. The pilot, Whitney Griffiths, was remarkably lucky to be able to eject and escape safely.

Other accidents could be said to have been attributable, in various ways, to particular Jaguar characteristics. For example a mid-air collision between two members of the same formation occurred in the late 1970s. This of course was nothing new in the RAF, for over the years a surprisingly high percentage of accidents had been of this nature. But in the Jag's case the aircraft's excellent navigation capability could be said to have had an input. Such was the accuracy of the NAVWASS that, early on, it was found possible to fly tactical formation on the 'same-way, same-day' principle – in other words with four aircraft in a square formation with anything up to a couple of miles line abreast between each pair and perhaps three to four miles between the front and back pairs. The idea, given the aircraft's limited self-defence capability (especially in its earlier configurations) and negligible chance of survival if engaged by an enemy fighter, was that the fewer formation members were detected the greater the chance of getting some through to the target. So the four Jags at the corners of the 'card' would, essentially, each be doing their own navigation and timing, providing mutual support only by way of lookout and radio commentary. But if one was engaged – well, he was essentially on his own.

This was a pragmatic tactic, given the Jag's small profile and excellent camouflage. But even with NAVWASS to help, it was demanding to fly. Especially for an ab-initio student with only the TWU's short intro to tactical flying behind him. And the reader will easily envisage the situation in an OCU formation when not all the aircraft were quite 'on track, on time'. For whatever reason – perhaps following weather deterioration or engagement by a simulated 'bounce' – they could get themselves into what was known as an 'over-square' situation, when the line-abreast distance became greater than the range between front and back pairs. When the aircraft now approached a ninety-degree turn requiring a cross-over, especially in less than perfect visibility, problems could ensue.

Other accidents were probably down to cockpit ergonomics and the NAVWASS, as related elsewhere in this volume. A couple of examples of accidents from the early period spring to mind.

First, given that the navigational capability was, for its day, magnificent, there must undoubtedly have been a temptation to 'press on' in marginal conditions. We have no real proof of this, but the professionals in the Jag Force are in little doubt that it was likely a factor in several accidents.

Then there was the question of NAVWASS management. The original system was definitely not reliable, while the cog-driven 35mm slide moving map display was even less accurate than the system that drove it. The lesson I remember learning very early on in training was that one must ensure that one always compared the hand-held map that we all carried with the outside world and NOT with the moving map display. There was certainly a tendency to become fixated on what was inside the cockpit rather than what was outside, a trait which would quickly ensure that one could become seriously 'uncertain of position' or, even worse, could seriously crash.

To the north of Lossiemouth airfield was Gordonstoun school, alma mater of a number of young Royals. During my later time at Lossie, HRH Prince Edward was sixteen years old and in the school's Air Training Corps. His squadron paid the occasional evening visit to the simulator as part of their training. With a little help, the prince became quite adept at flying the simulator and playing with the weapon system. I clearly remember one evening when he was 'flying' around the UK model bombing anything and everything he saw. I didn't point out that most of the targets he was attacking were schools, hospitals and churches – these were the most obvious buildings, easily picked out on the model because of either their size or vertical extent.

In 1991, a year after the end of the first Gulf War, 16 Tornado GR1 Squadron, then at RAF Laarbruch, was disbanded, and in November that year 226 OCU was re-badged as16 (Reserve) Squadron. Initially some were reluctant to shed the unit's original mantle, but when I took command in the summer of 1992 we had cast aside our short (OCU) history and were firmly and proudly the custodians of the longer-standing 16 Squadron badge. We quickly became closely connected with a very active squadron association, and the unit's buildings were soon adorned with this historic (formed in St Omer in 1915) squadron's paraphernalia and memorabilia. Also, as guardians of the squadron standard, for the first time the conversion unit had to undertake the additional ceremonial responsibilities that entailed.

There was also re-painting to be done. At one point during its existence, 226 OCU had adopted an attractive flash for the RWR fairings on the aircraft's fins. This was a tartan, applied in honour of John Lumsden, one of the unit's COs of the 1980s. But now the aircraft were re-badged with 16 Squadron's crossed keys, with occasional fancy paint schemes featuring 16's informal 'Saint' logo.

During its life, first as the JCT and then as 226 OCU and subsequently 16(R) Squadron, the Jag training unit had been firmly based at Lossiemouth, moving only once from the south to north side of the airfield to make way initially for the Buccaneer and then the Tornado GR1. Lossie was an excellent spot for training, with its fine weather and its adjacent wide-open and sparsely-populated countryside offering good low-flying opportunities without annoying too many people. However, as the RAF withdrew from Germany and units were re-allocated, a number of studies looked at moving the Jaguar OCU down to RAF Coltishall.

Lossie was a very particular location in that, being so far from anywhere, there were two distinct types of person posted there – those who loved it and those who hated it. If one enjoyed the great outdoors or was content to make one's life amongst the military community, one was happy there. On the other hand if one longed for the big city, or missed distant family, the place was less attractive. Similarly opposed views seemed also to manifest themselves among the staffs who conducted those studies, although early results tended to show that the OCU should stay in the north.

At about the same time, consideration was also being given to moving the Tornado GR1 OCU up from RAF Honington with, unsurprisingly, many of the reverse arguments being propounded – both professional and personal. Their OCU couldn't possibly manage without the weapons ranges of the Wash and the east coast of England, went their argument; they would be miles out of the mainstream; and many families who'd put down comfortable roots in Suffolk were dreading making the 500-mile move north.

I guess that's human nature; people in general simply don't like change. But in the end it came down to two things: the Jag OCU was shrinking in line with the Jag Force, and logistically it became less and less viable to have it out on a limb. While on the other hand the space at Lossie could be better used for Tornados. So in the summer of 2000 16 Squadron moved south to join the remaining Jaguar squadrons at Coltishall, ending twenty-five years north of the border.

The Tornados went north. But of course if there's one thing which never changes in the RAF it's that change will always be just around the corner. And at the time of writing the remaining Tornados are scheduled to leave Lossie, while Lossie will soon reverberate to the sound of Typhoons displaced from RAF Leuchars.

As for 16(R) Squadron, the unit finally disbanded in 2005, with any subsequent Jag training then being carried out on the remaining operational squadrons. It had been a marvellous time, and it's possibly true to say that Jaguar training had provided the template for future types.

CHAPTER 9

SHOWING IT OFF

As already recounted, ingrained on the minds of every Jaguar pilot from his earliest days on the OCU was the need to avoid pulling the aircraft into a situation of too high an angle of attack. First of all the heavy buffet would bleed speed off rapidly; more critically, the jet could flick and then spin with alarming rapidity. And the Jaguar was renowned for being well-nigh impossible to recover from a spin.

The machine was, nevertheless, flyable at incredibly low speed if one handled it correctly, as I found out one day when flying a currency trip following a month's absence on a staff course. My back-seater that day was Ian Smith, who had been, a couple of years previously, the Jaguar display pilot. During his seasons on the air show circuit he'd clearly learned a few new tricks. Thus it was, that morning, that he'd treated me to a demo of his 'confidence-building manoeuvres', during which he pedalled the jet around the sky at 100 knots or so using copious amounts of rudder. The trick was, of course, to keep the alpha very low and the wing un-stalled, but I nevertheless found the whole performance somewhat uncomfortable. It was unfamiliar territory for most Jag pilots.

Display pilots were a particular breed though. Despite the Jaguar's bomber pedigree they nevertheless managed to extract from the airframe the most impressive of performances, not to mention having incredible fun on 'the circuit'. Here, Smithy lets us in on a few of the secrets.

FLIGHT LIEUTENANT IAN SMITH (RETD)

Speed 100kts decreasing; top of wingover.

It's the 1979 RAF Innsworth display, and I'm operating out of Rhoose airport.

Fuel check; yes, just enough for the final high-speed pass. Hard pull back down, and there's the crowd line over my shoulder. Should get 600kts plus on this pass; not too much g on the pullout, don't want to bleed off the speed. Radalt height 300ft, 200, 100; push forward to stop it climbing as the speed continues to increase. Best not go too low on my first display; as well as all the brass, the aircrew appointers work here and I'd like a good posting at the end of this tour.

Background static coming through the headset: "Pitts positioning from hold to display point overhead at 8,000ft."

"Pitts, hold off. Jaguar high-speed pass and display climb complete in one minute, acknowledge."

"Roger."

Perfect; timing spot on. There's crowd centre; 7g; pulling like a bastard into the vertical; quick check left, right, yup that's vertical; boot full of rudder and aileron to get the vertical roll going; 5,000ft, 6,000ft, 7,000ft, 8,000ft; looking good. Where's Rhoose? There's the Bristol Channel, it will be somewhere over that way then.

Whoosh!

What the hell's that?

For a microsecond time stands still. The huge red letters on the top wing and fuselage of the Pitts Special spell the name of a well-known cigarette. They sweep past my canopy in slow time. An open-mouthed, white-faced pilot looks across the incredibly small gap between us. In an instant he's gone, leaving a shocked and very grumpy Jaguar pilot. I swear if it had been one-to-one aerial combat I could have shot him twice in the head with a 9mm pistol, it was that close.

The Pitts pilot had ignored display protocol and ATC's implicit instructions to hold off, and had manoeuvred, unobserved, into the overhead. The consequences of a mid-air crash over the display don't bear thinking about.

However, no time to dwell on that, I'll be able to have a frank and meaningful discussion with him later. I now need to head back to Rhoose, that high-speed pass had used up more fuel than I thought. A quick calculation; from my altitude of 20,000ft an idle/idle approach shouldn't use up much fuel. An idle run-in and break, and there'll be enough fuel to taxi onto the ramp where the ground crew wait to get the aircraft turned round for the Rhoose display in the afternoon.

"How did it go, Sir?" asks Mac as I sit as in a trance, locked silently in my thoughts at 8,000ft over Innsworth, musing about what could so easily have been my premature demise.

"What? Oh, no problems. Well, nearly no problems. Where are the bloody Pitts team parked?"

What a start to the first display of my first season of Jaguar display flying. During this and the following two seasons I can honestly say I never got closer to an early retirement to the big crew room in the sky. I learned my first lesson in display flying that sunny day; never ever relax until the jet is in the hangar and you are in the bar.

The Jaguar is a compact, well-muscled animal, adept at climbing, crawling and swimming. A solitary, opportunistic, stalk-and-ambush predator seemingly at the top of the food chain. However the RAF Jaguar appeared to lack the ability to meet some, if not most, of its 'Panthera' characteristics. At times overweight in its role, when fully loaded it preferred to stay close to the ground. Once, and only once, the French tried swimming off the carrier *Clemenceau*; however the Jaguar proved not to be a good swimmer. It works best in packs of four, being pretty good at sneaky tactics. But top of the RAF's food chain? Possibly not, although in its twilight years it certainly became a cat with a big bite.

As a display aircraft it lacked thrust, its underpowered Adour 104 hair dryers producing 7,500lbs reheated thrust each on a good day. With a high wing loading it had a distinct shortage of Bernoullis when fully loaded. However, when the Pussycat, as she was affectionately known to those who flew her and ridiculed by those who didn't, was given a Brazilian-style trim and tidy up, she morphed into a different creature altogether. Remove the Aden cannons and the stores – and things were different. Some display pilots liked to keep the pylons on – something about spanwise flow. Not being an aerodynamicist or a QFI I wouldn't know about these things, so I had the pylons off. I much preferred my display pussy to be clean and well trimmed!

Reduce fuel load to 1,250kgs (planning to land with 250kgs-ish) and you now had a TOW of 8,250kgs. With reheated thrust at 15,000lbs, you don't need to be a mathematician to see that you now had a real 'Panthera Onca', a 'Cat with Attitude'; more of a Feisty Feline than a Soggy Moggy.

Was it comparable to an F-16 or a Lightning? No, but it was fun and potent to fly. Ask the lead of a pair of Leuchars F-4s I mixed it with over Loch Shin. They got a surprise that day as we rolled and scissored from 20,000ft down to 250! With me locked in lead's 6 o'clock, a solitary predator, tracking, tracking, I didn't tell him 'til we met in a bar somewhere in another life that I was as clean as a whistle that day.

The Jaguar Force at the time had two display pilots from 226 OCU; the training unit, with no operational or reserve role, had capacity, whereas the operational squadrons were fully committed to their roles. I felt honoured and fortunate to be given the opportunity to be one of the display pilots that year by my then boss, Squadron Leader John Grogan. I was particularly grateful, having arrived at Lossie as a simulator instructor. But, because of enlightened OCU attitudes which permitted ground-school staff to fly, and also thanks to many good mates responding to my constant nagging for trips, I'd eventually graduated to a proper flying post. Pat Sanders was the other representative pilot, and we undoubtedly followed in illustrious footsteps.

Daily practice generally began around 0730 hours, providing an ever-popular wake-up call for the local population! Initial training started at 1,000ft, was then cleared down to 500ft by the station commander; the final clearance down to 100ft was flown in a T-bird with the OCU boss, Wing Commander Bruce 'Lumpy' Latton, in the rear seat, and watched by the station commander.

Whilst waiting to take off on that final clearance trip, a voice from the back seat piped up:

"Smithy, I know you know what you're doing. Would you mind if I flew the display from the back seat? I'm not likely to get another opportunity."

Without batting an eyelid I replied: "Fill your boots, Boss!"

And so I sat and watched in awe from the front seat as Bruce Latton, with absolutely minimum fuss, flew an immaculate display that fine morning. In the debrief I not only received plaudits from the station commander but also those of

'Lumpy' himself, with a sly, knowing twinkle in his eye. What a lovely man; now, sadly, no longer with us.

The Jaguar display was, at the time, restricted by the air lords to a rather tame and canned performance demonstration. The high attrition rate of Jaguar aircraft and pilots during the early years probably played a part in this decision. But the unrelated nature of those accidents made this, in my opinion, quite ill-reasoned. The aircraft was perfectly capable of performing a full aerobatic display.

During the 1981 season, the AOC took a bold step by authorising the aircraft for a full rolling display, including slow rolls, inverted runs and reverse, rolling wingovers. After weeks of practice I was duly cleared to perform this demanding display publicly. That was on a Wednesday. The clearance was withdrawn the following Friday.

Why? A totally unrelated flypast had tragically gone wrong elsewhere, resulting in a very public loss of the aircraft and pilot. So my full display came to a premature end without a solitary public performance. C'est la vie!

But I still completed displays at various venues throughout the UK and Europe, each one with a different tale to tell. Biggin Hill was always a favourite.

"Biggin Tower, Jaguar cleared to line up after the landing Sally B."

"Roger, Jaguar line up after Sally B." I look up and am transported into another era as the camouflaged B-17 floats past and touches down on completion of a display which had been interesting and exciting. A magnificent sight, and I watch as she disappears over the hump in the runway. I'm swiftly brought back to the present.

"Jaguar cleared for take-off."

Final check of ejection seat, five pins all there, I roll onto the runway directly opposite the VIP tents. Champers, Pimm's and G&Ts in abundance, their polite chit chat about to be interrupted by the sound of jet noise and a tasty infusion of AVTUR. After all, that's why we're all here isn't it, to inhale the sweet smell of aviation?

Wind is on-crowd, so will have to watch that in turns. Visor down, harness locked, power up, brakes holding full dry power, final check of temperatures, pressures, HUD brightness; brakes off, full reheat. Everything feels OK, acceleration normal, 145kts, stick back, wheels off, roll left 60° bank, stick hard forward, gear up, and keep it at 50-100ft, aircraft accelerating.

Steep wingover and Biggin's crowd line comes into view over my right shoulder – and wow, what a spectacular sight. Thousands of spectators, cars, courtesy tents and fairground attractions laid out below in a kaleidoscope of colour from one end of the 1,800m runway to the other. I can see the Ferris wheel, Dodgems, Waltzers, Hula Hoop stalls, and the smoke rising from the hot dog and burger stands. Can almost smell the family BBQs dotted around the cars parked for miles around, an extravaganza of aviation enthusiasts gathered below. As I float over the top I realise these spectators have paid a lot of money to enjoy the annual jamboree, and today it's up to me to display the Royal Air Force Jaguar to the best of its capabilities. Within the restrictions imposed by the nanny-ish group air staff, that is!

Back to work; get the nose of the aircraft pointing the way I want it to go. Height, speed and inertia are critical, nose buried too low and you leave yourself few margins. But there's scope for gamesmanship; with performance in hand an exaggerated pullout gives the impression that you and the aircraft are on the limits.

Heavyweight taxiing across the grass.

Regarding margins, though, someone allegedly once commented that, 'if you're not living on the edge you're taking up too much space'. In my opinion display flying is not about being on the edge, while ego has killed more pilots than I would care to mention. As a display pilot you are empowered and trusted with a responsibility to others, primarily the paying spectators. I was always conscious of the need to avoid the accidents which have historically littered air displays. So I always kept my ego in check and some performance in hand.

"Watch the alpha, China," registers somewhere in the recesses of my brain as the green angle-of-attack line accelerates off the scale on the left-hand side of the HUD. I'm on the low-speed pass now, and more power comes on to peg the alpha to something sensible. Then into a dirty 360° turn right; full reheat; pull to get established then back off power to hold the max rate turn; on the buffet; 3-4g; going well.

Normally I would clean up coming out of the turn for another wingover reversal into a high-speed finish. However, Biggin Hill's infamous dip lures me towards it like other aviators before me, the seductive, mythical Greek siren that it is.

The Rothmans aerobatic team's colourful corporate hospitality bus goes by on the left, the open upper deck complete with more alluring sirens and their captivated audience. Pilots who have finished their displays are now enjoying champagne, fine wine and the pleasures of real nymphs.

There ahead is the 10ft hessian security screen – or it was there before it was blown down earlier by the Sally B! Full power, clean up as I roll through 150° down into the dip. There is little enough lift off a Jaguar wing, never mind when almost upside down with the gear coming up, so no room for error here. Snap back wings level, accelerating, quick check, gear and flaps are up, full reheat, now well down in the hollow. 350kts – that should do. Snap stick back into what was then a small gut, 5g, should look good for the crowd as, hopefully, I will appear coming vertically out of the ground.

Now, from 2,000 to 3,000ft, I set up for continuous curved approach, looking to land on the piano keys and stop 800ft later. Alpha's up at 17, power on, getting ready to demonstrate the Jaguar's drag-bag. Rumour has it that, in an evaluation conducted in 1976 by the Israelis, they concluded that the brake chute was the aircraft's biggest asset!

On this day Raymond Baxter is in the tower commentating for the BBC, so I am hoping to demonstrate a really short landing. However, in Robbie Burns' immortal words: 'The best laid plans of mice and men gang aft agley.' And they certainly did.

A demo short-field landing was a high angle of attack, power-controlled manoeuvre, with the chute pulled at around 20ft radalt. The power would assist in filling the oversize canopy which, along with full braking, would bring you rapidly and impressively to a halt. But when I pulled this time the drag bag popped out like a scalded cat, still completely enclosed in its protective cover. I knew instantly what had happened, and a very disappointed display pilot vanished, cursing, over the runway hump in a clatter of brake smoke and bits.

Worse was to follow. Not, I have to say from my lords and masters, but from the discerning, critical and always piss-taking display pilot fraternity. Jaguar street cred zero, particularly as today I was parked right next to the Arrows, most of whom I knew and were renowned for taking the mickey. Needless to say I didn't appear in the BBC News item that night, nor did I feature highly in the Rothmans hospitality bus. Ah well, off to the display reception.

A shout across the crew room: "Smithy, somebody called Mick from 38 Group for you."

Mick was the display coordinator: "Hi Ian, how would you like to go to France? I've got a show for you in Roanne, Al Boxall-Hunt will go with you in the Hunter, the details are in the post."

"You bet, and where the hell is Roanne?"

"Somewhere north of St Etienne and west of Lyon, that's all I know."

So the planning started for the trip, with Dave Bagshaw acting as our recce and navigation expert. The four-ship comprised myself, Baggers (in the spare Jag), B-H and Keith Griffin, who would fly the spare Hunter. We duly set off from Lossiemouth one Friday morning for the high-level trip to France. The transit was uneventful, and we called up the display co-ordinator:

"Roanne, this is Jaguar formation, a mixed four-ship of Jaguars and Hunters, requesting an airfield recce and practice display."

This was met with an enthusiastic, Gallic: "*Bon, magnifique, excellente*! The celebrations are in progress in Roanne town centre this afternoon and Monsieur le Maire has asked if you could you do a low-level flyby over l'Hôtel de Ville?"

Don't you just hate it when someone asks you for a non-authorised, unbriefed, get-you-in-the-guano flyby? You can almost feel the horns growing out of the top of your head; you know full well how weak you are and that *merde* awaits. Ah well, it's only the depth that ever varies!

"Jaguar section, common, go."

A quick brief on common frequency as to the potential for *merde*. But my team came up with a unanimous "Go for it Smithy!"

So I brief: "Baggers, you're in the box, B-H number two, Griff number three. We'll start in loose finger to allow us a bit of manoeuvrability until we've had a look at the town."

The recce goes well; no large steeples or wires that I could see. And here's the town hall coming up.

"Tight box, go."

B-H slipped effortlessly into echelon starboard, Griff likewise into the port slot; within a microsecond Baggers calls 'four in'. So here we are, a mixed box of Jaguars and Hunters, briefed in thirty seconds. Not really so difficult, and we are RAF ambassadors in every respect!

"Rolling right."

It works a treat, we maintain close box over the town hall for 270° then reverse left back towards Roanne airfield situated to the west of the town.

"Loose arrow, go."

A quick rebrief to get us reorganised into our original pairs, a two-second break into the circuit, followed by a quick display practice.

The following day the *merde* developed the potential to get thicker and deeper. Seemingly the mayor was so impressed by our city flyby he wanted the same four-ship for the flying display. However, common sense prevailed. After much discussion and debate we decided that we would suffer the wrath of 38 Group and Strike Command if we pushed it. Not that there were many high flyers in the team, but it could have jeopardised any future overseas displays. So, just for once, discretion was the better part of valour.

One fine morning, as I taxied onto the stand I registered a Mini speeding towards me. It screeched to a halt at the bottom of the ladder and as the boss wrestled his large Kiwi frame out of the undersized car, he looked up at me and pointed accusingly skywards.

"Was that you?"

I followed his gaze and put on a nonchalant, perplexed and quizzical look.

"Who, me? Certainly not, Boss." Note: rule one is never admit to or volunteer any information.

"Are you bloody well sure? RSP (Group Captain Ron Stuart-Paul) is throwing a wobbly and I don't know whether the AOC is too happy, either."

It was the day of the AOC's parade. As an OCU we were not invited to play a part in this one (Lossie at the time had several AOCs, having units from 11, 18 and 38 Groups based there – this particular AOC wasn't ours). Thank goodness; I didn't fancy painting kerbstones for a week, polishing anything that didn't move, or making the grass greener. The OCU aircraft were required to be out of sight and out of mind for the duration of the parade, and to this end we had deployed many to different parts of the UK.

But I was there. Met brief that day had indicated that it would be an unusually clear day with little or no cloud and very light, westerly upper winds with a Mintra around 29-30,000 feet. Mintra, by the way is 'minimum trail altitude', the height above which condensation trails form. To mud-movers a figure of no consequence; they were likely to get nosebleeds if they ever went that high. To intrepid air defenders, though, trails meant the difference between being seen or not – by nasty persons wishing to do them harm.

I'd happened to be flying the only clean Jaguar on the OCU and had, as part of the training sortie, done a medium-level tour of the Outer Hebrides, Orkney and the Shetlands. As I'd topped out at 29,000ft overhead John O'Groats from the zoom climb departing Sumburgh I could almost see from one side of the country to the next, from Stornoway to Peterhead – the quintessential beauty of Scotland's Highlands laid out below me.

But now I was being challenged. I followed Lumpy's pointing finger. And there was the most magnificent contrail I have ever seen from that day until now. It traced a twenty-five-mile phallus, carved in intimate detail into the sky. It stretched from Nairn to Fochabers, with gonads the size of Inverness. An unbelievable and truly wondrous sight. In my previous life as a WIWOL I had often seen attempts at the task; however, none had compared to this Leonardo in the sky.

"You're an ex-air defender. And you were in the only Jaguar today that could get up there."

"It's a work of art, Boss."

It was, too. It's not as easy as it looks. You would have to know the Mintra and how to fly the turns, look at the orientation. To do it you would probably have to start a climbing turn to port on a southerly heading, roll out on a westerly heading for some time, then a level, probably 30-40 deg banked turn onto east, then back to abeam the tangent. Then possibly a steady left turn onto south, descending and accelerating rapidly out of the Mintra, then the *pièce de resistance* would be a high-level loop, popping in and out of the Mintra, a quick aileron roll level, another climbing roll into a vertical dive into a high-speed recovery to base, wherever that was. Plenty of theory. But Lumpy was still waiting.

"I would have been proud to have produced an *objet d'art* like that!"

"Bollocks, Smithy." He jumped back into his car and roared off towards the station commander's office.

Because of the slack upper level winds the phallus remained overhead Lossiemouth all day and late into the evening, causing consternation from the Outer Hebrides to Aberdeen. RSP was apoplectic, the Bothy Bar was buzzing. Dougie's chippy was doing a roaring trade in deliveries to the Bothy; "Brontosaurus ribs and chips please!"

And no doubt the AOC, Joe Gilbert, was chuckling under his breath. As it happened both he and RSP were ex-bosses of 92 Lightning Squadron. I, on the other hand, had been a 19 Squadron JP on the same station. Not, you'll understand, that there had been much inter-squadron rivalry ...

The newspapers were full of it, and across the Highlands several minor road traffic accidents occurred as perplexed onlookers tried to figure it out. Is it – isn't it? It can't be. Oh my god, yes it is! Then they'd run into the back of the car in front. Grampian TV, BBC Scotland, Radio Scotland, Highland Radio – all were inundated with calls. What does it mean? Was it aliens? A lady from Skye even asked if it was a Greek symbol.

Interestingly there was a multi-national joint exercise at Leuchars that week involving various air defence units, Jaguar squadrons from Coltishall and Canberra outfits from Marham and Wyton. I know of at least three pilots who could have been the culprit.

But no one has ever owned up, After all these years I still have my suspicions. But that's all they are.

"You sure it wasn't you Smithy?"

"Absolutely, Boss!"

Well, that last story was a kind of 'display flying'. But returning to the real thing I must close by mentioning all the men and women who made the display seasons possible. From the start of pre-season work-up, display pilots were an armourer's and a liney's nightmare, as stores went up and down, pylons went on and off, fuel loads went from light to heavy – and all this often twice a day. Early starts, late finishes; throughout it, all ranks were brilliant. Nothing fazed them, and all whilst dovetailing into the normal OCU daily task.

The travelling, hand-picked engineering support team; what can I say – dedicated, or what? Lossiemouth to anywhere takes an eternity by air or rail, never mind in an RAF Leyland Combi overloaded with the spares, tyres, jacks, chutes and tool kits required to keep the show on the road. The guys would set off southwards for the weekend, sometimes on Thursday night. To cheer them up we would, where possible, target a line search for the Combi, and often they'd be spotted on the A9 and acknowledged by a low flyby.

At the venue the guys would be just as keen as we were to get the aircraft quickly checked, prepped and put to bed so we could all enjoy the benefits of the display location's social and cultural activities – and especially, of course, the hospitality. For me, the three years of display flying would not have been possible without their tremendous support. I cannot thank them enough, and I salute them.

CHAPTER 10

EXCHANGING EXPERIENCES

The exchange programme was a marvellous institution, enabling RAF pilots to spend a couple of years with foreign air forces, while their overseas counterparts came to fly and live with the RAF. The aims of the programme were to cross-fertilise, to broaden understanding of other nations' operational procedures and areas, and to learn their strengths and limitations. The ultimate goal was to strengthen the whole, and the programme was focussed mainly on NATO and Commonwealth air forces.

Naturally there was a cultural aspect to all this. Families shared the experience of living in locations they might not otherwise have visited, with their children having the opportunity to attend foreign schools. Living immersed in a foreign community brings its own challenges, while differences in the social customs of nations which, on the face of it, have much in common, can be surprisingly large. Overall though, the experience was positive, and I returned from my three-year tour with the RNoAF with not only a number of lifetime friends and an enhanced appreciation of one of the Jaguar's main operating areas, but also full membership of 'det Norsk Øl Forbund' – the Norwegian Association for the Appreciation of Beer.

Due to national security caveats surrounding the strike role there were never any exchange pilots at Brüggen during Jaguar times. However, Coltishall had its fair quota of Dutch, Norwegian, Danish, French, Italian and German pilots, while the OCU welcomed USAF exchange pilots from time to time.

Language could sometimes be an issue. I did a linguistic course before travelling to Norway, took an exam and scored well. At a mess party early in the tour, emboldened by my alleged expertise with the language (or perhaps with the Aquavit) I asked a beautiful Norwegian lady whether she'd like to dance. "Yes please," she said; "I'd love a glass of wine." Was my Norwegian that bad? I certainly refuse to contemplate the possibility that she didn't, in fact, want to dance with me!

One of the Norwegians I served with, Jan-Otto Haugen, later came to Coltishall on a Jaguar tour. He subsequently told me that, on his Lossiemouth course, he'd been baffled at met brief by continual mentions of 'Cromarty Gales'. "Who are these women?" he'd eventually asked.

Arguably the most important of our exchange guests were the French, who brought with them an insight into their own air force's method of operating the Jaguar. One of those with whom I served certainly had no language difficulties, and now Bernard Molard tells, in his inimitable way, of his experiences in the UK.

GÉNÉRAL DE DIVISION
AÉRIENNE BERNARD MOLARD, FAF (RETD)

Bernard Molard, *l'Armée de l'Air*, meets HM the Queen. The station commander is Harrier-turned-Jaguar pilot Group Captain Richie Profit.

Having joined the French Air Force Academy in 1972, I qualified 'four-ship leader' on the French Jaguar in 1980 just before being selected for a three-year exchange tour in the RAF. After thirty-two years in the French Air Force, I can honestly say that my three best flying years as a fighter pilot are the ones I had the honour to spend on the RAF Jaguar, in the 6th Squadron.

The first thing I learned during my stay in the RAF is a lesson in modesty (which is not an easy task for a Frenchman!) Although I was a four-ship leader in France with some war experience in Africa, I had to demonstrate my aeronautical skill and restart the full training programme right from the beginning, just like any British 'baby pilot' coming straight from flying school.

That meant I had to start with a three-month course in RAF Brawdy for 'familiarisation flights' on the Jet Provost followed by the Hawk before having to learn all over again about the Jaguar airframe and procedures during the six-month course at RAF Lossiemouth.

Funnily enough, although the Jaguar was the fruit of a very positive cooperation between British and French industry, the two partners had developed two rather different versions and the operating modes were different as well. For instance, the French Jaguar was equipped neither with NAVWASS nor with head-up display and the engines were 10% less powerful than the British ones (Rolls-Royce Turbomeca Mk 102 for France instead of, later, the 104 for the UK). As a consequence, French pilots had to be extremely good to compensate for these technological handicaps.

After a very nice and sunny winter in Scotland (I'm not joking) I finally joined RAF Coltishall with my wife and our six-month-old baby girl, and a big lorry filled with our belongings. On the logistic side, everything was perfect and RAF personnel did look after us very well. A nice married quarter was allocated to us and we had a wonderful time in 27 Filby Road, Coltishall. Every need was anticipated: keys, electricity, gas, telephone and even milk. However, during the unloading of the lorry, our neighbour, the late and much-loved Al Mathie, came to welcome us with a toilet roll in his hands saying: "this is probably the only thing the RAF has not thought about!"

Some other amusing surprises on the way RAF British officers behave in their social life quickly became visible to my innocent French eyes. For example 'happy hours', which I had to survive after three or four pints of beer. This was awful for my nicely-educated French stomach and even worse the day after.

By chance, an old man, employed as a waiter in the officers' club, was the privileged observer of my Friday night distress. Perhaps because he fought in France during WWII and wanted to act once again as a hero towards a French citizen facing a critical situation, he proposed an escape door especially for me. Instead of drinking beer he offered me to drink his 'special Cognac' – which was one drop of Coke and additional water in a nice Cognac glass. The colour was fine and the illusion was perfect. The taste was not very good but it worked well and I managed to drink dozens of this Cognac during happy hour every Friday night. My reputation of being an alcoholic French pilot originated here, but I had no other choice but to accept it!

Another huge surprise was the contrast between the gentlemanly attitude during official dinners in the mess and the transformation of these officers into wild animals as soon as the PMC had left the dining room. Within a few seconds, just after the very official toasts to the queen and to the other "heads of states here represented", all the official silver trophies displayed on the table were secured in a safe place, all the uniforms taken off, and the elegant dining room was transformed into a dirty place open to all sort of silly games. Very silly games.

After this introduction, I wish to say that, during my three-year exchange tour I also had the chance to see RAF Jaguars and military personnel at work in a very operational way. I would now like to focus on two main experiences: the way they trained; and the Falklands War.

In the weekdays between those crazy Friday happy hours in the 1980-83 years, RAF fighter pilots used to fly and train very hard. At that time all the training was focussed on getting ready for WWIII and to fight against the Soviets and to avoid the Warsaw Pact invasion plan from the Baltic Sea. In the 6th Squadron our war mission was very clear since we knew that our war deployment base would be Tirstrup air station in Denmark.

Despite my very limited knowledge about maritime recognition, Mel Evans, OC 6 Squadron, decided that I would be the guy in charge of training the squadron in this very critical domain. So I had to study every physical and electromagnetic detail on Kara, Kashin, Krivak, Kirov … etc. Today, even thirty years later, I can still remember quite a few of the characteristics and performances of these famous warships.

At the same time, flight training started in order to quickly acquire my RAF 'combat ready' licence. Then, I was told how proud I should be to be a 6 Squadron pilot but, before being considered as a full member of this famous family, I needed to pass an exam to check my knowledge on the history of the squadron, the longest continuously-serving RAF squadron, formed in 1914. Very surprised (but positively impressed) by the importance given to history and traditions in the RAF, I spent many hours in the squadron history room in order to be up to the challenge.

As far as the flying was concerned, the basic training for young pilots was very similar to the French programme: a lot of navigation, general handling and strike missions, going through a shooting range for strafing or bombing, but only limited training in air combat missions and night flying. However, it was amusing to notice that the 'never exceed' limitations were different between the RAF Jaguar and the French one. For example, for an aircraft with a centre-line tank, the speed limit in France was settled at M 0.8 whereas in UK the speed limit was M 0.91. When I asked why there was such a difference, I received the following answer: "You must know that, in the RAF, when a limit is settled at M 0.91 it means that if you try to fly at M 0.92, the aircraft will probably not survive. British pilots are educated like that and they will never exceed a given speed limit. On the other hand, a Frenchman never respects the limitations and he will always try to challenge authority by going further than the deadline. This is why, in France, the speed limit is lower." No comment.

Another difference in the training at low altitude was the combination of speed and altitude limitations. In France, low-level navigation was limited at that time to 450kts at 500ft (down to 250ft for IP to target run-in specific areas). In the RAF, with the same aircraft, pilots were authorised to go up to 540kts at 250ft (down to 100ft in specific areas). This illustrates the fact that in the RAF, it was acknowledged sooner than in France that the best way for a Jaguar to survive in war missions was to fly as fast and as low as possible.

The best demonstration of this assessment took place during Red Flag exercises. I had the chance to participate in Red Flag 83 with the 54th Squadron (another Coltishall squadron, trying hard to compete with the 6th) and the preparation for the exercise took place in 'moon country' in northern Scotland. This very demanding training, the deployment to Nellis AFB, and the exercise itself gave me an excellent vision of RAF professionalism and team spirit. The Americans themselves could not believe how well we were performing with such a basic aircraft. The difference came from the combination of a good aircraft, very good weapon systems, excellent pilots and outstanding ground crew fully motivated for the mission. Back in France, I was selected for another two Red Flag exercises, and most of the inputs I introduced to the French team came from my British experience.

Another aspect of RAF Jaguar training philosophy was the combination of tough work and engagement of the crews with the possibility to relax in a professional way. How wonderful were these missions to Cyprus, where four Jaguars took off from Coltishall on a Friday morning to make a technical stop in Sardinia before landing in RAF Akrotiri for a terrible weekend of operational training and tactical concentration! I remember Bill Rimmer watching a beautiful sunset on the beach, declaring with an inspiration similar to a priest facing the Holy Cross: "Another shitty day in paradise!" I soon understood why the trip back to the UK on Mondays was very quiet and peaceful, and the oxygen selector was on 100%.

I now come to two special experiences of my time in Great Britain which are still very alive in my memory: Tirstrup and Taceval.

Tirstrup still rings like a very painful word in my memory. It was our war deployment location and NATO exercises were played in a very realistic way. We were accommodated in military tents, but Tirstrup was nothing like a holiday camp. The water was frozen in winter and we couldn't have a shower before the first sortie of the day. This was terrible for a very clean Frenchman! Mission preparation was looking like WWI pictures, where pilots had to draw maps on open-air dusty tables, then walk towards their planes under freezing rain, and react to air attack alerts by lying down quickly on the wet and dirty grass.

In a very demanding phase of a specific exercise, I was authorised to fly four missions in one single day. This was very demanding but quite exciting. Flying four sorties in a single day never happened to me again during my entire fighter-pilot life.

Taceval was another magic word during my exchange tour with the RAF. Thanks to the Strike Command organisers, I experienced not only the pleasure to be woken-up at 3 o'clock at night but also the delight of experiencing the effect of eating Heinz baked beans at 4 o'clock in the morning. I would recommend to Paul Bocuse (a celebrity chef in France) to introduce this delightful recipe in his restaurants – before the next issue of the Michelin Guide!

This was a really a crime against the French Republic's gastronomic tradition to force one of its officers to have no choice but to eat this food to survive. I could have complained to the International Court of Justice at The Hague but, in solidarity with my British colleagues, I didn't.

I would now like to comment on a very exceptional experience I had during my exchange tour: the Falklands War. I am aware that some information is still very sensitive and will only focus on unclassified issues.

After the first deployment of the Task Force protected by Navy Sea Harriers, our RAF Harrier colleagues were scrambled and they did their best with the operational constraints they had to face. But, at one point, things were not going smoothly down there, and 6 Squadron was put on alert just in case we would be needed to contribute to the fight with our very powerful machines.

At that point we were working under 'UK Eyes Only Secret' conditions. From the beginning of the conflict, the French government did everything possible to show full solidarity to its British allies and to train them to fight against the Mirage III aircraft and Exocet anti-ship missiles which had been delivered to Argentina. In accordance with the governmental agreements between nations exchanging pilots in peacetime, the four other exchange officers based at Coltishall received a red light from their governments, meaning that they would not be involved whatsoever in what was considered by them as a purely British war.

In opposition to this line of thinking, France did not want to show any restriction in its solidarity and I was invited to stay with the 6th Squadron team, should the

RAF authorities want me to stay. This was the case and I was fully integrated in the preparations for war. Day and night, different options were studied for deployment and for the strike missions. Our GLO was updating at 'secret' level the pilots' knowledge on the fast-moving tactical situation in order to be ready as soon as needed and be fully operational once deployed.

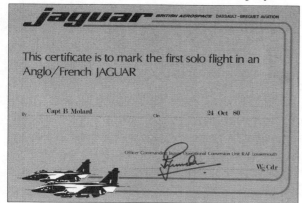

The solo certificate. It neglected to mention that Bernard was already a Jaguar fours-leader in the French air force.

The point I wish to make here is that, once the Union Jack was flying back in the Falklands, the CTTO team came to Coltishall for the official debriefing on the war, looking at it through different perspectives. This debriefing was, of course, placed under 'UK Eyes Only Secret' restriction but, due to the fact I had been declared ready to fight with the RAF Jaguar pilots, I was exceptionally authorised to listen to this debriefing. The self-criticism was very deep and honest and I was surprised to hear all those lessons learned from lack of preparation for this kind of war. But it was very different from the Warsaw Pact scenario on which we were all being trained. From this personal experience I know what the words 'British fair play' mean and I was very honoured by this demonstration of trust and confidence.

Another very exceptional experience was the Royal visit to RAF Coltishall on 5 May 1983. For the pure French Republican that I am, it was very interesting to observe the preparation for such a visit and to realise that HM The Queen is not just a VIP, she is 'The Queen', a very marked difference.

I saw quite a few of my colleagues getting more and more excited by the prospect of meeting her and to deplore the situation of their bank account after their wives came back from shopping to acquire the best dress, hat, shoes and bag for the occasion!

Everything was double and triple checked and quite a few rehearsals took place in the days before: ground display of all the Jaguars in two lines; flying display; reception in the officers' mess and lunch; but also the visit to an especially newly furnished and decorated married quarter ...

On that day, I met the queen on two occasions. The first time was on the tarmac, just when she walked out of her plane. I was wearing the British Jaguar flying suit with my French hat and I was standing in front of a Jaguar together with two ground crews. I was the first pilot on the line, and therefore the first one she was meeting. I did shake her hand in a manner befitting the protocol and we exchanged a few words in French.

From the front line, I then had five minutes to run to the officers' mess, change into my dress uniform and join the other officers in the reception room where I had another chance to exchange a few words before having a very formal lunch in the main dining room.

Many things seemed to me to be excessive in all that preparation but, I must admit that when I was facing the queen, I really had the feeling of meeting someone exceptional.

To conclude this short insight into my three years on the RAF Jaguar, I confirm that this unique experience has been the best one of my military career. Lots of good missions with more than 800 flying hours in a great variety of locations, the interesting discovery of many differences in the way to operate the same aircraft, and exceptional friendship with and confidence of British officers and their families.

The best proof of this long-lasting and extraordinary human experience is that I got very close to two excellent Jaguar pilots: I am the godfather of Max, one of Keith Rigden's sons, and Steve Randles is my son's godfather.

My final words will illustrate how much I enjoyed flying on the Anglo-French Jaguar aircraft and how exciting is an exchange experience. My son Julian, born in the UK, is also a fighter pilot (on the Mirage 2000D) and he is ready to volunteer for an exchange tour, hopefully on the RAF Tornado or Typhoon. The circle is completed and the handover is in process.

God Save the Queen! *Honi soit qui mal y pense!*

CHAPTER 11

WITH FRIENDS LIKE THESE...

As already related, the Jaguar suffered more than its fair share of accidents. In the early days these events contributed to a sorry record, with the Jaguar loss rate in percentage terms up in the same league as the Harrier and the infamous 'Widow Maker', the F-104 in Luftwaffe service. Thank goodness that things are different today. Aircraft are safer; aerodynamics and the associated stability systems are much smarter; engines are also much more reliable. Tactics are different, with far less emphasis being placed on the hazardous low-level environment. Military aircraft are fewer, reducing the collision risk; and perhaps the training is more cleverly controlled. All in all, given the colossal cost of today's equipments, it's a relief that we don't lose airframes and crews at the rate we used to.

Some Jaguar accidents could be described as 'normal' fighter events for the era, such as bird-strikes and engines suffering uncontained fires. But the ergonomics of the original cockpit and the potential for controlled flight into terrain accidents have already received mention in this story. Later we shall hear of Jaguar developments which went far towards alleviating that particular problem.

Other accidents occurred as a result of the Jaguar's particularly unforgiving handling characteristics if the alpha limitations were exceeded; by all accounts it spun much as a metal toy would spin if dropped off a high building, with the only successful recoveries being made in trials aircraft fitted with special spin-recovery chutes.

Many accidents resulted from collisions. As with CFIT occurrences, a number of these events happened over the flat North German Plain, where the temptation to press on in poor weather conditions was huge. The trouble was that others were doing the same, as evidenced by the friend of mine who landed to have the ground crew point out to him that half of his tailplane was missing. Simultaneously, a German Starfighter ground crewman at a nearby base was discovering corresponding damage to his F-104. Neither pilot, blundering around in the murk, had seen or felt anything.

One lucky individual actually survived not one but two head-on impacts with Tornados. If this book was a novel it would be panned for having such an unlikely storyline – but I promise you, it's true.

But even so we can out-do that story. Amongst all those Jaguar losses, none resulted from enemy action. But the unfortunate Steve Griggs did nevertheless find himself shot down in what was arguably the most bizarre incident of recent RAF times. This accident preceded, by the way, Steve's second ejection (following a double-engine fire), by three months. He had also earlier made a single-engined landing at Decimomannu following an engine fire on the range at Capo Frasca, as well as having had to force-land a Chipmunk in a cornfield during his training days.

I've known Steve for many years, and marvelled at how he eked out his nine lives. Even during our later careers, when we flew from the same base for a large UK regional airline, not content with just flying those safe-as-houses airliners, Steve on one occasion had to land his machine, full of passengers, on one engine following the failure of the other powerplant.

Do we detect a trend, here? Anyway, to relive the extraordinary event of the shoot down, we'll join the unfortunate Steve (later to command RAF Valley) as he meandered inbound towards Brüggen following a training mission one fine day in 1982...

GROUP CAPTAIN STEVE GRIGGS (RETD)

Second to 1,000 Jaguar hours. Jeff Morgan (just left of centre) celebrates with Group Captain 'JR' Walker. On the station commander's other side is Steve Griggs. Second from left is OC31 Squadron Wing Commander Terry Nash.

Bang! The aircraft was yawing violently to the right, and not responding to the controls; I heard the canopy shattering. I hear Paddy's voice from the other aircraft yelling "Eject! Eject!" Thought process – he must know what is going on because I certainly don't! Result – I eject.

There was a violent explosion, my head was driven down to the breast plate of my lifejacket, I had a vision of the floor of the cockpit dropping away, a snatch of parachute opening, a wrenching pain in my right hand (fool, let go of the seat handle!), then a moment of blissful quiet before the ground below began approaching rapidly. Now what did the physical training instructors tell us about parachute rolls on landing? Can't remember in time and – thump, I land completely out of control in a field – and it hurts. Look up and think, momentarily, that I might be in heaven (I was a young, bachelor flight lieutenant at the time) as a blonde vision of loveliness dressed in tight-fitting jodhpurs ran over to me, followed by her father (blast!).

"It must be your birthday," Gerd Mölleken (ex-cavalry officer) said.

Still distracted by the vision of Germanic loveliness peering (fondly?) at me, I somewhat confusingly replied, "no, that's not until September", which seemed to perplex them both.

I was being helped to my feet and gathering my parachute and various bits together when a lone Phantom flew overhead, very low down.

"Did you see what happened?" I asked the farmer.

He did not, and neither did I know what had happened, except that I thought that it was odd for the F-4 to be alone – they normally flew as pairs. Could I have had a mid-air with his mate? They were questions for later, since a bottle of brandy had now been produced and hospitality offered (not by daughter, unfortunately). Pausing only to make a quick phone call to Brüggen to relay the news (apparently disturbing the station commander during the annual formal inspection lunch) we attacked the bottle. Remember, this was in the years before compulsory 'medicals' following accidents; i.e. I would have compromised the blood test. Still, morale, welfare and not offending the farmer were much higher priorities in my mind at the time – as well as his daughter.

The farmer seemed quite unperturbed by the whole event. Little did I know that he was quite used to having aircraft crash into his fields. A Harrier had ended up there a few years earlier and his cash register was already ringing up the latest invoice for compensation. Several glasses of brandy later (not sure if they went onto the bill), the sound of a chopper was heard and a lift back to Brüggen given courtesy of the German air force. I was rushed to the medical centre for a quick check up, to be met by Paddy and other members of 14 Squadron (I was Staneval Weapons at Brüggen and was flying with 14 Squadron that day) with bottles of beer stuffed in their pockets. I was waved off for a rather wobbly ride to Wegberg hospital for X-rays, etc; at that point there was still no news of what had occurred. Even Paddy was in the dark; he had just happened to look back at me in time to see the aircraft explode, and had had the presence of mind to immediately call for me to eject.

Wegberg hospital was worse than useless. Having arrived in casualty covered in mud and with a cut chin, there was not a soul in sight even though they had been told to expect me. Finally, I found someone who told me to go down the corridor and book in for an X-ray. That over, I sat around seemingly for ages waiting to see a doctor. I was getting bored and feeling in need of another beer, when on cue in walked Flight Lieutenant Brian Newby (I had been flying his 'named' aircraft Jaguar GR1 XX963). Giving up on the medics, we decided it was time for the bar and he offered me a lift home. Only on the way back to Brüggen did I find out what had happened. The Phantom I had seen fly over the farmer's field had shot me down!

So how did it happen? There I was minding my own business at 1,350ft, returning to Brüggen after a forward air controller training sortie as number two to Paddy Mullen, when the radar unit we were using warned of conflicting traffic ahead. The RWR lit up, which was not an unusual event in the corridor routing aircraft to and from the training areas to Brüggen and Wildenrath. Aircraft went out at 750ft and back at 1,350ft for deconfliction. The F-4s from Wildenrath often 'painted' aircraft to ensure their separation. What was unusual this time was that the CWI-band vector moved from front to rear. "Might not be a Phantom then," I thought, "I could be picking up the Hawk surface-to-air missile site to the north – although that would be a fair distance away." In the meantime I saw a German F-104 pass down the starboard side – more of him later.

Hours before this the hooter had sounded at RAF Wildenrath (the Phantom FGR2 base) in the early hours of the morning for a station exercise. Aircraft and crews had been generated, and the aircraft loaded with live weapons in accordance with normal policy for exercising quick-reaction forces in NATO. Once the required number of live-armed aircraft had been achieved, the aircraft were then de-armed and prepared for training sorties loaded with acquisition rounds (inert missiles but with real, heat-seeking heads). Crews were then to stand by to fly missions as directed by the SOC for training. For the purpose of such exercises, other RAF Germany aircraft were generally regarded as hostile targets, with fighter controllers scrambling the F-4s to intercept targets for training.

One crew, who shall remain nameless, were scrambled for such a mission in Phantom FGR2 XV422. They took off from RAF Wildenrath to mount a combat air patrol under the control of the SOC. At approximately 1247 hrs they were vectored onto a pair of Jaguars and told to engage the 'hostile' aircraft. Following standard procedures for a simulated attack, the Phantom closed on the Jaguars and, when in an ideal position to complete what until that moment had been a typically routine engagement, the pilot pulled the missile release trigger. This should only have produced a witness mark on the radar film to record the intercept. Instead, as the pilot said later, the growl from the missile seeker transferred to his other ear (now indicating the missile on the other wing) and the first missile launched.

Dumbfounded he watched, powerless to influence the outcome, (the Sidewinder being a fire-and-forget weapon) as the missile exhaust trail headed off towards my aircraft. He was not even on the same radio frequency as me, and we in turn had not been made aware that we were to be intercepted for training. The AIM-9G missile hit my aircraft, with my complete tail section behind the wing breaking away, and the front part of the aircraft (with me still inside) entering a flat spin.

I cannot begin to imagine what was going through the poor guys' minds on their way back to Wildenrath; it is a bit difficult to explain away returning to base after a training flight with one missile fewer than when you started out! Indeed, on the way back I understand that they had some difficulty in convincing other agencies of the reality of the event. At least they had the reassuring knowledge that they had seen me eject safely.

Since I was well, with only a slight cut to the chin and not even back pain (I would be able to play golf the next day – albeit with a sore head), I decided to celebrate my lucky escape in the traditional way by putting on a barrel of beer in the mess. Since I did not know the F-4 crew, I invited them to attend to show that there were no hard feelings. To their credit, they entered into the lion's den and came along to apologise. It was later that evening that the Brüggen station commander discovered they were in the bar with me, and pointed out that this would not look good for the subsequent board of inquiry – since we could be accused of collaborating. Indeed the 'party' was subsequently mis-reported in the press as us 'celebrating' the loss of one of Her Majesty's aircraft, a fact I tried to correct by a letter to *The Telegraph*.

At any rate we split from the mess, with members of 14 Squadron taking the F-4 crew away for beers at the married quarters, and me being royally entertained by the combined efforts of members of 17, 20 and 31 Squadrons elsewhere on the patch.

Obviously the accident was the result of a monumental cock-up. The board of inquiry found the crew of the Phantom to be negligent, but were they solely to blame? Having read the accident report, and spoken to those involved, the crew seemed to me to be the last link in an unbroken chain that was destined to result in an accident.

The crew had been called out late and had missed the start of the exercise. They were briefed hurriedly, and were the last to be allocated an aircraft, which was live armed. A simulated bomb incident forced them to evacuate the aircraft shelter and they were allocated another, which was also still armed with live weapons. The navigator noted that this aircraft had no red tape over the master armament switch, which would have denoted that the aircraft was live armed. Halfway through a pee-break (flying and NBC kit hindering a speedy execution of this manoeuvre) they were scrambled by the SOC, which was also on exercise. The accident train was underway.

The report of the board of inquiry revealed that all of the safeguards provided for in the command and station operating and engineering orders relating to the carriage of live missiles were either ineffective or had not been complied with. The circuit breaker for the firing circuit was found not to be an effective safety device, even though it had been pulled to render the system inactive. The SOC fighter controller had not made a 'check switches safe' call because he had not been informed that the aircraft was carrying live weapons. Indeed, the operations officer at RAF Wildenrath had not passed the information to the SOC because he was not aware of it himself.

Despite these factors, and the absence of the vital tape on the master arm switch, the crew were deemed by the board of inquiry to be negligent and (eventually) faced a court martial which resulted in them being found guilty of negligence. The severe reprimand given by the court, which was the lightest punishment possible, suggested the court acknowledged that the crew was not solely to blame. The organisation behind them was seen to be at fault, and following a comprehensive review numerous changes were made to procedures.

The accident may seem unbelievable, but vividly illustrates how pressure on individuals, combined with poor organisation and inadequate orders, can lead to mistakes being made.

On a happy note, and to show what a small world it is, I met a number of the key players in the accident chain over the next few years. The pilot of the German air force F-104 (remember he passed down the right side of my aircraft shortly before the accident) saw the missile leave the F-4 and hit my aircraft. He turned round and flew back to his base at Nörvenich where his story that "... the Brits have gone mad and are shooting each other down over the Lippe river ...!" was not believed initially. I met up with him some years later in a bar on weapons practice camp at Decimomannu.

The SOC controller turned up, funnily enough again in a bar, as an AWACS controller on a Maple Flag exercise in Canada. Needless to say, I met the Phantom crew on a number of occasions over the later years – with no hard feelings.

The ejection was good practice for my next 'adventure' when I left the burning wreckage of Jaguar XX760 (another 14 Squadron aircraft) in a peat bog in Scotland some four months later. This resulted in OC 20 Squadron at Brüggen issuing a squadron flying order: "With immediate effect, Staneval (W) is not permitted to even taxi any 20 Squadron aircraft." But that is all another story.

CHAPTER 12

DESERT JAGS

One might not have imagined the Jaguar, given its alleged shortage of oomph, as an aircraft ideally suited to red-hot climates. But BAC/BAe (not SEPECAT, for the French side had opted to devote their energies to selling Mirages) nevertheless managed to secure notable overseas sales. Ecuador bought a number of aircraft, and India many more. India, indeed, must have many fascinating stories to tell, not least of their two-seat operational variants and their single-seaters fitted with radar for anti-shipping ops.

Nigeria, too, bought the aircraft, and we shall hear shortly of their experiences. But first Oman, a country with which the RAF had been associated for many years in connection with the Strikemaster and the Hunter, was a very significant overseas market.

Many British pilots have flown with Omani forces over the years. Some were seconded from the RAF, while others were on contract. In the early days the Dhofar War brought combat, but later the balance shifted – reflecting more Oman's strategic position at the mouth of the Persian Gulf.

My own limited experience of the country started in the early 1970s with Hunter 'flag-waves' from Bahrain, down across the spectacular Jebel Akhdar mountains to Masirah Island. Later, I staged through Masirah again in a Phantom en route to Singapore.

Some years on came a two-week Tornado detachment to Thumrait. Our next contributor, Ian Ord, had at that time just left, so denies all knowledge of the in-brief which sticks in my mind. We were in the main station briefing room, and representatives of all the resident squadrons were there to assist. The briefing officer, from the Jaguar squadron, was describing deconfliction procedures designed to avoid accidents when flying in the notoriously hazardous wadi to which Ian refers in his piece.

"It's one-way traffic," he said; "On Mondays, Wednesdays and Fridays we fly down it, and on Tuesdays and Thursdays up." "Hang on," interjected the representative from the Hunter squadron. "Surely that's not right; we fly down the wadi on odd dates and up it on even." "No, no," put in a helicopter rep; "We alternate; we fly down the wadi one week, up it the next!"

At least that's what I think I heard, although time might have scrambled my recollection. But the image is typical of the many, slightly off-the-wall tales which have emanated from Oman over the years. Whilst they provide a chuckle, it would be a mistake to underestimate the professionalism of the Omani operation. So to put the whole situation into perspective, I turn over to one of the most experienced of the ex-pat officers.

WING COMMANDER IAN ORD, RAFO (RETD)

One fine day, two Jaguar pilots (Tiger formation) brief up for a Rubkut Range sortie, to be preceded by some low-level stuff, then into an FRA (first-run attack) on the range. The RSO, Dave, a Hunter pilot, travels the 12km to the range down the main road towards Salalah in his trusty old green Toyota Corolla saloon, followed closely by two friends (Paul plus a visiting female teacher) in another Toyota. Dave, being a wise sort of chap, keeps his eyes on the rear-view mirror ready for the inevitable Jaguar bounce. Sure enough, the lead pilot, known for his derring-do and low-altitude skill, is spotted in the mirror. No problem; he looks to be at about fifty feet or so. Whoosh! Now a quick look back for his number two.

Bloody hell! There's no discernible gap between the jet and the cars. Dave ducks. "Bang – whoosh." "Shit ...!"

Dave's now driving a Toyota Corolla convertible – which is ready for the scrap yard. Both cars stop, Paul thinking Dave has been decapitated. The teacher is in a state of shock; Paul shouts to her to stay in the car. Meanwhile, the attackers circle around for a second pass to make their point. Now the three car occupants lie flat on the road. The teacher is screaming hysterically; she thinks they are being attacked by the Yemeni air force.

Tiger formation head off on their planned trip, pleased that they have scared the pants off the bumbling Hunter RSO and his friends. There is no-one at the range to clear their planned FRA, as the RSO is back at Thumrait nursing his – luckily only – superficial battle damage.

As Tiger 2 taxies in at the end of the curtailed sortie he can't understand why there is so much activity under his jet as he shuts down. What's all the fuss about, he wonders? He is completely unaware of the conversion treatment he has rendered to the Toyota, but the green paint and missing panels on his underside gave a clue. "I thought the thump was a bit of jet wake from my leader's aircraft," he says during the subsequent debrief.

The jet needs a centre-line pylon change, but otherwise only minor repairs. The police report on the collision states that the vehicle speeds were 100kph and 600kph respectively. Tiger 2 leaves Oman shortly afterwards. Dave stays for a while, continuing to fly Hunters.

They are now both aging captains with a major and respected airline, seeing and talking to each other occasionally. I was the Jaguar squadron commander, but was away at the time of the incident.

The story will chime well with many people's perceptions of Jaguar ops in Oman, but I promise you there's another side to it. Let me paint the true picture for you.

Following two Hunter tours I was well placed to join the Jaguar Conversion

Team as it started up. Then, after an extended USAF exchange flying the A-7D and the A-10, I returned to the RAF for a tour as deputy OC 54 Squadron at Coltishall. I retired in 1982 with airlines in mind, but at the time pilots were being laid off around the world. So now I was looking for an interim job to see me through until the airline business picked up. SOAF Jaguars fitted the bill; I was experienced and had always been fascinated by Oman. I knew some of the guys out there and I'd loved the desert flying in the States. So, decision made, off I went, to arrive in the sultanate in April 1982 on contract.

At Thumrait, tales and myths of the Dhofar War were still being related in the bars by hairy old veterans from helis, Strikemasters and Hunters. The place was full of characters and the interaction, both professionally and socially, between the SOAF units – 8 Squadron Jaguars and 6 Squadron Hunters – and with the army regiments and Sultan's special forces, absolutely outstanding. There was, though, a somewhat wild west flavour, including the holstered, loaded gun.

Thumrait lies 80km north of the southern city of Salalah, which is on the coast of Dhofar; frankincense country, the southern governorate of Oman. The base is situated on the edge of the mountains to the south and the 'empty quarter' (Rub Al Khali) to the north. It is ideally positioned with almost year-round sunshine. It is 150km from the Yemen border, where historically the main threat lay. Until the 1990s Oman's border was in dispute with Yemen and also, in certain areas, with the Saudis. The Yemeni troops had no reservations about shooting at us as we flew along the border. But this blind shooting towards the sound caused more of a problem for the Omani army border positions than ourselves, as the rounds mostly landed on them; so we tended to steer clear unless tasked.

SOAF had taken delivery of its first single and two-seat Jaguars in 1977. The aircraft were 'international' variants, similar in most respects to the RAF's but with slightly more powerful engines. We still could have done with more grunt in the heat, though. One or two of them were tired by the time I got there, including XX138, which I had already flown with the JCT. It had been loaned to the Indian air force, subsequently arriving in Oman as a replacement for another lost in 1979. It was somewhat bent and leaking like a sieve – a shadow of its former JCT self. The seeping fuel tanks were discovered to be patched up by sealant slapped on from the outside. This was eventually sorted by Airwork Services, who maintained SOAF's aircraft extremely well, under the direction of RAF loan servers and contracted SOAF uniformed officers. Airwork was joined at the hip with SOAF, as it had started up at the same time as SOAF formed in 1959. It survives today, but with considerably reduced numbers as the majority of engineers are now Omani nationals.

We operated the Jaguars from HASs, whereas poor old 6 Squadron had to be content with umbrellas over the cockpits to stop their bums being burnt as the guys strapped in. It was pretty hot at times, although tempered in summer by the Khareef monsoon hitting the coast. Nevertheless I recall a Hunter T-bird's ejection seat catching fire on the ground one day.

In 1983, 8 Squadron split into two as the second batch of aircraft arrived from Warton. 20 Squadron eventually moved up to Masirah Island, where the old RAF base had been newly prepared with HASs. There they joined 1 Squadron Strikemasters, SOAF's basic flying training unit. 8 continued to operate as an operational and training squadron, while 20 held the fort in northern Oman. The country was to test the Jaguar to the limits without the restrictions that the RAF had necessarily imposed upon it and its pilots. It was a dream to fly in the desert and in the mountains of Oman despite the high temperatures.

I very quickly fell into the SOAF expat trap of enjoying good money, few written flying regulations, seemingly unlimited budgets for fuel and weapons, and an almost complete freedom of the desert skies. This combined with living in a fascinating country amongst the delightful Omanis made for a dream fighter-pilot posting. It was the stuff of former RAF operations, still alive and kicking in the 1980s. My interim one-year plan for SOAF thus extended to ten.

Social life revolved around the officers' messes. No computers, DVD players, or satellite TV in those days. BBC World Service radio was our contact with the outside world apart from the one international phone line from the mess foyer. So lots of liver destruction! With the superb flying there was an air of controlled professional unruliness about the place.

The only tedious task for us was the daily QRA, which we took in turns with the Hunters. The lads got it off to a fine art, the ability to move from totally relaxed mode somewhere on base, to being airborne in fifteen minutes or less. Even from the bottom of the officers' mess swimming pool complete with diving kit! We would intercept the odd Russian IL-38 flying up from Socotra or, when the Yemen border got a bit tense, we would launch to help the army units.

During the 1980s and 1990s the USAF and USN regularly operated over Oman, so we hosted many and regular exercises with them and with the RAF – sometimes all three at the same time. SOAF's experiences in Dhofar were looked upon by others with envy. Oman was for a time the USN's best overland operating area, and the only place overseas where they could expend live ordnance. SOAF of course took full advantage of these exercises with DACT, CAPs, mass attacks against Masirah and Thumrait, and of course against the USN carrier task groups. We also did a fair amount of AAR from the USN's various types and from the RAF's tankers. Good sport for all and tremendous training value. Red Flag on our own doorstep.

While 20 Squadron preferred to use a centre-line tank, mainly to extend their range from distant Masirah, quite often we would fly really clean with just the two outboard pylons and AIM-9P missiles. It made the aircraft into quite a nippy air defence fighter, although we were under no illusions about its lack of agility. However, with some cunning we could acquit ourselves well. The mark-one eyeball, together with very low-level flying at high speed for surprise, worked invariably against the foreign fighter aircraft – until they caught on. On the second or third days our artful tactics didn't do so well.

The Hunter was also a good adversary; staying in a turning fight with them was death, but we learned to employ the Jaguar's strengths. All this dissimilar combat was immensely valuable training, and led to the aircraft being flown to its limits regularly – and to the pilots knowing the aircraft's limits as well as their own.

In the early days, at the end of the week we would occasionally launch all available qualified pilots and aircraft, Hunters and Jaguars, apart from those on 'Q', at the same time. We had a cylindrical area centred on a feature just a few miles west of Thumrait, 20nm radius, ground level upwards. Inside the tube and you were fair game. We would start with all v all and, after fifteen minutes or so, the appointed leader of the Balbo would shout, "like aircraft friendly". Then it would turn into Hunters v Jaguars; it was an interesting and revealing exercise. Hunters of course would wheel around inside the tube looking for trade thinking they could out-turn anything, whilst the Jaguars would tend to rush in at warp ten from the outside, missiles growling, picking off whatever they could get into missile or guns kill position without bleeding off too much speed. Normally attack film was a plan view of a very surprised Hunter. Of course it would inevitably end up with combats inscribing the inside of the tube like cooked spaghetti. It certainly sharpened you up. Of course there were loads of false claims, as always.

Occasionally we would carry out one v one or two v two in Thumrait's overhead, with no low-altitude restriction. Wheels in the well – "outwards turn for combat – go". It was a great spectator sport for the ground crew below.

We flew some interesting firepower demonstrations for HM the Sultan, as well as for visiting VIPs including King Hussein of Jordan. We weren't shy with the weapons expenditure: 400kg retards, 1,000lb ballistics, CBUs, rockets, LGBs and of course HE 30mm. All in a couple of passes with large numbers of aircraft fully loaded. On one occasion I think we probably dispensed the equivalent of the RAF Jaguar fleet's three-year training allocation of live weapons in about five minutes! Not only was it great sport and impressive from the ground but it taught us the business of safe separation from preceding attackers for fragment avoidance as well as target obscuration (visual and laser) problems due to smoke and dust.

In time I took over command of 8 Squadron, which then comprised a bunch of very experienced ex-RAF contract and RAF loan service pilots, and the first of the young Omani pilots. One or two of the latter were already well trained on the Jaguar. I knew most of the RAF guys. In fact two of them during my time as OC were ex-JCT members.

With the few Omani Jaguar pilots there were, naturally, even fewer Omani senior officers then. However, within ten years almost all the executive positions in RAFO (renamed from Sultan of Oman's Air Force to Royal Air Force of Oman) would be Oman-ised without degradation of quality in the force – an indication of the quality of the training that the young Omanis experienced. The responsibilities that they were given and enjoyed in the cockpits came much earlier in their training than normally experienced in other air forces. Strikemaster and Hunter training was a truly sound basis prior to the Jaguar. By the time they came to 8 Squadron, flying at 100 feet and being bounced by dissimilar aircraft was not a new experience to them. Most had dropped a big HE bomb or two and fired an AIM-9. They had even got to smell cordite with the Strikemaster guns. The young lads were let loose at a very early stage in their flying, and they matured quickly.

Not surprisingly, running the squadron was much along the same lines as in the RAF, and this was not difficult because almost everyone was ex-RAF or still serving. Keeping discipline was not too difficult either – and not just because of the lack of regulations. The one golden rule was that once you took command of an aircraft it was your responsibility to be safe and stay within your own limits and those of the aircraft. And the realistic bottom line was that SOAF/RAFO operated close to the limits of aircraft and pilots. Our operational flying training was little different from that we'd carry out in anger. We didn't need a Red Flag scenario to 'work us up', as 'fully worked-up' was the norm. The air force was better for it; it was a very punchy and competent outfit.

The unique and refreshing conduct of operations and training was solely due the SOAF commander (CSOAF), Air Marshal (later Sir) Erik Bennett. His command was total and all-embracing. He had his finger on the pulse of SOAF and trusted his subordinates in their cockpits. His approach to accidents, of which there were remarkably few, was realistic and philosophical. Accidents did not deter him from operating to the limits, which we did all the time. On the contrary, he insisted on more practice to those limits if accidents showed the need. It was good stuff, and everybody enjoyed life to the limits too.

However, as you read earlier, unwanted incidents did happen. New Year's Eve 1985/6 brought them in spades.

The first involved an RAF loan service pilot who managed to display his lack of flying skills and discipline. Prior to a range detail he briefed the RSO: "Take my camera to the range and I'll do some steely flybys so you can get some good pics of me. All right? Thanks a lot."

An hour later I'm sitting in the station commander's office as deputy doing some admin before flying a sortie myself. I get a call from the tower:

"Wildcat 86 is returning from the range with airframe damage."

"Roger. What's the damage?"

"He wouldn't say. But he's doing a straight-in approach."

Probably picked up a ricochet, I think. I dash down to the Range Rover and spot him on approach as I head down the taxiway. That's interesting. The jet looks a bit asymmetric. One wing looks shorter than the other.

Indeed it was. Moreover the shortened wing had bits of angle iron wrapped around the leading edge, with gravel dropping from the jagged wing tip. The man had managed to scrape a wing along the ground on the little jebel atop of which was the RSO's hut – no doubt whilst smiling for the camera. Not content with that he had brought back ten feet or so of the handrail that was alongside the steps leading up to the hut. A comprehensive job.

I get on the phone to CSOAF.

"Urr. Morning Sir, we've had an unfortunate incident on the range ...!"

"Umm. Not a good New Year's Eve is it?"

"No Sir."

"OK, I'll send Wing Commander Rod Harrison (OC 20 Squadron) down from Masirah to run a unit inquiry."

"OK Sir. Happy New Year."

"And to you."

Click.

Two hours later I'm in my jet with Paddy Mullen as my number two, on the same range – but with a different RSO, the original having gone home to recover his composure. We dropped some bombs, fired the guns, and I pulled up from the last strafe pass.

"Switches safe."

Paddy responds: "Switches safe. Urr. Lead, I felt a bit of a thump on my last pass. Slowing down for an inspection."

"Roger, come left onto north so I can cut the corner."

No response.

"Paddy come left."

No response. I'm now closing at about 1,000 yards in his 8 o'clock. We are level at about 1,000 feet over the range. All of a sudden Paddy's jet does a rapid hard turn away from me and continues in a spectacular spiral into the ground. There is a huge explosion and lots of bits and smoke. Holy shit. Where's Paddy?

Russ Peart, the RSO, says something like "Paddy's crashed. Oh no. He's OK. He's in his chute. I'll try to pick him up in the car."

After a few frantic seconds trying to spot him, there's the little Irishman dangling on his chute, descending nicely to the desert. His ejection had been blanked off to me by his airframe. I call a Mayday to Thumrait Tower.

Russ then gets his car stuck in the sand trying to reach Paddy, who is by now standing on a rock and waving at me with only one shoe on as I circle. Desert boots come off when you eject! He's OK though.

So, thirty minutes later I'm on the blower to CSOAF again.

"Urr, Sir. You're not going to believe this but Paddy Mullen has just ..."

"Umm. Definitely not a good New Year's Eve, is it?"

"No Sir."

"I think I'll upgrade the unit inquiry to a board. I'll send Group Captain Porky Munro down to you, he can do both."

"Yes Sir. OK. And, urm – Happy New Year!"

"Yes!"

Click.

You'll be unsurprised to hear that the loan-service wingtip scraper left Oman shortly afterwards back to the RAF. What stuck in my throat was that the guy didn't have the decency to say sorry after climbing out of the cockpit. His aircraft was grounded awaiting a new wing for over a year. I never did get to see any of the steely flyby photos.

The board found that a round from Paddy's aircraft had exploded about a metre in front of the barrel, blowing open the side of the fuselage and damaging the comms and hydraulic controls. Hence no radio, no control and only one option. Manurhin, the French manufacturer of our 30mm HE rounds, (we always fired HE at the ground to reduce the ricochet chances), was sued as it had sold us defective ammunition.

In 1985 I led a diamond sixteen of Jaguars, a diamond nine of Hunters, four Strikeys and four helis for the national day parade flypast over Muscat. In a jam-packed stadium, HM the Sultan and about six other kings and heads of states (and CSOAF) would cast their critical eyes upwards at formation symmetry and timing. We were due overhead as the SOAF marching contingent on the parade were saluting His Majesty. Royalty, however, does have its prerogatives, as the following radio exchange indicates:

"SOAF combine lead this is stadium control."

"Go ahead."

"We've just been informed that the Sultan's speech is not the planned fifteen minutes but forty. Will you be OK?"

Wonderful! I have twenty-nine aircraft, including flying spares, orbiting in the holding area. So we all stumble up to altitude. Me thinking, is this going to save us any fuel or use up more? It probably did neither. It turned out smartly in the end, and twenty-nine thirsty and nearly empty jets eventually landed safely. HM and CSOAF were happy. All's well that ends well.

Another royal task, escorting King Hussein of Jordan into country, was always a pleasure. We would join up with the Royal Jordanian jet at the border as a 4-ship on either side, two Jaguars and two Hunters (the latter important, as they were the king's gift to Oman) and escort him in close formation for punchy flybys at 100 feet over the airfield with the king at the controls of his jet. He would always call us 'Sir' when chatting on the R/T. What a true gentleman he was, even when a lesser mortal called up with a friendly wave from one of the Hunters on one occasion with "Wotcha, king. 'Ow goes it?"

Being out on a limb gave us some independence in adapting innovative equipment for the Jags. The Bristol CRV7 rocket was one, a very effective weapon which was eventually adopted by the RAF and used successfully during the Gulf War by their Jaguars.

SOAF managed to procure a number of very special recce cameras from a 'source' overseas, and our innovative SOAF engineers designed pods for them from drop tanks. BAe didn't get a look in at the flight clearance that followed. The pod was bolted to the centre-line pylon, and we checked it to some reasonably realistic limits within a day or so – free of charge. These cameras took beautiful, high-definition pictures at long slant ranges of various border positions of Oman's neighbours. Once we disguised a three-ship close formation as an airliner (call sign and all) as we took some interesting snaps.

Not so successful, though, was use of a Pakistani fuse for 500lb bombs. Before my arrival there was an accident when one triggered directly after release, about nine feet under the wing. Rick Lea, the unfortunate pilot, ejected but was severely burned by a fire caused by bomb fragmentation cutting a LOX pipe in the cockpit as the aircraft split into bits. He miraculously survived. Suffice to say those bombs and fuses were discarded.

Flying in the desert is not without its hazards, particularly when the sun is at its zenith and in hazy, dusty conditions. No shadows, no relief, and merging sand dunes with sandy skies – it's killed more than one low-level-experienced soul. But in the main the Jaguar was a great aircraft to fly in the deep rocky canyons of Dhofar and northern Oman. One favourite valley was Wadi Rabkat, which we called the 'Grand Canyon' ; the USN knew it as 'Star Wars Canyon'. A spectacularly scenic place to demonstrate the aircraft to visitors, with a 4g chicane towards the bottom end. Unfortunately there's an F-18-shaped scar there made by one USN pilot who didn't quite make the chicane.

This place intrigued us so much that one day a small party of us asked 3 Squadron helis to drop us at the top of the escarpment entry point. From there, at about 4,500 feet amsl and 120nm SE of Thumrait, we would walk the 30km of wadi we had so often flown down. We had three days to do it.

The first day was laborious but we progressed pretty well 15km down into the wadi. The second and third days were interesting to say the least. We swam, abseiled, climbed, descended, and fell in this amazing jumble of house-sized boulders, smoothed by centuries of water flow. It was painful and at the same time spectacular, with the sides of the canyon towering 2-3,000 feet above our diminutive, shattered figures. On the morning of the third day Dick Manning flashed down the canyon in a Jaguar to check on us. By then we were exhausted and only two thirds of the way down; our three days was up so we called for a lift out. 3 Squadron hauled us out very professionally, and not without some risk. The chopper then dropped us at the point we'd been attempting to reach – where the wadi spills out into the Arabian Sea at Hasik. From the old strip near the beach a trusty Skyvan (with my wife and son aboard) took us back to Thumrait and a rest.

The first Gulf War was a big event. Oman didn't participate in combat but Thumrait hosted the work-up for USAF and RAF units prior to their move north. The base went from a quiet 1,000 personnel to 5,000 almost overnight. 6 Squadron RAF's Jaguars came, and tent cities sprang up everywhere. In fact just about the whole of Seymour Johnson's USAF F-15 wing was there, including the base hospital, nurses and all!

It was incredibly noisy during this time, with constant day and night air traffic landing and taking off for weeks. Earplugs at night were indispensable. Thumrait, Seeb and Masirah had become repositories for prepositioned US equipment from the early 1980s, and now all this kit was going to be used in anger. We had everything from runway repair equipment to 'meals ready to eat' (MREs), otherwise known as 'meals rejected by Ethiopia'. Somewhat unfairly, I felt, as they were superior to some of the junk I had been forced to eat in the RAF in the past! Despite the tension, the discomfort, the noise and the collapsed mess tents from the occasional low flyby, we all got on very well. The flying experience was unique and serious. When our visitors at last deployed north and the war started we felt that RAFO's significant help had contributed to RAF and USAF preparedness.

The odd aberration you've read about which gave SOAF/RAFO a sometimes undeserved reputation for hooliganism may perhaps best be seen as growing pains. The RAFO, these days, is a mature and very effective air force. Today the aging RAFO Jaguar mirrors the RAF aircraft in final form with all sorts of cosmic kit I don't begin to comprehend, Advanced LCD map and MFD, GPS, obstacle clearance and warning system, an integrated nav solution, wide angle one-to-one HUD, full night vision suite, TIALD, Sky Guardian RWR and refurbished engines. A far cry from the NAVWASS and radalt of 1973.

The Jaguar continues to fly and do sterling service in Oman and will do so until 2015/16 when it will retire gracefully from RAFO service. It will be replaced by the Typhoon, which will equip 8 Squadron. A worthy successor to a very capable and much-loved aircraft.

CHAPTER 13

DEEPEST, DARKEST AFRICA

We all need our friends and contacts. In previous times it was known as 'old school tie', a phrase which, these days, bears something of an unacceptable connotation. Nowadays it's known as 'networking', which is apparently quite OK. Whichever, it came in useful in my relationship with Mike Crook. I had hardly known him in the RAF; even when I'd taken over from him as a flight commander on 6 Squadron we'd had no handover, as he'd left before I arrived. But we knew of each other, which later came in handy as I sought to begin my civil flying career. For, when ordered to attend an airline assessment session in some dreadfully-unstable old link trainer, I was relieved and delighted to find that Crooky was the checking officer. I'm sure my performance in that horrible-to-fly machine was appalling, but I got away with it. And later I was grateful to Mike, as my trainer, for teaching me much of what I needed to know before being let loose with passengers.

Nowadays I meet him regularly at the lunches enjoyed by our group of knackered old Norfolk Jaguar pilots, and I'm delighted that he joins us here in recounting a tale of a little-known aspect of Jaguar ops – that of the Nigerian air force.

SQUADRON LEADER MIKE CROOK (RETD)

Boom! It was lunch time; an enormous explosion rattled the doors and windows of our family bungalow. We rushed outside to see a large mushroom cloud rising into the hazy, dust-filled sky from the general direction of the bomb dump, which lay 5km away at the far end of the airfield. In the early evening, as we ex-pats met up as usual in the central club house for the usual G&Ts, there was a series of further explosions and the whoosh of rockets departing skywards. We were instructed not to report for met brief over the next few days and to remain in our compound, but eventually the dust settled and we restarted flying. It was New Year 1986 and the location was Makurdi, the Nigerian air force Jaguar base, so how on earth had I ended up there?

By early 1982 I'd accumulated 3,700 flying hours in eight years on Hunters and seven on Jaguars, all without the slightest hint of a ground tour. But I knew things were finally coming down to earth when I was summoned to RAF Barnwood, the RAF's equivalent of an HR department. I was to have my tea leaves read, and to discover why my planned fast-track promotion seemed to have been diverted into the slow lane. I knew full well that I'd need to get a successful ground tour under my belt, but had been only too happy to continue roaring around the sky in those wonderful jets, hoping that nobody would notice. It was a pleasant surprise, therefore, to be told I had been selected for yet another flying tour, the prestigious job of senior British instructor and deputy chief instructor at the Tri-National Tornado Training Establishment (TTTE). "What about the necessary ground tour?" I asked. "Not to worry," was the reply; this tour would "... involve a lot of PR work and would be counted as a ground tour for your assessments."

In my eagerness to stay flying I swallowed these weasel words hook, line and sinker, although the parting shot as I left the office was slightly worrying: "By the way, Mike, you were our third choice..." However, I thoroughly enjoyed my three years on Tornados. By the end of that, though, the reality hit that I had peaked in career terms, so I opted to leave; on the bright side, I could point to not having had a ground tour during twenty-one years of RAF service.

What next though? I was in contact by virtue of my TTTE job with BAe's chief test pilot at Warton, and with the Tornado contract being formulated with Saudi Arabia I knew they were bound to need instructors. Unfortunately, that deal came too late for my leaving date, but as it happened BAe were in need of a Jaguar pilot for the on-going contract in Nigeria. And thus, after a short discussion with my wife, our African adventure began.

We arrived at Lagos airport in November 1985, and what a place it was. Immigration queues which would make Gatwick look like a stroll in the park; noise and bustle everywhere; baggage inspection on arrival to search for interesting or attractive items; and vast numbers of touts to persuade you to let them porter your baggage, ride in their taxis, or who were simply begging. BAe had set up a 'gofer' who made the hassle fade away and thus, after a few days acclimatisation at the company house in Lagos, we travelled up country to Makurdi.

There I found my new employment. Of the five Jaguar T2 trainers supplied by BAe the previous year, one had already crashed when the crew, a couple of young Nigerian pilots, ran out of fuel – while reputedly doing flybys at a university town where they were known to have had girlfriends. About half of the thirteen single-seaters were still serviceable. The BAe aircrew comprised one pilot, Rod Dix, the other two having left for various reasons after only about six months in country. I had come across Rod many years before at RAF Wittering when I had been flying Hunters. He had moved on to fly Jaguars in Oman, before finally ending up in Nigeria. In addition there were about thirty assorted engineers and support staff.

We were all accommodated in individual prefabricated, but very comfortable, bungalows inside a small, fenced compound within the confines of the base. The buildings were located around the periphery, with a small club house, swimming pool and tennis court in the centre. The site had its own water supply, power generator and medical facility. I warmed to the situation and looked forward to getting stuck in. Following a quick dual check and a solo I was into the swing of things.

There were some six or seven Nigerian pilots of somewhat variable abilities, five of whom were ex-MiG-21 pilots and had done some training with the RAF at the Jag OCU. The remaining two had come through the Nigerian training system in country, having flown Bulldogs and Alpha Jets. Apparently, before I arrived, the initial concept of training, as seen by the Nigerians, was that all they required was a quick Jaguar type-conversion. However, they were eventually persuaded that it would make better sense to do a full operational conversion course such as the RAF had offered. Fortunately I had brought out all my notes and guides from my days at Lossiemouth, so I was able to slot in without too much difficulty. But in the two years of my contract no other Nigerian pilots materialised.

Flying around Nigeria was of course very different from the UK. The north of the country was essentially flattish scrubland, while the south was well-forested, undulating tropical terrain. There were highlands around Jos in the central northern area, and a high plateau in the south east near the Cameroon border. There were two distinct weather patterns. In the winter the Harmattan wind blew sand from the Sahara, reducing visibility to a maximum of five kilometres, and in the summer the monsoon brought heavy rain and thunderstorms. Since the only maps available to us were rather inaccurate and at a scale of 1:1,000,000, and the cockpit PMD had many areas which were blank white with the statement 'no map data', we welcomed the good weather in the changeover from one system to the other.

There were virtually no low-level restrictions other than flying directly over the big cities, and almost no air traffic control. Makurdi air base, which had been constructed by Dornier several years earlier, had an excellent 10,000ft runway with parallel taxiways and an impressive ATC tower that would have graced any European airfield. Unfortunately, the two very fine generators installed in the tower's basement had been flooded early on in their life and had never recovered. It was rumoured that a MiG had flown through the ILS aerial on a less than precise landing; from personal observation it certainly was useless. An NDB beacon operated intermittently, and the only local air traffic facility was an old, Russian-built, valve-driven FAC radio, powered by a small camping-type generator at the end of a long power lead dangling down the outside of the tower.

So that brings us back to that explosion at the bomb dump. Even now it is difficult to establish exactly what was going on; the Nigerians would only tell us what they deemed necessary. But it would appear that this was some part of the seventh Nigerian coup – which failed. It seems likely that part of the plan was to load some 250kg bombs onto the MiG-21s at Makurdi to use against the ruling military council. Speculation was that the bombs might not have been properly maintained. The first bomb had exploded during the handling process, setting off several others – as well as old Atoll missiles some hours later. In any event the

Nigerian MiG squadron commander and some of his pilots disappeared from the base, and we understood that the boss and other coup leaders were eventually executed. When I later flew round the bomb dump, which was near the finals turn to the runway, the devastation was quite clear. Even beyond this area large numbers of the traditional, circular Nigerian huts were missing their roofs. The official comment was that there had been an accident, but no injuries had been sustained. Eventually we resumed our training programme and the only outcome was that, for a while, the aircraft were dispersed up and down the taxiway as a counter-measure against attack from elsewhere.

The line-up at Makurdi, the Nigerian Air Force base, shows Jaguars head-to-head with MiG-21s.

Our rate of flying was rather hit and miss depending on a variety of factors. To put it into perspective I flew about 108 hours in the two-year contract, whereas in the RAF I was flying about 230 hours a year. Fuel supplies were one issue, which certainly affected progress for the Nigerian pilots. Although Dornier had installed proper fuel storage when constructing the airfield, by the time I arrived this was no longer functioning, so fuel was stored in a series of bowsers parked along a peri-track. The amount available at any one time was relatively low; as I recall there were some six or seven bowsers. Despite suggestions that some form of planned flying rate might be appropriate, the MiG-21 squadron decided to use it up as quickly as they could, and thus there was a bit of a race for us to get our flights in as well before it all disappeared. Once it had gone we had to await replenishment by road from the oil production area in the south of Nigeria several hundred miles away; this took anything from two to five weeks to happen. The delivery problem was exacerbated by the probability that the bowsers used to pick up the fuel were designed for low-speed operation on airfields – perhaps lacking the baffle plates necessary to prevent fuel surging in road tankers. In any event, on a recce flight along the road down to Port Harcourt I noticed several bowsers on their sides in the bush, having rolled at bends owing to instability and, perhaps, over-enthusiastic driving.

No doubt as a result of the attempted coup, we were not allowed to carry weapons on the aircraft. However the Nigerians did decide that they would like a bombing range, and I was tasked to set this up. Once again my handy notes from the OCU at Lossiemouth came to the fore, and I dug out the section on Tain Range layout, procedures and so on. Having completed the design it was with a certain amount of trepidation that, one day, I was told that a Bo105 helicopter was on its way up from the south to take me out to the assigned area to start making the range a reality by flying some simulated attack profiles. A ground party had been sent ahead, established a white-painted VW as a target, and set out barrels in the prescribed pattern. The ride was, as you would imagine, both exciting and nerve racking, as the helicopter pilot was determined to show me that this was 'no problem for him'. I was mightily relieved to return in one piece.

Our next involvement with the Nigerian helicopter force was somewhat more traumatic. We had suggested that the lack of any search and rescue facility was undesirable, and I had already taken to wearing one of those day-glow orange flying suits sported by the Luftwaffe – which I had acquired on a squadron exchange years earlier. A short while later, a Bo105 helicopter appeared from the south to be our SAR ally. After a brief discussion with the pilot it was evident that this was not one of his specialities; in fact he had never done any winching at all. We suggested that he might like to take a willing volunteer from the many Nigerian ground crew and do some practice winching from a sandbank in the nearby River Benue. Having successfully completed that exercise, he could then try his hand at winching the survivor from water.

We will never know the full story, but it seems likely that the helicopter descended onto the survivor rather than the survivor being pulled up to the helicopter. The helicopter was written off and, for a while, was set on the airfield with some crashed MiG-21s as a decoy. Not reassuring and, from a survival point of view, if I had parted company with my aircraft I'd have felt I'd be better off taking my chances with local villagers. These I greatly admired for their ability to smile through all sorts of poverty and deprivation. Indeed we met many while taking part in hash runs, the sort of paper chase fun run through local villages which takes place all over the world.

Progress on the look-alike OCU course continued rather slowly but we did eventually get to the air-to-air combat phase. Initial sorties consisted of tracking exercises and tail chases, before we got to the standard one v one set up. But at this point we encountered a problem. The Nigerian engineers had been in the habit of covering the cockpits with sheets to keep the heat from the direct sun off. What with the dust, a very fine sandpaper abrasive process had taken place and it proved impossible to see out clearly over the top of one's head. This made combat manoeuvring an interesting proposition, and the phase was scrubbed.

Another area of the course which came to grief was range firing. Whilst, following the coup attempt, the army generals had very sensibly banned live weapons for the air force, simulated attacks were still possible. The MiG-21s were making use of the new range and early on, one of the two Russian instructors was giving a steep dive demo on the range in their only two-seater. Because he spoke little English, his flight briefs apparently required an interpreter – and then he hoped that the flight proceeded pretty much as briefed. Obviously, though, this one hadn't. The first we knew of a problem was that both Rod and I were asked to get airborne and go and search for an overdue MiG. It wasn't too long before we found the smoking wreck with no signs of survivors, just beyond the target area. We of course again never heard officially what had happened – indeed it is probable that no-one really knew for sure. But the range was put out of operation and the MiGs stopped flying for several months.

I had had a lot of sympathy for the Russian pilots, they were there essentially to do the same job as us but without the benefit of comfortable living, guaranteed water and power supplies, regular visits home and a very good salary. Despite the fact we shared the same hangar and were parked opposite them on the ramp we didn't have too much contact. They were, at the time, of course, still the Cold War enemy, and although this didn't bother us they lived under the careful scrutiny of a political agent who was part of their team. We did invite them to our clubhouse during our first Christmas and, once out of sight of the agent and a few drinks down the road, I had some very interesting discussions with the one guy who spoke reasonable English. We also had an international football match on one occasion. I was coerced to play, but having run up and down the pitch for thirty minutes in the heat and humidity without ever actually touching the ball, I sent myself to the bench, exhausted!

One event which sticks out clearly in my mind takes much longer to write about or even recount than the real time that passed. I came in one morning to be told that I would be needed to supervise some engine runs that were scheduled to take place. This was not particularly unusual apart from the fact that the person to carry out the runs was to be a Nigerian engineer who had recently joined the unit, having, it was rumoured, not completed the flying training which had been his preferred option. The aircraft was parked on the parallel taxiway, fully chocked and connected by an umbilical cable to a test unit from which various readings of fuel flow, engine jet pipe temperature, and so on could be recorded by the Rolls-Royce engineer who was to be in attendance.

As I neared the squadron I heard the well-known resonance of Adour engines being started; clearly the engineer had reckoned that supervision was unnecessary and decided to proceed before I got there, so I leapt into my car and drove the 300 yards or so from the squadron towards the parked aircraft. The next few seconds seemed to be frozen in time. As I approached I saw the reheat petals in both engines open up and the characteristic blue flame of full reheat lighting up. The Rolls-Royce rep, who was standing by his test unit and just off to one side from directly behind the aircraft, fortunately had the presence of mind to dive flat on the ground as the aircraft shot forward, washing some very high temperature air over him. The umbilical cable stretched out and then parted as the aircraft gathered momentum across the intersection heading for the bush. It left the taxiway and passed across a monsoon ditch some two to three feet deep, which neatly broke off the starboard undercarriage leg and caused the starboard wing tip to buckle upwards as it manfully took the weight. Full reheat continued and the Jaguar was not about to give up yet. It slid on into the scrub as I rushed up on one side, frantically giving the 'cut engines' signal to our erstwhile engineer. Fortunately it seemed he had come to the same conclusion, as suddenly there was silence as the engines shut down.

In the nanosecond during which I considered what to do next, the appearance of fuel leaking from under the aircraft left me in no doubt and I departed in considerable haste. The engineer, who had come to the same conclusion, also made a rapid exit from the scene. There was some speculation that he did eventually reappear some time later as an admin officer, but I certainly never saw him again. The Rolls-Royce rep suffered some minor burns, lost his eyebrows and singed the hairs on his arms, but was otherwise undamaged. The briefing had been to test only one engine at a time, and then only at minimum reheat, so one can only speculate as to the sequence of events in the cockpit. I thought perhaps the aircraft had jumped the chocks, but in fact the wheels had not rotated at all but had simply slid forward, planing down the metal eventually to the axle stubs. Who said the Jaguar lacked thrust?! Needless to say that aircraft never, as far as I know, flew again. It had only achieved some fifteen to twenty hours flying time over and above its delivery hours.

Time passed and a plethora of events came and went, interspersed with a bit of flying. Some of these situations were amusing, some were frustrating, some were tragic and some quite dangerous. The oxygen plant eventually failed and, whilst we didn't really need oxygen for high level operations, it would have been handy to keep our anti-g systems operating (in the Jaguar, unusually, dependent on oxygen).

Even after my two years in country the simulator still languished in the docks at Lagos awaiting customs clearance and special charges. Its building had still not been erected at Makurdi base.

It was always imperative to make a careful check of fuel in the drop tanks during the external checks, as this was seen as a ready supply for many of the local town inhabitants to power lights and cooking. On the other hand it was always good to get airborne with freedom to fly almost anywhere, with the only real hazards being large vultures. One of the Nigerian pilots collected one of these at high speed, which destroyed both the intake and engine on that side. He did a good job of getting the aircraft back in difficult circumstances.

We enjoyed the opportunity to travel round Nigeria on our R&R weekends and to experience a completely different life style, dramatically removed from our life in the UK, but eventually the time came to move on. The Tornado contract in Saudi Arabia was coming together and so, in September 1987, we returned to the UK to get our life sorted to move out to the Middle East. Thus it was that I said goodbye with much regret to Jaguar flying, with a last flight on 2 September 1987. I was saddened to learn that after I had left, the situation generally continued to deteriorate with more aircraft losses and that, by 1991, Jaguars in Nigeria were no longer in service.

CHAPTER 14

SYSTEMS (MIS)MANAGEMENT

GROUP CAPTAIN IAN HALL (RETD)

Most fighters and fighter-bombers have the potential to bite those who take liberties, with the Jaguar being no exception. Some of its systems seemed purpose-built to catch out pilots. The fuel jettison function was a good example, being a new idea to many; used, as a rule, when an early landing was necessary following a problem of one sort or another, it sometimes got switched on and forgotten in the heat of dealing with the original problem. Or, following switching on, the unlucky pilot would discover it was malfunctioning and couldn't be de-selected. The result would be the same in both cases: red captions and clangers indicating very little fuel left and imminent disaster. The upshot was flying orders prohibiting use of the fuel jettison system more than ten miles from a suitable landing strip.

Unlike some of our other illustrious contributors, I never had to step over the side in a hurry. But I still had exciting moments, of which some could have been termed unlucky. My own carelessness undoubtedly played a part in others, while still more had their origin in the idiosyncratic nature of some of the Jaguar's technical systems, of which the fuel feed and engine reheats were but two examples. The worst culminated in my finding myself in a very tricky situation far out to sea, but before we get to that let me describe an earlier adventure.

Ferrying fighters long distances was always a welcome variation to the routine although, in the case of the Jaguar, it could be hard work, as the aircraft had no autopilot and was reluctant to trim out at altitude. Anyway, this memorable journey, made when I was on 6 Squadron, was from Nellis Air Force Base Nevada, to Goose Bay Labrador, leading a flight of three Jags on return from Exercise Red Flag. Although it was warm in Nevada, we were dressed in rubber immersion suits for the trip, for it was still deep winter in eastern Canada. Thus we were dripping with sweat by the time we got airborne. Nevertheless, we safely made the first rendezvous with the Victor tanker over Omaha, Nebraska, and were soon established on our accompanied route.

Now, the Jaguar's piping had a peculiarity in that it had to take fuel at a lower pressure than most refuelling systems generally provide. Simple enough to regulate on the ground, but reputedly not so easy to sort out from a Victor. It was not uncommon for Jags to spring leaks when air-to-air refuelling, and so it proved this time; before long, two of my three aircraft were streaming fuel from the seals at the drop-tank attachment points. Not a life or death problem – we could refuel more often – but it soon became apparent that the total fuel available wasn't going to get the formation to its destination. The Victor could make it (they always, it seemed to us, looked after number one first) but we'd have to land somewhere short. Bagotville, Province of Quebec, was the nominated diversion, and as we reached the overhead the Victor cast us off and we were soon safely on the deck.

'Bag Town', as the base was known in the fighter trade, was at that time home to the French-Canadian CF-101 Voodoo Wing, and we found the crews of that awesome two-seat fighter incredibly welcoming. A couple of them were deputed to see us into a local hotel, and after we'd showered and changed they returned to escort us out for our evening's entertainment. This comprised a trip to the local town, Chicoutimi; a substantial place, but one which undoubtedly had about it the wild and woolly atmosphere of the Canadian wilderness. The highlight, indeed the only thing I remember of the evening, was a visit to a nightclub where, according to our hosts, ... the dancing girls were so unattractive you paid them to keep their clothes on ...!

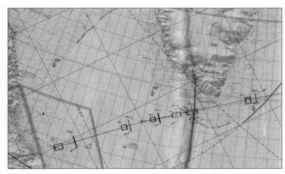

Trailing across the Atlantic (trailing being the term used for a refuelled transit). This particular one is a part of the 'clean-wing' crossing referred to here. The refuelling 'brackets' came thick and fast.

We continued to Goose Bay the next morning without further incident, making the short and pleasant trip along the St Lawrence Seaway. For this stretch, by the way, it was sufficient to fill up only the internal fuel tanks, thus avoiding the difficulty of the ruptured drop-tank seals. These were replaced at Goose for the subsequent Atlantic crossing, but I do recall further problems for one of the aircraft on that last leg. With burst seals and no convenient diversion available, the pilot's solution that time was to jettison the drop tanks into the ocean and continue 'clean wing'. It stopped the leak – but was rather a drastic remedy.

All this set me thinking, and some time later I made a case for getting round the seal problem entirely by planning future Atlantic crossings without external tanks. Quite apart from the problems of diversion and jettisoned tanks, a drawback of standard Jaguar AAR was that the heavy aircraft could not refuel at more than medium levels, increasing both its and the tanker's fuel burn. This was exacerbated because, even at those modest altitudes, the Jags needed to use a touch of reheat in order to plug in and remain in contact. So the fuel intake seemed at times to be almost offset by the fuel usage during refuelling. The whole performance reduced the range, or increased the tanker requirement.

My alternative was simple; with the Jaguars 'clean' the formation would be able to fly much higher, markedly improving fuel economy. At first sight the basic aircraft's range seemed all too short, but a few calculations suggested it might be otherwise. Having made my pitch to group HQ, they were sufficiently interested to permit me a trial. And so it was that one fine day soon after found me trundling around the UK for a couple of hours behind a Victor, refuelling at 31,000ft, without reheat, and measuring the total usage of the whole formation. The results were favourable, although group staffs made minor objections based on marginal diversion capability in the event of, say, a broken refuelling probe. But the clincher for the eventual 'no' finally turned out to be that the drop tanks, being required on the other side of the pond for the subsequent exercises, had to be got there one way or another. If they weren't ferried under the Jags' wings, they would have to be transported in extra Hercules aircraft. This would incur its own costs, zeroing the net saving – so that was the end of my bright idea.

Curiously, as I compiled this volume another of my contributors commented that my 'clean AAR' wheeze was not as original as I had thought it to be. Indeed he produced a map confirming that his squadron had crossed the Atlantic clean-wing some eight years before the event I've been describing. Which goes to prove that nothing is new. But the fact that I was allowed my trial doesn't say a great deal for the corporate memory at group HQ.

Anyway, all that is by way of an appetiser for my 'big one', and for this we'll shift the scenario to Gibraltar and a detachment of three Jaguars. This was one of a series which started at the time of the Falklands conflict – the Spanish having supported the 'wrong' side and, at the same time, having made unfriendly noises regarding what they perceived as the UK's colonial occupation of the Rock. Now, not long after the conflict had ended, the Royal Navy was still heavily involved in policing the South Atlantic. Whenever relief ships transited southwards towards the operational theatre, they took the opportunity to get in some defensive training against incoming jets by calling up Gib and arranging for simulated attacks by our Jags. On this occasion a flotilla would be passing at good speed to the west of Gibraltar, with its nearest approach to the Rock being some 200 miles. There would be only a very short window when they would be within range, and timing would be crucial.

The Jag's Gibraltar performance was slightly problematical. The runway, at 6,000ft, was not over-long for the aircraft, especially when both the under- and over-shoot areas were the sea. There was an arrestor wire, but not of the conventional type. It was a CHAG, a 'chain arrestor gear', whose braking effect came from the engaged wire taking up heavy chains link by link. Its characteristics differed from the usual, hydraulically-braked hookwires, which altered our permitted take-off limits; indeed it was normally best to operate Jaguars from Gib without drop tanks. The aircraft was always pleasant to fly in that configuration, so nobody minded – not least because clean-wing meant increased manoeuvrability and higher g limits. So we would often enjoy the opportunity while there of practising air combat training – dog fighting.

On this particular occasion, though, I can't remember why, we were operating with external tanks. In this fit, because of runway and performance limitations we would normally take on less than a full fuel load to ensure we were within the stop/go/CHAG limitations in the event of a problem on take-off. Our three aircraft were tasked with some other mission early that morning, and the plan was that two would make a quick turn-round and then launch towards the ships. For reasons lost in the mists of time, things went wrong; we were delayed, and were also left with only a singleton to do the naval sortie. The ships were already past their predicted nearest approach, and if we didn't get a move on we'd miss the RV. I'd selected myself to fly the solo sortie (being the DetCo, it was my privilege to hog the hours!) and stayed in the cockpit of the only available aircraft while it was readied for its second trip. Join me there as I spend the time pointedly studying my watch and tossing out occasional words of 'encouragement' to the techies who are toiling to hasten the turn-round.

While we're waiting for them to finish I could usefully describe another of the Jaguar's odd technical features. Most reheated military jets have the reheat or 'afterburner' facility tacked on top of the normal power range. However it was found during Jaguar trials flying that, following an engine failure, max 'dry' power on the remaining engine was too little for a single-engined approach, whereas min reheat was too much. This interesting area was fully investigated by a French test pilot, who duly crashed a prototype aircraft in the process. He ejected safely – but it was an expensive and painful way of finding out about the problem. The innovative solution was to install 'part-throttle reheat' as well as the normal system. As the name suggests this gives the ability to select reheat at less than full dry power. PTR is selectable by a couple of small switches on the cockpit wall up behind the pilot's left shoulder – and is embodied on the fleet. In fact, as PTR also offers a way of fine-tuning the power in the range necessary for AAR, it's useful there as well as during a single-engined landing.

Now then; turn-round and refuelling are complete, and I can still just about make it. A brief check around prior to engine start and – ohmygawd – the tanks have filled completely and I'm now heavier than permitted for take-off in the conditions. The only solution is to defuel a bit, but that's easier said than done. It's an operation rarely performed, the first show-stopper usually being the lack of an empty bowser to take the unwanted fuel. But miracles do happen, and my trusty troops quickly locate a spare truck behind the hangars; perhaps our luck's changing, and we quickly plug it in. The external tanks are not gauged, except by dolls-eyes indicating 'full', 'partly full' or 'empty'. So the best way to get rid of the precise amount needed to achieve the desired take-off weight is to leave the drop tanks full but to meter the fuel out of the gauged, internal tanks. The switches are arranged accordingly, and I sit drumming my fingers on the cockpit sides while the decrepit bowser's ancient pump inches the fuel out. After what seems an age, the cockpit gauges indicate correctly and we detach the bowser. Pausing no longer, I give a thumbs up, slam the canopy shut, crank the beast into life, and roar out to the take-off point. I can still just about hack the task.

On lift-off I automatically correct a strong wing-drop as I pull into the air – that's not unusual for Gib, where the Rock can induce remarkable gusts and turbulence. Hang it left down Algeciras Bay, turn right through the Straits, and set course at low level with best speed out into the Atlantic towards the latest estimated fleet position. Let's hope all this effort hasn't been wasted.

Some fifteen minutes later I begin seriously to scan ahead for our nautical friends. The RAF Jaguar, lacking a radar, isn't really equipped for the maritime role, and it wouldn't be at all surprising if my DR is out after all the delay. But no – I'm in luck. The odd whiff of give-away smoke appears on the horizon, soon reinforced by tell-tale grey smudges of superstructure – and then the more substantial bulk of hulls. I increase to attack speed. There's nowhere to hide over the sea. Not only do the ships have their own powerful radars, but I know that if I can see them in the prevailing good visibility, they can certainly see me – especially as they're looking directly along the smoky trail of the Jag's engines in dry power. They must think they've got me on a plate. But they don't reckon on the boundless cunning of this expert fighter pilot – and I flick on the two switches that control my stealth defence. PTR! Reheat instantly kills the smoke, and I know the tiny head-on cross section of the Jag will now be harder to pick up. Not an approved technique – but one which most Jaguar pilots would admit to using in circumstances where invisibility is a factor and neither noise nor fuel a problem. I adjust the throttles within the 'dry' range to avoid over-speeding, weave a little, and drop some chaff – just to move the aircraft out of the obvious line of approach and to give the ships' computers something to think about.

There is still some distance to go, and I've time for a brief check around the instruments. My eye is caught by the fuel gauges. Can't be! Should still be on the external tanks – dolls-eyes cross-hatched. But no. One of them is white and the corresponding side of the internal tanks is indicating far lower than it should be. Instantly it all falls into place. It's that fickle fuel system again. The bowser, unbidden, must have sucked some out of one of the drop tanks. That, rather than turbulence, might explain the wing drop on take-off. In my haste, I hadn't cross-checked the bowser's contents before rushing off – and I guess my impatience had distracted the ground crew from making their usual checks. A brilliant deduction. Pity I hadn't been that brilliant thirty minutes ago. But never mind; what can be done about it now? A quick re-calculation says I can still complete the run-in. It'll leave me a little short, but we mustn't let the RAF down by not turning up at all for the naval task, eh. I'll have to climb to high level for the return immediately after the attack, so they'll certainly claim a 'shoot down' as I egress. However, the primary aim of giving the fish-heads training against inbound targets will have been achieved.

Confront problems; solve them instantly; execute the mission. The razor-sharp brain is finely honed for moments such as this. OK, back to the job in hand. The ships are looming large and my radar-warning receiver is lighting up. I weave increasingly aggressively to get right down on the deck and push the speed higher. Atlantic rollers are really whistling past my ears now so I select the largest and juiciest target and home in on her. A blur of funnels, superstructure, and white faces are peering up as I flash across the decks. Whoops – mind those masts and wires! I crank it round on course for Gib and point skywards as my rate of breathing reduces. Mission accomplished, despite everything.

Time, now, to take another look at the fuel/miles equation. It ought to be relatively easy to sort out the imbalance; the total should, according to my earlier estimate, be tight but manageable. I coolly scan the gauges and transfer data to my lightning-fast mental calculator – but the answer doesn't come out right. I have another look, hang on now – the fuel's even lower than I'd expected. An uncomfortable feeling descends on me. What the hell is going on? More urgently – and considerably more carefully – I scan the instruments. The total contents are reducing far too quickly; I can almost see the needles moving round the dials. Could it be a leak? It is unlikely to be leaking from both sides, surely. We're climbing at a tremendous rate, which is good news as we'll be in the more economical upper atmosphere sooner. But I still can't work it out – and the fuel is relentlessly draining away.

At last the penny drops. Those reheat nozzle indicators have been gazing, stupidly, at me all this time and I hadn't registered. PTR is still gobbling fuel at a ridiculous rate. I reach around behind my shoulder and snap the switches off – but by now the damage has been done. I start to curse blindly – but that doesn't help either. After recalculating the options, and continuing to climb as high as it will go in order to conserve what little fuel is left I put the throttle back to maximum range speed. We're only crawling towards Gib now, and the engines are still relentlessly burning gas. The ocean looks cold.

A possibility would be to jettison the drop tanks into the sea to reduce drag, but then I'll certainly have to explain to 'them'. Divert, instead? 'They' would certainly question that – but need they know all the damning details? What's en route? Spain, in the context of the Gibraltar operation, is out of the question. The only Moroccan airport known to be remotely friendly is Tangiers, which is little more than twenty-five miles short of Gib. But my calculations tell me that those miles might make all the difference, so that's the way I'll have to go and just concentrate on saving fuel in every way possible. I trim the airframe to the n'th degree to minimise drag and plan the most economical descent possible. I feel I might just make it, so I shift my sweat-soaked body into the most comfortable position possible. On second thoughts, better tighten the ejection-seat straps. Dear oh dear; what a mess.

Well, from there on in luck began to smile on me. And my brain focussed properly for, perhaps, the first time in the day. Tangiers' weather was fine, they had no other traffic, and I was cleared for a straight-in approach. I virtually glided the last hundred miles, only applying a little power to check the descent after the gear and flaps went down for landing. The wheels touched and I breathed a huge sigh of relief. Taxied on the fumes to a distant corner of the airfield and shut down to a lovely, deafening silence.

It was siesta time, and even the flies were dozing. What now; call the air attaché? Phones were problematical in those days, especially from remote parts of Moroccan airfields. While I was still mulling over the options and consequences, my decision was made for me. To my surprise a fuel truck hove into view and the driver gestured his willingness to give me a little fuel – enough to hop across to Gib. I jumped at the offer, and signed the proffered chit. I called Tangiers ATC on this sleepy afternoon for clearance to Gib, and they approved the unplanned request as though it happened every day. I gratefully departed North Africa, touching down on the Rock barely ten minutes later.

What an idiot. All those mistakes. There was nothing for it now, I realised, but to face the music, and I prepared to phone hierarchy back home. But before I had a chance to do so I bumped into a flight commander from another squadron – whom I knew well and who just happened to be staging through. I told him the story and of my intention to come clean. More detached from the incident than I, he thought it over for a minute. "You know," he said, "we're an awfully long way from base and the truth's never likely to come out. Sounds like a transient fuel snag you've had there, sensibly dealt with by a precautionary diversion. Then quickly sorted out on return to Gib. No need to confuse them with unnecessary detail, I'd say." Well, it wasn't his head that would roll if I took his advice and the truth was subsequently to emerge. But the more I thought about it, the more attractive this way forward seemed.

And so it was. I made the phone call, spoke the necessary weasel words, and no questions were asked. And when, at the next morning's Gibraltar ops briefing, the air commander mentioned that there had been an appreciative signal from the RN for my simulated attack, I merely smiled modestly. "Had a fuel problem as well, I understand?" he said. Secure in the knowledge he knew little about Jags, I murmured about it being of a minor nature and that all three jets were now serviceable. Content with that, he turned back to the main business of Gib's day, which I seem to recall as being the planned tour of the airfield by the local Rotary Club – or something along those lines. As for me, my initial reaction was to curse those Jaguar systems. However, on mature reflection, and to borrow the title of that fine old *Air Clues* series of articles, I had to admit that 'I learnt about flying from that'.

CHAPTER 15

THE OLD MAN OF THE DESERT

Now, away from trivial training incidents to the real thing: operations. The man to tell of these is Dave Bagshaw.

I meet Baggers regularly at lunch with that same bunch of retired Jaguar pilots. Well, mainly Jaguar pilots, although we are periodically joined by retired aircrew from just about any type the RAF ever based in East Anglia. Although Baggers and I both had long RAF careers flying similar aircraft, chance ensured that we were stationed together for only the briefest of periods. So it is only in recent years that I've really got to know him.

Whilst we both served on Middle East Hunters and then Jaguars, Baggers' times were considerably more exciting than mine. I was just too late for the action in Aden, and then spent the Gulf Conflict bravely manning my MoD office. But he managed to be in the front line on both occasions.

War is supposed to be a young man's game but, by the time of the Iraq business, Baggers could fairly have been described as elderly by fighter pilot standards – albeit hugely loved and respected in the Jaguar world by virtue of his years of experience. The stories of both conflicts have oft been told, but nevertheless let's hear Baggers' unique slant on his desert service.

SQUADRON LEADER DAVE BAGSHAW (RETD)

It's an incongruous setting. The Doubletree Inn, Austin, Texas, and it's mid August 1990 as I awake in my hotel room. I turn on the TV. CNN gives an update of happenings around the US and the rest of the world, concluding with a short piece on Saddam Hussein's invasion of Kuwait. This includes a clip of RAF Coltishall Jaguars taxiing out as part of the UK's rapid reaction to this Iraqi aggression.

What? Am I seeing things? I'm right out of the Coltishall information loop in my capacity as detachment commander/team leader of the 41(F) Squadron element participating in the USAF's Reconnaissance Air Meet 90, now in full swing at Bergstrom Air Force Base just a few miles away.

But no, I'm not imagining this, as confirmed by the other aircrew team members; my room suddenly fills with potential mutineers. "We don't wanna do any more of this recce stuff! We need to get back to Colt, join the rest of the lads and get doin' the real thing – like dropping bombs and strafing!"

With a little application of tact and diplomacy I manage to persuade them that perhaps we should first win the recce competition and then return to base and take it from there. Little did we know that three-and-a-half-months later

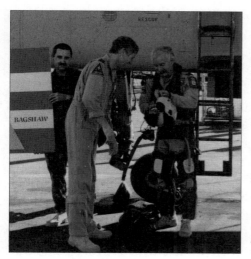

Dave Bagshaw's 4,000th Jaguar hour, celebrated with OC 41 Squadron, Bill Pixton.

all four of us, plus SEngO and many of the engineering and intelligence team, would take over in the Middle East from those we'd just seen on TV at the end of the 'diplomatic' stage of Operation Desert Shield and just in time for the action of Desert Storm. Meanwhile, we concentrated on the exercise, pipping the RAAF F-111s and taking home the Foreign Air Force Participants trophy.

That initial Gulf Jaguar effort primarily comprised Wing Commander Jerry Connolly and his 6 Squadron crews, who initially deployed on Operation Granby (the UK element of the coalition operation) to Thumrait in the Omani desert. In spartan conditions, all aspects of theatre acclimatisation and training were addressed, including NBC training – Saddam was widely suspected of possessing and planning to use WMD. Gas masks and charcoal suits were made doubly uncomfortable by the 45° heat of the Omani summer.

However, because Thumrait was somewhat remote from Kuwait, the AAR 'bill' to get a Jaguar mission there and back would have been unsupportable. So in October, as Iraq continued to defy UN resolutions, the Jaguar Boys were redeployed to Bahrain International Airport. Great joy abounded among the troops when they learned that Thumrait's tent city, especially its thunderboxes and field kitchens, were to be replaced by plush hotels. Sadly, though, it was during this period that 54 Squadron's Keith Collister was killed when his XX754 hit the desert.

Once they had settled in they were tasked with pre-planning war missions. Their initial targets were expected to be Iraqi assets such as the Chinese Silkworm SSMs located along the Kuwaiti coastline, which posed a threat to ships of the coalition naval task force. The plans were for low-level approaches to deliver BL755 CBUs or 1,000lb retard bombs from level or shallow-dive attacks.

Timing was such, though, that there now needed to be a roulement of personnel. When the original team were informed that they were to be 'rotated' back to their home base at Coltishall, they very likely had mixed feelings; relief to be rejoining loved ones and returning to familiar environments, but also disappointment that they were leaving unfinished business behind.

But that was where we came in, for in November 1990 the new set of Jaguar Boys arriving in Bahrain comprised an augmented 41 Squadron. In fact we had known of this from September, when Wing Commander Bill Pixton had been told to prepare his squadron. This had triggered a compressed but intensive work-up:

OLF against simulated targets in the tactical low-flying areas and the EW range at Spadeadam; fighter affiliation; live 1,000lb bombs were dropped on the Garvie Island 'rock'; and some of us were lucky enough to launch the AIM-9D AAM on Aberporth Range from our new overwing pylons. It's amazing how the approach of war facilitated training opportunities.

The same could be said for aircraft enhancements, for those overwing missile pylons weren't the only improvements which suddenly appeared. As had occurred during the Falklands conflict, RAF aircraft were rapidly up-graded to overcome known deficiencies in operational capability. For the Jaguar, the most welcome was a vastly improved RWR. The first-generation receiver, which gave only quadrantal directional indication and audio threat identification, was replaced with Sky Guardian, which projected the actual threat, e.g. SA8, and an accurate threat direction in the HUD, as well as an easily identifiable search or lock-up audio warning. Additional defensive aids which were dusted off and tweaked included the ALQ 101-10 radar jamming pod and the Phimat chaff dispenser, carried on the outboard wing pylons, while ALE-40 flare-dispensing units were 'scabbed' on underneath the engine access doors to provide infra-red decoy defence against heat-seeking missiles.

Secure radio communication was ensured by fitting Have Quick frequency-agile radios to protect against jamming or interception. A state-of-the-art IFF/SIF system, compatible with coalition weapon systems, replaced the Jaguar original fit, thus ensuring a minimal risk of 'blue on blue' incidents. For accurate interpretation of weapons delivery effectiveness, a HUD video recorder produced a colour record of the operational aspects of a sortie.

Initial attack profiles were in level flight to simulate dropping the BL755 or 1,000lb retard bomb, but when we found that retard bomb tails would be in short supply, 20° or 30° dive attacks became the norm. As it would turn out, the medium-level environment would soon become our favoured operating level, and here would come in useful two weapons which were new to us: the American CBU-87 and the Canadian CRV7 high-velocity rocket.

In late November, the air and ground personnel earmarked to relieve the initial team travelled to their designated operating base by luxury (!) RAF Hercules. I stepped off the Herk and was immediately struck by something familiar. That smell – the unmistakeable scent of a Bahrain night – for its international airport was formerly RAF Muharraq, and I had been there during the RAF's previous Middle Eastern life prior to the 1971 withdrawal. Indeed, had I been on the original Operation Granby deployment to Thumrait, I'd have felt on familiar territory there too. This is how it had all happened.

Following completion of half the day-fighter/ground-attack course and then the fighter-recce stage on the Hunter at 229 OCU Chivenor, I was posted, in April 1967, to 1417(FR) Flight at RAF Khormaksar, Aden. I seemed to be old even then, having spent an earlier life in the RCAF and the instructional world. Eventually escaping to fighters and joining as a thirty-year-old 'junior pilot', I immediately raised the wing's average age by a considerable amount. Strike Wing ('Attack' in current parlance) comprised 8 and 43 Squadrons with Hunter FGA9s, with 1417 Flight operating the FR10 version to provide tac recce.

The start-early-finish-early working day (colonial hours!) was particularly civilised, as we could then enjoy a full afternoon at Tarshyne beach, including the on-going beach volleyball tournament. (Chaps only – no twenty-first century amazons togged in abbreviated bikinis!) Sun-downers in the Khormaksar jungle bar were obligatory – with the routine being to recycle one's empty Amstel or Carlsberg cans via adjacent palm trees.

Accommodation varied from the camel-shed bungalows (fans only) for new boys, to Shangri-La, an air-conditioned barrack block for those having got their knees adequately brown. Sadly, I never reached this dizzy residential height as we were all transferred to the Dhobi Lines married quarters vacated by families repatriated to the UK when the security situation worsened as the date for the withdrawal of British forces approached.

When we were declared to be on active service in August, all missions tasked by HQ at RAF Steamer Point were deemed to be operational, and were entered in log books in green ink. One of mine was a pre-strike recce for the last-ever fort attack by Aden's Hunters. But post-strike recce photos indicated that weapon-to-target matching had left something to be desired; three-inch rockets versus a stone fort only knock a few blocks off the corners.

In early September, Strike Wing numbers rapidly diminished; 8 Squadron was gradually re-deployed to the Gulf, via Masirah and Sharjah to, eventually, Bahrain. 43 Squadron was disbanded, to re-form soon afterwards in the UK with Phantoms.

My 1417 Flight would be absorbed by 8 Squadron, but for the time being remained the last RAF tactical presence in Aden. As such we flew a total of sixty operational missions through to November. We encountered little hostile ground fire, although on one trip my wingman observed a lone chap taking pot shots at me with his trusty musket.

Our final task was to escort the Britannia carrying HE the Governor Sir Humphrey Trevelyan to the FIR boundary; from there we carried on to land on the rolled sand runway at SOAF Base Salalah in western Oman to refuel. Resisting the entreaties of the resident aircrews to remain overnight, we departed in the gathering dusk for a night landing at RAF Sharjah to join our 8 and 208 Squadron colleagues (208 having temporarily been displaced from Muharraq), who welcomed us with copious quantities of cold, foaming beverages.

There was little time to catch my breath, as next morning this recce pilot was airborne in a two-seat Hunter to learn, on Rashid Range, how 'attack' was done. All attacks were dummy, as we weren't carrying weapons, but I still managed to 'pickle-off' the 100-gallon drop tanks. They landed 'unplottable at 6 o'clock' of course – a small matter of the bombs/rockets switch having wrongly been selected to 'bombs'. Red faces all around. My instructor on that trip was from 208 Squadron, and would later become a knight of the realm – so plenty of top cover!

By December 1967, as the Aden withdrawal airlift through RAF Muharraq was complete and ramp space was now available, 8 and 208 Squadrons were able to occupy their permanent base.

So that had been my initial brush with the Middle East. Now, RAF Muharraq had become Bahrain International Airport, where I now found myself in November 1991. My late-night arrival this time had precluded much immediate re-orientation with the old Muharraq topography, but on walkabout the next day I was able to locate the former RAF officers' mess – well overgrown and obviously unfit for purpose in its original role. There was no trace of our accommodation huts, but the Hunter hangar was still recognisable.

Sunshades on the ramp Muharraq, Bahrain.

The formerly wide-open space of the apron was now extremely congested, with temporary structures as well as those inherited from the Bahraini Air Force – which had moved down-island to the newly completed Sheikh Isa (ruler of Bahrain) Air Base. Although there were no hardened facilities for people or aircraft, the Muharraq ramp area sported sun-shaded revetments, partially protected against blast effects by stacks of sand-filled 45-gallon fuel drums. Their size and limited number decreed that only Jaguar, Tornado and Buccaneer aircraft could be protected. On the bright side, the aircrew home for the coming period would be the four-star Diplomat Hotel.

Our work-up commenced on 29 November. As pre-planned war missions we had inherited specified low-level attacks against coastal targets in Kuwait. Our first training sorties were flown at ultra low level in south-west Saudi Arabia. It was on one of those that I clocked up my 4,000th Jaguar hour.

We learned that on every mission we would operate as part of a large 'package' – 100-plus aircraft – so we rehearsed being small cogs in a very big wheel. Mission format included refuelling from our Victor tankers and then joining the package at the correct place and time. Among the other players were USMC F-18s and USAF Phantom F-4G 'Wild Weasels'; the latter, which could detect and destroy enemy missile radars, were to be one of our most valued support assets.

As we got up to speed operating at low level in the desert and became more aware of the Kuwait/Iraq tactical situation, we began to realise that the ULL environment in which we had trained for a generation might not be appropriate for the targets we were likely to be given. In consultation with 'our man in Riyadh', Squadron Leader Tom Mallorie, who represented our interests at the coalition operations centre, we learned that we were now likely to be tasked against Iraqi artillery batteries and their supporting facilities. These were believed to possess a chemical/biological capability, which greatly concerned coalition ground forces. After intensive tactical discussion, we concluded that, for the best chance of early target identification and accuracy of weapon delivery, the steepest possible dive attack was the best option. Therefore, as the New Year dawned, we practised mainly 30° dive attacks to simulate dropping our WWII vintage bombs or the CBU-87.

These tactical discussions naturally continued after work, and the Diplomat's penthouse bar, which was pretty much earmarked for detachment aircrews' exclusive use, proved to be the perfect venue. Many thorny problems concerning the switch of emphasis from low to high level were gradually ironed out and then evaluated and fine tuned on the final work-up sorties.

Security wasn't a problem at the Diplomat, but word nevertheless got out that these 'Brit Jaguar guys' were lording it in their own penthouse bar. Shortly thereafter we received a deputation from the F-18 Squadron, normally carrier-based but now part of the large US contingent at Sheikh Isa Airbase. Although ostensibly confined to camp, they could 'spring' themselves by embarking on an authorised laundry run to Manama. On this and subsequent visitations, tactics were discussed at some length, and their opinion confirmed in no uncertain terms that we should move up to medium level: "You guys must be out of your minds to plan to go in at low level!" Iraqi defensive capability, together with the protection which could be given by other coalition assets, was their driver towards the upper air. Given that our own ideas were beginning to align with this wise counsel, we were grateful for their contribution.

Our friends from the 192nd Tactical Reconnaissance Squadron ANG from Reno, Nevada, now also at Sheikh Isa, had also climbed on the laundry bandwagon, and they and the USMC pilots must have had the cleanest 'flite soots' in theatre. The 192nd and their RF-4Cs, by the way, were well known to us, as we had conducted a series of unofficial exchanges with them following our first meeting in Norway in 1978. Other visitors to our 'Diplomat tactical symposia' were RAF escapees from the 'dry' environment across the causeway in Saudi Arabia.

During early January 1991 it became apparent to dedicated CNN viewers and recipients of regular intelligence updates that the frenetic shuttle diplomacy of various foreign and state secretaries wasn't going to change Saddam's mind, and that we would all be going to war. This gave me much cause for thought. During our work-up, I had found that two of my fifty-four-year-old bodily sensors were not performing up to scratch, namely my mark 1 eyeballs. I had worn bifocals for some time to read the fine print on the switchery and black boxes located in the ergonomic wasteland of the Jaguar side consoles, and was awaiting an updated set of specs from the RAF Central Medical Establishment. I shared my misgivings with the boss and we agreed that I would be best employed for the time being as operations officer and detachment 'uncle' until my vision deficiencies were rectified. Somewhat later, when we were well into the first week of hostilities and after a frantic series of phone calls to the UK, the 'magic' specs duly arrived. They were trifocal format with the 'tri' bit at the top of the lens – which turned out to be totally useless when operationally evaluated. I was more than somewhat disappointed, but read on.

As our work-up progressed through its final stages, detachment resources were organised on an operational footing. We were established with twenty-two pilots who were assigned to constituted four-ship formations. We had twelve Jaguar GR1As, two army GLOs, two additional ops officers, a SquIntO, and an EWO, plus of course the essential engineering and reconnaissance personnel.

Ah yes, remember tactical air reconnaissance? 41(F) Squadron not only had a conventional attack role; 50% of its effort could be devoted to recce. So two aircraft were configured for this role with the normal recce pod on the centreline. Usually this was fitted with four F95 cameras (later versions of the three in the Hunter nose cone) providing horizon-to-horizon photo cover, and an infra-red linescan sensor which could be manually slewed left, vertical or right. But the rotating drum which normally mounted two F95s could also be fitted with an F126 vertical 'survey' long-focus camera with a twelve-inch lens. I flew a single F126 trial sortie grafted on to an early work-up four-ship to provide photo coverage of bomblet dispersion of a JP233 airfield denial weapon dropped by our Tornado colleagues. Although we could expect recce tasking if the balloon went up, because of the emphasis on attack and the availability of other recce assets, this was the sole use of the recce pod pre-hostilities.

But a new toy arrived soon after action commenced in the form of the LOROP camera pod on loan from the Army Air Corps. They had reputedly mounted it in the doorway of Beaver aircraft to peer through the bedroom windows of IRA terrorists, employing the stand-off capability of the camera's thirty-six-inch lens to avoid detection. We had other ideas for the pod, but first we had to integrate it with the Jaguar systems and then fly trials to discover if and how it worked. Someone who was not otherwise involved with the constituted formations would have to fly the LOROP – and guess who? In discussion with the chain of command it was decided that my slight visual impairment would not preclude me from flying the trial sorties. So thankfully, on 29 January, I flew my first Desert Storm mission. Flying above the expected AAA level, I slewed the LOROP camera to port, switched on, and flew a line search of the Kuwait and Saudi coasts until the film ran out. As I had learned from my colleagues' previous mission debriefs, the Sky Guardian HUD and audio 'warble' in the ear phones indicated some interesting threats, but with the ECM pod on 'active' and loosing off some chaff, radar lock was broken,

Top: Desert camouflage is effective. Jaguars over Nizwa, Oman.
Above left: 'He went thataway!' Thumrait, Oman.

Above right: Hapless Hunter pilot 'Wiz' Wilson and a bemused local airman review the effects of (too) low flying in the Omani desert.

Opposite top: Even royalty joined in the low flying! RAFO Jaguars and Hunters escort King Hussein of Jordan's Boeing 727 over Nizwa, Oman.

Opposite bottom: They liked to fly low in Oman. Kicking up the dust at Thumrait.

Top: Omani Jaguars refuelling from a KA-6D Intruder of the USN.

Above: The Gulf War team. Dave Bagshaw sitting on the front of the intake, Mike Rondot is three to the right of him.

Right: Gulf Conflict nose art.

Below: A T2 of the training unit vents a little fuel as it runs up for take-off (not unusual).

Opposite top: In desert colours and in typical Gulf Conflict fit, a GR1 shows off its overwing Sidewinders and dumb bombs on tandem-beam carriers. A centreline drop tank, together with a Phimat chaff dispenser on the starboard outer station, completes the fit.

Opposite bottom: Third from left, Jerry Connolly (OC 6 Squadron, who led the initial Gulf deployment); fourth from left, Andy Sephton (ex 54 Sqn – RR test pilot); fifth from left, Terry Lloyd; on the right, Graham Wright. The occasion was a stopover at Filton in 1991 following a flypast over HMS *London* at Plymouth. The ship, as part of the naval task force during the Gulf conflict had provided the 'radar eyes' for the Jaguars.

Top: The camouflage isn't just useful over open terrain. A Jaguar over the city of Norwich.
Above: The Jag where it's at home – hugging the contours (Nick Short).

Opposite top to bottom: XX830, XX955-EK and XZ356-EP on the ground at Boscombe Down, July 1990. (Ray Deacon)

THE REAL THING!

Everett Aero

For those of you that have the finances, and land — how about buying a real ex-RAF Jaguar? Everett Aero offering a number of Jaguars, both GR3s and T4s, for sale.

- ■ **Prices:** starting at £7,500
- ■ **Availability:** www.everettaero.com

Above: A sad end, but you can buy anything now! Scrap Jags for sale.

Below: 'Jaguar Sunset' by Mike Rondot. (www.collectair.co.uk/01362-860890)

either by my own efforts or more likely by our Wild Weasel friends.

The film was processed, but when viewed on the light table the PIs began to scratch their heads. "Where's the coast Baggers? Are you sure your eye-sight is up to flying and navigating?" Following further learned cogitation, we twigged – looking at my map and comparing the film with terrain features to starboard of my track, we realised that LOROP had been pointing west instead of east; therefore, no coast! We re-consulted the sketchy bumff that had accompanied the kit and deduced that what we had thought was a rear view of the pod in the un-annotated diagram was in fact a front view. So LOROP had been looking the wrong way.

With left and right hand sorted, I flew trials on the following four days, again grafted on to a four-ship or a pair, flying at 25,000ft and experimenting with differing angles of LOROP depression. On the fifth and final trip, my log book records, 'mega cloud – acquisition by SA2/SA6 radars – o'head Kuwait International'. When the results of the trials were assessed, the imagery indicated very high-definition cover of target areas from a stand-off distance of 7 to 8km at 25,000ft, making it a really useful tool for pre-attack updates and, later, battle damage assessment.

I've jumped somewhat, to the point where Desert Storm was raging. In fact in the early hours of 17 January, as I snuggled under the protection of my Diplomat Hotel 'scud-proof' blanket, I had heard the first RAF Tornado mission taking off. And then as I and the rest of the ops team reported for duty later that day, we had met the leader of that mission. He'd reported that all had gone well, as they had encountered only light AAA defences and all aircraft had returned to base. Sadly, such good news for the Tornados was not to be repeated on subsequent mornings.

Later, the Jaguar Boys had had their turn, with the first mission being flown by Squadron Leader Mike Gordon's team. They were tasked with interdiction in a kill zone just across the Kuwait border, and had attacked enemy vehicles, dropping BL755s and strafing with 30mm HE. All weapons expended, they'd been egressing the area when they'd encountered AAA. Feeling somewhat aggrieved and having no other means of retaliation, 'Strike' Gordon turned about and let them have it with one of his AIM-9L air-to-air missiles. After landing, they were met by the clamouring media; during his TV interview, when asked for his reaction to his first confrontation with the enemy, Mal Rainier replied with his oft-quoted phrase: "I ran away bravely!"

As the first week of Desert Storm operations had progressed, it had become apparent that, in order for the aircrew to cope with an extended period of combat flying, an effective R&R programme would be required. To this end, a system of 'four days on, one off' was implemented. In practice this worked very well, as the off-duty bunch were able to savour the cosmopolitan delights of downtown Manama ranging from the Thai Uppa Tree Cuppa Tea to the Londoner Inn Bar & Grill offering traditional roast beef, Yorkshire pud and two veg. The social life of the on-duty lot was understandably somewhat restricted, but at the same time quite surreal. Breakfast or lunch at the Diplomat or all-ranks' feeder on base, plan, brief, go to war, land, debrief, mini-bus back to the Diplomat to relax over suitable refreshment whilst being entertained by the resident Filipino heritage band belting out seventies and eighties hits in a disco atmosphere. Magic! Longer term R&R plans were also put in place; selected aircrew would spend a week or so sampling the delights of Muscat and the eastern Oman riviera. As it happened, success in the ground advance and the consequent reduction in air operations made visits to this local Utopia unnecessary. Pity!

One day poor weather forced the morning mission, as well as their Victor tankers, to divert to Dhahran in Saudi Arabia. For the next couple of days, similar weather conditions curtailed all but one afternoon mission, which was tasked to attack a suspected ammunition store. Weather improved later, permitting successful attacks on AAA, artillery and SSM sites. During week two, inclement weather again affected mission success, causing many attacks to be aborted and alternative targets to be bombed instead. During these early missions, the 30° dive profiles placed the aircraft well within the AAA lethal envelope during recovery after weapon release, as evidenced by shell bursts seen above the 'bottom out' altitude. Fortunately, little damage was suffered by aircraft or pilots, but a lump of spent shrapnel dented the underside of the boss's aircraft pretty much in line with the base of the ejection seat.

To lessen the risk, steeper dive angles would ensure a higher recovery height after bomb release and also potentially offer better accuracy. The QWIs suggested 45° – then 60° – and went off to crunch the numbers to come up with the correct depression and required HUD sight picture. In order to achieve a stabilised 60° dive with the HUD 'bomb fall line' tracking the target, it was necessary to tip in from the highest possible altitude. The technique was to select PTR approaching the IP, and maintain a gentle climb until target acquisition. I can vividly recall seeing 32,000ft in the HUD as I rolled (gently, gently) over into the dive. Who could ever have imagined the Jaguar being used in such a fashion? (Notwithstanding the test work described in the first chapter.) Anyway, with the target so far below, what a good job my visual difficulties had been resolved!

I might not have imagined, either, this old recce pilot flying combat attack missions. But now, although the trifocals had been abandoned, the boss had invited me to join his team. I think he had been a bit wary of this recce 'splitter' swanning off to do his own thing on the LOROP trials, but on 5 February I flew my first attack mission as 'Wicket 01C' – number three of what was now a five-ship dropping 1,000 pounders on a radio mast. As I hurtled down with all relevant switches made (I think) and with the planned recovery altitude fast approaching, the bombs hadn't released, so I hastily reverted to the 'live jettison' procedure. Off came the bombs and I heaved into a recovery, well inside the AAA envelope. Looking over my shoulder I saw the bomb bursts, fortunately in the target area, and for me and my Jaguar (XX733) no obvious damage. Not a great effort first time out, but much-improved results were achieved on my next missions. These included further attacks on artillery batteries with 1,000 pounders, and two CBU-87 attacks on an ammunition storage site and more artillery.

Whilst I was getting my teeth into the attack business, developments loomed on the recce scene. A 'recce pair' was constituted: myself, plus former 'recce puke' Pete Livesey, flying one aircraft with LOROP and one with F126. The plan, as agreed with our man in Riyadh, was for us to be tasked as part of a Jaguar attack mission to provide post-attack BDA as well as updated photos of targets to be tasked for the next day's missions. By leaving the cameras running as we departed the combat area, our PIs might also locate on film 'targets of opportunity' which could be allocated to future missions.

The recce pair first took to Kuwaiti skies on 11 February. Thick cloud in the target area, but we filmed as much of the visible terrain as possible. Post-mission interpretation showed that the F126, when operated at 25,000ft, exposed the terrain at a scale very nearly that of the 1:50,000 maps used for target planning, whilst the LOROP produced excellent target detail, albeit covering a much smaller area. The following day the weather was excellent and we covered all our planned areas.

While the recce pair were getting their act together, attack missions continued to be flown at intensive rates. As well as the twice-daily four or six ships tasked to attack interdiction targets, pairs were usually tasked on CSAR or SUCAP, but on one memorable occasion a pair was directed to an air defence standing patrol and then vectored to intercept a 'bogey'. When the leader advised the controller that, although they carried self-defence AAMs, Jaguars were not really interceptors, the error was acknowledged and they were let off the hook.

SUCAP missions were armed with CRV7 rockets which, on one occasion, were effectively launched against enemy fast patrol boats. The next day, the Boss and Pete Tholen attacked a Polnocny landing craft and left it blazing and abandoned. On their 31 January SUCAP mission, Dick Midwinter and Simon Young were directed to attack enemy vehicles on the main highway near Kuwait city. They identified a ZSU 23/4, probably the most lethal Iraqi AAA asset, but, selecting gonads to 'Giant' mode, they duly attacked it – and lived to tell the tale.

From mid February, Saddam implemented his 'scorched-earth' policy, setting many Kuwaiti oil installations alight. The resultant plume of oily black smoke was amalgamated with the extensive spring cloud cover by the cold Shamal wind blowing down the Gulf from the Persian mountains. Not only were Desert Storm missions severely curtailed, but post-mission sun-tanning sessions around the Diplomat outdoor pool became impossible. However, the Jaguar Boys were still able to continue chalking up missions; generally at least one each day.

The weather also made it necessary to plan AAR slots to ensure sufficient fuel was available for an instrument recovery at Muharraq and possible diversion. Of course this also included the recce pair; but Livvo had only done the AAR ground school and one 'dry' demo in the probe-less T2. So he completed the AAR syllabus 'in anger', with two of his conversion sorties being flown in turbulent rainy/oily/smoky air at 5,000ft! The second of these, our penultimate mission, was flown through and above solid cloud as we followed our planned route on the PMD – no possibility of getting anything on film. Our final mission on 27 February suffered the same fate, but recce results were not completely zero. As we were walking out one of the PIs intercepted us. "Hey, Baggers! HQ staff want to know if the Kuwait City water towers are still standing. Can you have a look?" "OK," says I, "if the fuel holds out." Our planned route took us near the city, so as we approached I told Livvo that I was about to take the plunge, and that he was welcome to stay above cloud and head on home. He wisely decided to take no part in this madness, so I rolled into the dive and pressed on down through 20,000ft of grotty cloud. I broke out at 2,500ft just east of the city centre. The towers were still standing and apparently intact, so I rolled belly-up to point my F126 and F95 vertical cameras in their general direction. Just in case any trigger-happy bad (or good) guys might take a final pot shot, I effected a rapid recovery back into the murk, climbed back on top, and made an uneventful recovery to Muharraq.

That day's efforts were the last Desert Storm missions to be flown by the Jaguar Boys. After a series of temporary cease-fire declarations, on 28 February the final cessation of hostilities order was issued. This just happened to coincide with my fifty-fourth birthday; the double celebration therefore degenerated into the 'Mother of All Parties'.

Over the next fortnight while preparing for recovery to Coltishall, we had ample time to reflect on our achievements. Our Jaguars (and ourselves), originally optimised for the low-level environment, had proved to be eminently adaptable and effective dive bombers. We had flown 618 'war' sorties, and aircraft serviceability had been 98%; outstanding. The few sorties lost to aircraft snags could have been flown if 'war goers' had really been called for, so huge credit to our marvellous engineers. The supposedly fragile Jaguar had been flown to all corners of (and occasionally outside) the flight envelope, but airframe and engines had stood up to this hard usage. The minor battle damage, attributed to bits of 'flak' shrapnel, suffered by three aircraft, was easily and quickly repaired. The RIC PIs and processors had provided the HQ with imagery enabling them to assign the most lucrative targets in Kuwait to coalition air forces. Most importantly, we had suffered no combat losses. So, job done – as far as our political masters would allow. But that's another story.

The collective mood following the declaration of 'peace in our area' was inevitably anticlimactic; after six weeks of intensive combat, the relative idleness induced a feeling of 'get-home-itis'. But as we took our place in the queue for the services of the RAF's AT and AAR resources, the wait was not unpleasant. Paradoxically, the weather which had adversely affected the second half of Desert Storm cleared as if by magic – the Shamal stopped blowing, the oily smoke cloud dissipated and the sun reappeared. So when the pack-up activities allowed, unrestricted social and leisure pursuits resumed.

On 13 March our number came up and the Jaguar Boys' return to base commenced. The twelve jets, manned by those at the top of the seniority ladder, would fly non-stop to Coltishall using most of the RAF's tanker fleet. The third four-ship, comprising the recce pair plus Chris Allam and Steve Shutt, provided airborne spares for the first and second formations, but everything went according to plan for the first eight.

We landed back at Bahrain for a fuel top-up and took off again to RV with our TriStar, then proceeded in company to the first refuelling bracket somewhere south of Tabuk in north-west Saudi Arabia. Livvo and I were first in, got our fuel and made way for the second pair. Chris and Shutty were flying the heavier jets fitted with recce pods, and had difficulty plugging in. At the end of the bracket the TriStar set up a mandatory 'racetrack' to keep Tabuk within diversion range should they be unable to take fuel. They eventually cracked it, but as we set off westwards again the tanker captain announced: "Sorry boys, you've run me out of gas. We'll have to divert to Akrotiri so I can get some more."

We landed, refuelled Jaguars and TriStar, and pressed on homewards, arriving at dusk to break and land at a now quiet and subdued Coltishall. We were over four hours behind everyone else and had missed all the razzmatazz – bands, media frenzy, flag-waving – but nonetheless received a suitably warm welcome from patiently waiting families, friends and colleagues.

The Gulf War Jaguar Boys were back home: aircrew, ground crew and RIC personnel – and after a few days of 'make and mend' to get squadron organisation back on a peacetime footing, we went off on four weeks well-earned leave. For most, the knowledge of a job well done was just beginning to sink in. For some, re-adjustment to the 'horrors of peacetime soldiering' would take time. But for us all, the experience of the previous months would be unforgettable.

CHAPTER 16

A BLOODY NAVIGATOR

Each Jaguar squadron had, as well as its complement of single-seaters, a 'T-bird' for recurrent training and checking. The RAF two-seater was a non-operational aircraft; although it had a gun, together with all the weapon-aiming and carriage capability necessary to drop bombs, it lacked a few important elements. It had no refuelling probe; no RWR; no laser ranger and marked target seeker; and it was not strike-capable. These elements were not crucial for the peripheral mission set for the T2s, although a probe would have been very useful. For, after a fatal accident in which a Buccaneer collided with a Victor tanker, it had been made mandatory for pilots to receive AAR dual checks before going solo. And in the Jaguar T2, this was a somewhat limited exercise without a probe!

But the lack of operational capability was a pity in other ways, especially once NATO began to go for big, mixed, attack packages. As leading one of those was a substantial task, an extra brain on board would often have been advantageous. In fact the Harrier Force (although you won't catch many Harrier pilots admitting it) was not above putting a T10 at the head of its big packages from time to time for just that reason.

Anyway, partly with this in mind I came up with a scheme while I was working in the MoD in the early 1990s to make Jaguar T2s operational. The necessary modifications would cost money, so would have to be paid for by withdrawing one single-seater from each squadron and declaring the T-bird 'operational' to maintain declared numbers. But once the new state was established, the smaller squadrons would be cheaper to run, and that was always an attraction to the bean counters.

So I, together with appropriate Civil Service colleagues, set to and got the whole thing feasibility-studied and costed. Lo and behold, the savings were potentially realisable and the operational capability would be maintained, so the plan went into the programme. And thus it was that we might have seen, by the mid 1990s, our T2s sprouting refuelling probes, RWRs and so on.

A while later, though, some bright spark noticed a fundamental glitch in the financial calculations; which was that, as things presently stood, the T2s were not established on the squadrons at all. In other words the number of airmen on strength, together with the monthly flying hours, the fuel allowed and the spares held, were all based solely upon the number of operational GR1s. So T2 flying was currently being funded and managed from within that allowance. Reducing the overall number of aircraft on each squadron by one, as envisaged by my scheme, would not reduce the bill because operational numbers would remain unaltered – and therefore no saving would accrue. So the whole idea was thrown in the shredder, and that was the end of it.

But still there are T2 tales to tell. By necessity, RAF Jaguars were flown mainly by single-seat pilots. But a variety of other characters got a chance from time to time to 'have a go'. Almost without exception, they enjoyed flying in the Jaguar T-bird. Which, incidentally, was an aircraft whose back seat was set nice and high, so offering a most magnificent view of the world around – in stark contrast with the back seat of, say, a Phantom or a Tornado.

The following three chapters are by 'outsiders' various, starting with a navigator friend of mine who commanded Tornado units at squadron and station levels. But during his career he came up against Jaguars in various situations ...

AIR COMMODORE DICK BOGG (RETD)

What? A bloody navigator writing about the Jaguar and its boys? Absurd!

My first contact with the Jaguar Boys? That should have been in April 1970. I had just converted to the Phantom as the weapon system trials officer at Boscombe Down, and had become a de facto member of 'A' Squadron, which had a variety of aircraft to play with. Including, I originally imagined, the Jaguar, so I guessed there'd be the chance of the occasional trip. But I was wrong; although the squadron's Jerry Lee was flying the Jaguar, he spent most of his time in France and it would be some while before the Jag would arrive at Boscombe for its test programme. Ah well, cross that one off the list, I thought; now I'll never get a Jag trip. But fate, chance and a flight test entry into the MRCA/Tornado project led me to Laarbruch on my return to the RAF a few years later for a flight commander tour on the Buccaneer. And there at Laarbruch, in mid-1978, I found a squadron of Jaguars in the south-west HAS site. Perhaps, after all, I'd get my Jag trip.

Professionally, there was initially very little contact between the Bucc boys at Laarbruch and the Jag team. They had a completely different role, and apart from on our occasional visits to the RIC, we seldom saw them. Socially it was a different matter though, and many pints of German beer were shared in the mess. But professional contact would develop in several ways as my tour progressed, including by way of a forced marriage.

In early 1979 the Bucc acquired a new role. The 'Pave Spike' laser designator

The age-old argument about one seat or two, as 54 Phantom Squadron hands over to 54 Jaguar. Nowadays a more relevant discussion might be 'one seat or none?' The cartoonist 'Pez' was Chief Technician John Woodcock, 54 Phantom's engineering ops controller.

pod was being introduced into the RAF, and a few Buccs were modified to allow us to evaluate the system and to work on suitable tactics, either for self-designation or third-party designation for either Bucc or Jag bombers. By chance, our squadron had an exchange at Spangdahlem with the USAF, their Phantoms having a very similar Spike system to that purchased for the RAF, and so three or four navs did some familiarisation flying while on exchange. This is easy, we thought; what a beautifully-stabilised Pave Spike television picture. But the RAF's system was not stabilised, and the nav had to mark the target using his left hand, continuously 'ackling' the cross hairs on the target – all the while head down monitoring the TV screen between his legs as the pilot performed an uncomfortable manoeuvre at low level to keep outside target defences.

Not easy, but come the new year we were deemed 'ops ready' so we set off for Exercise Red Flag with a Brüggen Jag squadron to work up a co-operative attack profile, the Buccs designating for the Jags. With sixty or seventy aircraft on the Nevada ranges at the same time, there was need of a 'quiet' corner for us to develop our emerging tactics. We were granted this, and practised several 'dry' attacks, with 'designator' and bomber flying in tactical formation towards the target and closing together at an IP a couple of minutes short of the target. Soon after, we would split, the Bucc breaking left before flying an arc some 5nm from the target; the nav would pick up the target and track it like a god. Meantime, the Jag bomber would continue towards the target and, at the appropriate moment short of the target, pull up into a loft manoeuvre and release the bomb, the idea being that the bomb would enter the laser 'basket' just after the Bucc nav energised the laser.

On the assumption that both squadrons were satisfied that sufficient work-up had been achieved, a few HE 1,000lb LGBs were earmarked for the RAF's first live drops, and naturally we all wanted to be on the case. In early February 1980, Norry Bell and I took off from Nellis for a live drop to be made by a Jag – great excitement all round! The Americans clearly didn't want a 'high-value' target being destroyed, so we were allocated a clapped-out truck instead, but it was metal and we reckoned it would be a good reflector.

So at the appropriate point in the Flag mission, the two aircraft broke away from the main formation to attack our allocated target – at least I'd have the joy of watching on television as the truck was blown to smithereens by the Jag. Visions of Norman Schwarzkopf's subsequent 'luckiest man alive' video spring to mind! All went well, the Bucc and the Jag splitting as planned, and I soon found the target and tracked it without difficulty. So there we were in the Bucc, underneath the flight path of a live 1,000 pounder as it rushed upwards to apogee and then descended towards the target. But no problem; everything was worked out to the second. I switched on the laser just before the bomb was to enter the acquisition basket – it was then simply a matter of time as the bomb was guided eerily towards its target, arriving in ... 5, 4, 3, 2, 1 seconds ...

Except it didn't! Speak to me Jag boy – did you release on time and at the right point? I tracked the target for a good twenty seconds after calculated impact time but saw nothing, neither the bomb itself nor the expected explosion. With a live 1,000 pounder, we should certainly have seen the latter. But nowt! So where the bomb went was anyone's guess – perhaps it's still airborne? There was utter frustration all round. The best guess was that the bomb never entered the laser basket – a few red faces but, luckily, no serious recriminations or consequences. We bought the Jag pilot a beer and he bought two for us.

The same Red Flag exercise saw mixed formations of Bucc and Jag, six aircraft apiece, it was great fun and great learning. We were at the top of our game and we felt very comfortable operating with the Jag boys. But sadly all this was to come to a halt a couple of days later. Just before the end of the exercise, a wing fell off Ken Tait's Buccaneer during a Flag sortie, with him and his nav being killed. Metal fatigue was the problem, and the Bucc was grounded. The fix would take a long time, so Bucc/Jag LGB cooperation was put off indefinitely. Ironically, however, the event would lead to me seeing even more of the Jaguar.

On return to Germany, the need emerged to keep Bucc pilots and navs current while the 'system' worked out what to do about the Bucc's fatigue problem. Keeping current for the pilots was relatively easy as there were Hunter T7s on base already (Buccaneer squadrons used them as instrument-flying trainers). And mothballed single-seat Hunters were wheeled out, several arriving at Laarbruch in short order for the pilots to fly.

Currency for the navs was a different matter. Hunter T7 second seats were available, although there were not enough to go round. Suddenly the Jag boys became our greatest friends! OC II(AC) Squadron at Laarbruch (Wg Cdr Bob Fowler) willingly offered his T2 for continuation training for the Bucc navs, and we were very grateful for his help. So, ten years after trying to cadge a trip at Boscombe, I finally managed to fly in a Jag, and very enjoyable it was too. The cockpit felt small compared with the Bucc (and certainly the Tornado) but I was pleasantly surprised by the quietness inside, it was much less noisy than the Phantom and Harrier.

All that of course was at the height of the Cold War, and everybody in RAFG believed they were the bee's knees. There was intense rivalry between Laarbruch and Brüggen, particularly so after Brüggen achieved its unbelievable string of straight 'ones' in their Tacevals. Wow, we thought at Laarbruch, perhaps they know something we don't. There was an obvious way of finding out, as every exercise had its evaluators provided by other bases. Taceval was the end-result, but as most of us realised, Maxevals were reckoned to be more difficult, mainly because the RAF scrutinised itself during this 'dress rehearsal'. Given the roles of both Laarbruch and Brüggen, the Maxeval involved a great number of Bucc and Jag boys on each other's evaluation teams – so 'constructively super-critical' is perhaps the kindest way of describing the oversight given to these internal evaluations.

I was often co-opted as a member of the Taceval team, and I remember being told to report to Rheindahlen at 0100hrs one dark night, with no idea who we were going to surprise – as was the norm. The in-briefing soon disclosed that it was to be Brüggen, and we piled into a convoy of various vehicles led by a Taceval team car that 'blocked' the guardroom from announcing our presence to the COC. I had been allocated to 14 Squadron, in the south-east corner, arriving there at about 0240hrs and left waiting for the action to start.

Suddenly, round the corner came an RAF Police Land Rover on a routine patrol, whose driver spied me and my non-RAF colleague. The vehicle drew up alongside. "Mornin' Sir, a bit early aren't we?" "Yes," said I, struggling to keep a straight face; "we've got an early start, the boss'll be here in a few minutes." And off he went, clearly not having spied that my flying suit sported a nav brevet. A few minutes later, the Land Rover returned, the policeman observing that we were still hanging around. "Can I see some ID please, Sir?" So I passed over my F1250. Seeing that he was about to radio his supervisor I told him to stop. Luckily, at that very moment, the hooter sounded; it was 0300hrs and I said: "Taceval." "You bastard, Sir" he replied, speeding off to do his duty!

So I spent several days with 14 Squadron, whose boss at the time was Joe Sim, ironically a former Javelin navigator turned pilot. The squadron showed itself to be very proficient at playing the Taceval game, with many right noises being made at the right time by the boss. Chase sorties were pretty well handled, as indeed was the whole operation. I was impressed, so perhaps there was some power behind Whisky Walker's famous signpost on entry into the base which exhorted his people never to forget that they were preparing for war. Above all, I learned a lot about my own role as a warlord on a Bucc squadron, and I changed several things about the way I did business to reflect those of this Jag squadron.

Later, I was posted to MoD to find that I had successive Jag men working for me, Nobby Grey and Mike Gray, both of whom proved to be excellent weapons project officers. During this period I came across Joe Sim once again, working together on the offensive ops desk in air force ops as the Falklands War progressed. It was an amicable relationship – which was just as well as our paths would cross again.

Soon afterwards, I was sent for one day and asked, if I had a completely free choice of next posting, what I would like to do. Brashly I said, "be the boss of a Tornado squadron". To which the reply came, "You're going to be the boss of the first Tornado squadron at Brüggen". I was over the moon, but elsewhere (from the whole of the Brüggen Jag Wing) there was a resounding: "What? A bloody navigator here, as a boss?" Hang on a minute, I thought, you're already getting a (former) bloody navigator as station commander! Yes, Joe Sim was going back to Brüggen as station commander, to oversee the transition to Tornado.

Eventually this master plan became a reality, and I hoped I'd not upset Joe too much while he was OC14 and in MoD. But as I went through Tornado conversion at Cottesmore and Honington he couldn't have been more proactive, and we had several conversations about the initial introduction of the Tornado. He sought my advice on many aspects, suggesting that I should come out to Brüggen for a few days to see what they were doing. Being on OCU courses, I pointed out that missing a few days might not have been welcome, to which he responded: "OK, come out for a day from time to time – I'll send an aircraft to pick you up." And that's exactly what he did. On several occasions, a T2 Jag would arrive as soon as Cottesmore or Honington was open, and I'd enjoy a low-level trip across the North Sea to Brüggen, with a different taxi driver each time.

Dick Wharmby was OC 20 Squadron at the time, and I was to occupy the site he was vacating, right next to the golf course, which was very convenient. Dick proved to be an absolute star and gave me invaluable help and advice about the site and many other things about life at Brüggen. As a result of these visits, the modifications to the site, the hard and soft accommodation, and HAS extensions, went very smoothly.

On one occasion, I even managed to return to Honington via a route around northern Germany – it hadn't changed. I enjoyed those trips in the Jag, which was a joy at low level – although the NAVWASS seemed to need a bit of nursing. Now, if you had had a second person in the cockpit ..!

During this time I was invited to HQ to discuss the composition of my new squadron (which was to be 31). Hitherto, new Tornado squadrons had been 'experience heavy', so would I please accept some first tourists – and what about former Jaguar pilots? On both counts I had no reservations, so long as I had a core of experienced people, no more than 30% first tourists and, yes please, "... as many Jag pilots as you can find!" I had seen the way they operated and had no doubt that they would be worth their weight in gold – provided they could adapt to working with a bloody nav. The complement was agreed, and I was to receive ex-Jag pilots Martin Mahoney, John McBoyle and Peter Thornton from the outset. More followed later, and boy, was I pleased.

This bloody nav's eventual arrival at Brüggen was a strange experience. Some greeted me with good-humoured scepticism, but the vast majority could not have been more welcoming. And so began perhaps the best year in my life, as four Tornado squadrons arrived and four Jag squadrons left Brüggen.

31 Tornado (designate) ran in parallel with 31 Jaguar (20 Jaguar Squadron having now vacated their site and gone to Laarbruch with Tornados). The camaraderie between 'des' and 'real' could not have been better. At each squadron's succession, there was a joint standard hand-over parade and mixed flypast. The banter between the two teams was magnificent, and the mature approach to what must have been a rather sad period for the Jag boys during the loss of several of their squadrons was very well handled and much appreciated all round.

Socially, there was a healthy approach as the Jag wing gradually wound down – the various Jag bosses had agreed that the new kids on the block should be given their heads and so, too, the outgoing Jag squadrons were allowed to go in style without fear of disruption to their ceremonies and parties.

There was of course plenty of good-natured rivalry, which led to some great times in the mess. As, for example, with a three-cornered soccer match, three teams, three goals, no referee, each team ganging up on the others throughout the afternoon; the quality of the soccer being inversely proportional to the amount of alcohol consumed. Great stuff.

As each Tornado squadron arrived, the new boss was given the date of his Taceval, but the 'Staish' had decreed that, as each new squadron was Tacevalled, so the whole station would be exercised at the same time. So there was a lot of pressure throughout that first year, but with the whole station behind the squadron that was being 'done'.

There were two notable crises during this period, both involving my 31. We were the first to be evaluated, and everyone had worked really hard. But thirty-six hours before the Taceval, my SEngO was rushed to hospital and a replacement was needed urgently. The second Tornado squadron, 17, was already re-forming; they had taken over 31 Jaguar's former SEngO, Ken Harris, so he was rapidly seconded back and a seamless engineering organisation was presented to the Taceval team.

As it happened, a few months later when 17 Squadron was being 'done', their GLO was taken ill, so we loaned our GLO (the former 31 Jaguar's Major Martin Timmis) for the evaluation. So the debt was repaid!

After we'd been declared operational I became deputy station commander, and the next time Joe Sim went on leave, in fact before 0900 hours on my very first morning in the chair, Garry Brough stepped over the side of a Jaguar – just what I needed. But magnificently, immediately after I had advised the deputy commander at RAFG, OC 14 Squadron, Dave Henderson, came to the rescue and took over all the arrangements relating to the accident. Broughie had almost spoiled my day, but I was to come across him again when he was posted to 31 as a Tornado pilot later during my tour.

During that hectic first year, each Tornado squadron worked its socks off and flying hours were at a premium. There was virtually no chance for any outsider of ever cadging a ride in the all-electric jet – it was like finding rocking horse manure. It was even difficult for OC Operations Wing, Dave Phillips, another Tornado nav, to get a trip, and he soon realised that his best route to flying hours was to tap each Jaguar squadron before they left for T2 trips. As a result, he probably has more Jaguar hours than any other navigator.

With Taceval behind us, attack training became the order of the day and the main aim was to find suitable formation leaders. As boss, I flew with all the pilots, whatever their background and experience, and it soon became clear that the ex-Jaguar boys were pretty close to the top of the pile. They were very capable aviators, had been brought up on 'hard rules', and they stood no nonsense from anyone, not just the first tourists. I liked what I saw and they soon became most competent formation leaders, with lots of common sense, and airmanship second to none. I was lucky to have them on my team. That said, having flown previously in the Jaguar, it was interesting to note in retrospect how much Jag pilots had missed. This is not a criticism, merely an observation that, in a single-seater, when the pilot's grappling with the aeroplane, navigation, NAVWASS and lookout – a second pair of eyes would have made all the difference. Anyway, the ex-Jaguar pilots I had all adapted magnificently to the two-seat environment and became invaluable members of the squadron. Interestingly, though, I had one first-tourist pilot who craved the single-seat environment and longed to go to the Jaguar. Unusually, after two Tornado tours, he got his wish.

He was the exception, though. Jaguar pilots in general did very well on the Tornado, while from my point of view their airmanship and professionalism led me to accept them with open arms. High praise indeed from a bloody navigator.

CHAPTER 17

THE FLYING SPANNER

Clearly our engineers couldn't be classified as 'outsiders'. They were an integral part of the team, and it's self-evident that no air force could function without them. It's also clear that a squadron's own engineers would play a full part in the unit's activities. What's not so obvious is how much the second and third-line engineers felt a part of operations, tucked away in a hangar as they were, carrying out deep servicing of front-line units' aircraft as they flowed through the scheduled process.

As always with such things it depended to some extent on the individuals, as well as on the set-up at any particular station. In the case of Coltishall, not just the squadrons but virtually the whole station would have deployed forward in the event of conflict – incidentally leaving the base vacant for the planned deployment of a Phantom unit from Continental USA. So Coltishall's second-line engineers were, perhaps, closer to the squadrons than on other stations. And any engineer who enjoyed flying managed to become closer still, as is apparent in this tale from Les Hendry.

The wing is off! Indeed the right engine is out, as
well. Les Hendry (with beard) looks on from the left.

SQUADRON LEADER LES HENDRY (RETD)

I joined the Jaguar Force in March 1985, having cut my fast-jet teeth on six years with Harrier GR3s at Wittering, Belize and Gütersloh. Now I was a senior flight lieutenant waiting to be picked up for promotion, and the posters sent me to Coltishall as OC Aircraft Servicing Flight to wait my turn.

The Coltishall squadrons had a war role to deploy to NATO's flanks, and most of the second-line personnel were allocated to the squadrons to boost their complement to war-manning levels for deployment. My role was to act as an additional engineering officer in support of 6 Squadron to supplement the SEngO, JEngO and WO Eng. During my twenty months at Coltishall, as well as participating in on-base exercises, I deployed mainly to RDAF Tirstrup (now Århus airport), which was our likely base allocation in war and our best exercise training area.

Compared to my Harrier experience the Jaguar was a far easier aircraft to maintain. I had four servicing 'lines' in ASF, each run by a chief technician who oversaw a team of half a dozen troops. There were also several specialist teams for engine and armament work. The second-line maintenance regime was straightforward and, unlike today's air force, there was a lot of flexibility in the use of the manpower and spare space in number two hangar, with its prime position overlooking the flightline on Coltishall's 'waterfront'. I got into the habit of wandering round the squadrons picking up pieces of first-line work where we could help them out. Windscreen changes, for example, were a nightmare to the squadrons, as they took an inordinate number of man-hours to replace. Also, because the squadrons' hangar doors were almost permanently open, even in winter, it took far longer for the sealant to set. My hangar doors, on the other hand, were rarely opened and we lived in a well-heated environment, so the repair could be completed faster and the jet consequently put back on the line in the shortest time. This attitude was well received by the SEngOs, but my troops would hold their heads in their hands

Mission complete at Coltishall, ready for re-loading.

when they saw my smiling face approach with another 'small job'.

When, beginning in 1983, seventy Jaguars were upgraded to GR1A and T2A standard by replacing the NAVWASS with the improved Ferranti FIN 1064 inertial navigation system, the move to a far smaller and lighter digital fit released a lot of space in the nose of the Jaguar and necessitated the fitment of lead ballast to maintain the centre of gravity within limits.

41(F)'s Squadron Leader Glenn Torpy (later to become Air Chief Marshal Sir Glenn, chief of the air staff) had an idea to improve the capability in one of their operational recce tasks. He called me over to 41 to have a chat about his idea, which was in essence quite simple – to use the space and weight freed up by the FIN 1064 fit to house a long focal length, oblique camera. Even though the camera was large (we were still using wet film in 1986), there was sufficient space. The operational task, which was a covert one, could then be achieved by flying past the target at low level and far enough away not to alert the opposition. My part was to construct a ceramic glass panel within the nose-bay door to allow the camera to see out.

Glenn had been in touch with RAE Farnborough and RAE Bedford to have the drawings made and structural checks carried out. As was usual with Glenn he wanted everything done quickly, and the easiest way was for the two of us to visit both establishments. In those days T-birds were abundant and it was a simple matter to fly a round sortie Coltishall-Farnborough-Bedford-Coltishall, so off we set. Discussions were had, drawings picked up, together with a glass panel. Back at Coltishall we reworked a spare door and the fittings for the camera, and off it went on trial. My role ended at that point and I was posted away from Coltishall before I could find out if it worked, but I've little doubt there was a successful outcome.

One of the main issues with the Jaguar at second line surrounded fuel leaks, and there was one particular tank behind the cockpit and under the wing that could be a real nuisance to fix. One aircraft had had ricochet damage (from air-to-ground firing) to the tank, and it was proving to be extremely difficult to repair and seal in situ through the available access panels. In my Harrier days we were taking wings off left, right and centre, since it was the only way to change the engine, so I asked my troops why we couldn't remove this Jaguar's wing to gain better access. The answer came back that it was only done at third line (at a specialist maintenance unit such as RAF Abingdon or RAF St Athan). But we did remove Jaguar wings for road transport, following major accidents and so on, so we must have been able to do it. Nope, a third-line team from Abingdon would have to be sent to remove and refit this wing!

Not content with this response, and after getting agreement from OC Engineering Wing, we set to and removed the wing, which came off in one piece, being held on by a mere six bolts. I was posted away to Yorkshire before it was replaced. I did, however, later get a message to say: 'Wing replaced, fuel leak fixed, airtest satis.' A good result all round.

As a senior flight lieutenant I was often used by Wing Commander Dave

Anderson, my OC Engineering Wing, for extraneous tasks. During my time at Coltishall I was the engineering member on three boards of inquiry and president of a unit inquiry. Two of the boards concerned a mid-air collision in Cumbria on 7 October 1985 and a wire strike on 16 May 1986 in Sicily during a deployment to Brindisi. Both these accidents occurred on 6 Squadron, and you will recall my war role was to deploy with them. So there was probably a perceptible sense of relief on the squadron, particularly from the SEngO, when they saw me roll up as the engineering member on the boards. I had a reputation amongst the 6 Squadron aircrew and ground crew alike for being a pragmatic engineer, and they knew I wouldn't be lifting stones I considered irrelevant.

For the first, Dave Anderson called me into his office about lunchtime on the day of the accident to inform me that the board was forming that afternoon and that I was on it. Flight Lieutenants Len Stovin in XX728 and Steve Friday in XX731, in the same formation, had collided near the appropriately named Black Fell. The devastating news was that Len had been killed, while Steve was injured but alive. I have lots of memories, good and bad, from that inquiry, and I will share two of the lighter ones with you.

We were keen to get up to Cumbria quickly, and a Royal Navy Heron was tasked to pick us up at Coltishall to take us. All my gear was stowed in various places in the aircraft, along with kit belonging to the other members. The door was shut and then there was a voice from the cockpit: "Can a couple of you move behind the main spar, doesn't matter where, just spread out – it helps with the c of g." This was my first experience of naval flying, and I couldn't help but smile at their apparently casual attitude.

I had been issued with a 'mobile' phone to assist with the comms, since we were going to have to climb most of the way up a Cumbrian fell to reach the impact area. Remember, this was 1985 and mobile phones were in their infancy; if I'd been issued with it today it would be outside the limits of weight and volume for carry-on luggage. It weighed about 15kg, with a huge battery element which had a life of about thirty minutes. It even had a 'proper' handset. In the absence of a Sherpa to act as a porter on the climb, it stayed in the Land Rover and never got to the actual crash site!

A learning point from this inquiry was that we interviewed about twenty members of the public who had witnessed the accident and got – yep, you've guessed – twenty different versions. This was also my first experience of behavioural scientists and their way of looking at life and human reactions in particular. Their analysis gives one a completely new perspective on life.

Moving on to the board for the wire strike in Sicily, it will long be remembered for its very 'Italian' nature. Dealing with them and getting recorded evidence was all fun and games. As tends to be the case, the accident happened on a Friday and it was mid afternoon before news hit Coltishall. Again Wing Commander Anderson called me in, this time to send me off to RAF Lyneham. I was due to be having dinner that night in Norwich with Pete Dye, an old friend and later to be OC Engineering Wing at Coltishall during the Gulf War, so quick phone calls to cancel were made, together with fast packing.

The board president was Wing Commander Steve Jennings, who I knew well from my Harrier days; Flight Lieutenant Mike 'Strike' Gordon, who was based at Coltishall with 54 Squadron, was the aircraft specialist.

I met Steve in Lyneham mess and we caught up with the latest Harrier news, before getting into the process we would be going through. Although this was his first board it was my third, so I was able to help keep us on a good track. The following morning, together with Strike, we got a C-130 out to NAS Sigonella, which is where the aircraft had made an emergency landing.

It had been early on a detachment to Brindisi. The accident aircraft had been number three in a three-ship, and was on a familiarisation trip around southern Italy when it had hit a high-tension electrical distribution cable spanning a gorge. The jet was in a mess, with some of the top guard wire still embedded in its port inboard pylon. The port leading edge, port inboard pylon, the underside of the fuselage and a gun door were damaged. The starboard strake was missing, while the port engine would also need to be replaced as a precaution.

As the jet, GR1A XZ398, was badly damaged and there was little or no engineering concern with the inquiry, it was decided, since I was in position, that I should take on the responsibility for getting it into a safe condition to fly it back to Coltishall. We were well practised in battle-damage repairs, exercising regularly in the art, so I carried out a full assessment and sent a list of spares and the tradesmen I would need to be sent down from Coltishall. This in hand, I rejoined the board to fly across to Brindisi to interview the squadron members. The USN were extremely helpful, providing a P-3C Orion to take us on the short hop to the heel of the Italian mainland. An in-flight lecture on the use of the radar in the Orion was interesting and helped pass the time.

Interviews completed, we flew back by civil air to NAS Sigonella, together with the accident formation aircrew, who would now be part of our investigation. Again, back at Sigonella the USN were very helpful in supplying a CH-53 Sea Stallion to take us up to the gorge at NAS Sigonella to inspect the impact site. Hovering within feet of the power lines, we were able to gauge the viewpoint the formation pilots had had as they'd flown down the gorge towards the sea.

Next it was a visit to the Italian electricity company, who were outstanding in providing evidence on the exact time of the impact and where it hit on the span across the gorge. They even provided detailed maps of the powerline and details such as wire construction. Great, we thought, if you would please sign this statement we will be on our way.

"Ah – iiiisss problemo!"

The engineer helping us felt he had to get permission from HQ at Palermo before signing any official document.

"So how long will that take?"

"Very quick, probably within two to three months!"

Steve agreed he would take the evidence and sign it off himself, since clearly we were not going to wait two months to complete our work. We pressed on.

We had secured a map of the area showing the wire and were trying to get some sense of the scale involved. Strike pulled out this wacky gizmo, which unfolded to provide a magnified grid which could be placed over the map to aid scale assessment. Steve and I asked him how he had reason to have one of these natty devices. "I used it during my degree going through uni," was the response. We looked puzzled; what possible degree course would require such a device? "Textile management," came the response from one of the air force's best fast-jet pilots!

Back to Sigonella then, and completion of interview paperwork. Steve and Mike set off for the UK and I turned my attention to recovering the jet. My team had done well and the aircraft was ready for return just one week after the accident.

A problem was that we were now on the Whitsun bank-holiday weekend, and there was no Herk available to get the team home or a pilot down to fly the repaired aircraft to Coltishall. So a plan was hatched for the repair team and me, to sit in Sicily over the bank-holiday weekend. On the Tuesday a Herk would recover the repair team and the damaged parts, engine and so on. Meanwhile Andy 'Mos' Morris and Alex 'Musky' Muskett would arrive in a T-bird. Mos, a qualified air-test pilot, would fly the battle-damage-repaired jet back to Coltishall. Thinking ahead, I had asked for my flying kit to be sent down so I could travel in the back of the T-bird in case of issues staging through France.

We flew home as a pair via Nîmes-Garons, without too much difficulty, although particularly strong headwinds on the first leg and no underwing tanks on the repaired jet gave us a little concern with fuel. Safely landing, we were treated to the sight of a French Wren heading off to get us a baguette for lunch! All in all a good trip home with nothing to worry Mos. The repairs to the jet held up well and it was back on the front line with the squadron within a couple of months of the accident, having had 'proper' repairs carried out.

You may ask how an engineer could hop into the back of a jet at a moment's notice. Both the Harrier GR3 and Jaguar fleets had numerous T-birds available to each squadron, and back in my days at Wittering I had managed to get the top certification for passenger flying from the RAF Aviation Medicine Centre at North Luffenham. This basically removed the need for an individual medical prior to each flight but, more importantly, allowed the pilot to fly the entire envelope with me on board without restriction. Back in the 1980s there were not the same pressures on flying hours, and over the twenty months I spent at Coltishall I amassed some forty hours flying in the Jag, together with a shed load of Chipmunk hours when the ATC held their training camps over the summer.

Such back-seat trips included a very interesting time on the Tactical Leadership Programme at Jever in Germany. Coltishall routinely sent two students from each squadron, and six aircraft, including a T-bird. I was the engineering officer on one of these detachments, which was led by Flight Lieutenant Gus Donald from 6 Squadron. The primary reason for taking the T-bird was that we were the nation responsible for flying the supervising staff members. But after a quick chat with Gus I secured the empty back seat to Jever and back.

The Jaguar being an easy aircraft to keep serviceable, I again had plenty of flexibility, so I helped out the aircrew where I could; they were running around with their hair on fire during a very busy flying programme. In those days mission maps were hand drawn; as time was tight between briefing and flying, I got into a routine of helping to draw copies of the maps.

So my overall perceptions of serving on the Jaguar Force was one of easy maintenance, with lots of peripheral activity to keep life interesting. Detachments, deployments, and boards of inquiry all made my time at Coltishall flash by all too quickly, but gave me excellent experience which stood me in good stead for my later life as a SEngO, taking the Tornado into combat for the first time during the Gulf War. And all this exposure to flying and airmanship were also to come to the fore when I trained for my private pilot's licence later in life.

Thank you, Jaguar.

CHAPTER 18

BROWN AMONGST THE BLUE

A character found on most RAF attack squadrons was the GLO (ground liaison officer). These army gentlemen were largely majors, and were a disparate bunch. Most of them found the change in culture and routine on moving to the blue side challenging initially. I well recall the GLO on one of my squadrons becoming flustered during his first Taceval to the point that he repeatedly addressed the chief evaluator, a German, by the wrong rank. "Major," eventually said the exasperated German officer: "Why do you keep calling me captain? I am a colonel." "I'm sorry sir," came back our quick-thinking GLO. "Pressure of work. If it happens again you may call me lieutenant for the rest of the exercise!"

A lovely man, for whom we developed a great affection. He, like many GLOs, found happiness with the RAF, never returning to his regiment. Others, though, found it more difficult to fit in with light-blue life, and escaped as and when they could. To a man, they were known for hardly needing a radio or a telephone, having been brought up with stentorian voices so they could communicate in the din of the battlefield. We also loved them for the important additions they brought to both the on and off-duty life of our squadrons: invariably they had dogs; and each had a Land Rover with its dedicated driver/clerk and its own ration of fuel.

When Pat King (pictured below behind Glenn Torpy) delivered to me the chapter I'd asked him to contribute to this volume, I was delighted to discover on my first read-through that he'd instinctively touched on virtually all the points and attitudes I've mentioned in this introduction. So we'll now enjoy his GLO's-eye view of life on a Jaguar squadron.

MAJOR PAT KING, ROYAL ANGLIAN REGIMENT

I arrived at Coltishall after a three-year apprenticeship with IX(B) Squadron at RAF Honington. There, I had been ordered to get a dog to fulfil expectations: "... as all majors have a dog". Sadly, because of bad behaviour, the dog had to go after a while – but the RAF Police acquired a lovely Springer as a result.

Having learned a little from that, I arrived on 41(F) Squadron with a Lurcher called Clancy, who fast became a star, loved by all the squadron. My first interview with the

'Grey Fox', 41's boss, Wing Commander David Norris, began with, "at least you won't have to talk to navigators ever again, Pat". I had arrived in single-seat country!

In fact I had first encountered the Jaguar on my forward air controller course some years earlier, where I had given an instruction for the jet to come lower. The result then had been that I had looked straight up his engine intakes and had had my map blown away.

I could not have asked for a better station than Coltishall. It was such a happy place, with many people extending there for years. I myself managed six years before my army endex. Our military Land Rover was a much-prized squadron asset, and we did trips all round the area for my RAF friends, including collecting beer-call barrels from Reepham and spare parts for various people's vehicles. The GLO on one of the other squadrons was sent out to purchase a wooden piano each week for it to be sacrificed on the concrete circle made for a ritual burning outside the officers' mess during happy hour. I always felt sorry for the people who placed small ads in the local papers requesting a 'good home for a much-loved piano'.

It was great to deploy to the Arctic again, as I had earlier spent three winters there with the AMF(L) with my battalion. Then down to reality, as on my first RAF deployment we were grounded for five days by bad weather. As a soldier I had always, of course, been aware of weather, but I quickly learned that failure of squadron ops to keep an eye on the Norwegian weather could be disastrous.

The scenery at Bardufoss was spectacular, and something I shall remember to my dying day. Early starts were the norm, and my clerk and I were first in to get all the tasks for the day. Keeping the Land Rover's battery charged was a major preoccupation to avoid the embarrassment of being late, as overnight temperatures could be as low as -25 degrees. I developed massive arm muscles (well, relatively!) humping the blessed thing into my accommodation to keep it warm. On Sundays I allowed myself the luxury of a morning's skiing, as Norwegian military flying didn't start that day until 1400 hrs.

I had numerous hours at the wheel of the Land Rover or the crew bus taking others floodlit skiing in the evening and for pizzas in Bardufoss. The Norwegian MPs were mustard, and would book you for two mph over the limit. And of course for excess alcohol, I'm glad that I didn't drink at the time, as beer was £5 a pint!

On the squadron, and particularly in Norway, I tasked the pilots and gave them all the updates necessary for their missions. On one occasion Greg Monaghan was the pilot; he flew his sortie successfully and came back with good film. Later, all flying was stopped as an avalanche in the area had killed twenty-three Norwegian army engineers. The exercise was cancelled and a huge memorial parade took place at Bardufoss. In Norway, with such a small population, such an incident was shattering.

Prior to our return to Colt I remembered what my predecessor had told me: "Keep all tasks filed for three years as there may be the odd comeback." There certainly was on this occasion. Interpol came to interview Greg and suggested that he might be charged with murder, accusing him of starting the avalanche. Luckily, our tasking record showed that it could not possibly have been him, so he was off the hook.

We had so many Tacevals in north Norway that I lost count. The squadron always did extremely well, and the pilots and ground crew grafted away – all working their socks off. It was hugely hard work for all, but so rewarding. The pilots flew an average of three missions each day, and could have flown more but for the short daylight hours. Taceval plots were fiendish, and at times I think that we felt like murdering the whole team.

There were a lot of VIP visitors, and the ops room got so full that it became very hot – and there was nowhere to sit. But relations between GLO and ops were excellent, and also between GLO and RNoAF HQ. Back at Colt we had long Taceval debriefs, and Clancy summed it up one day with a massive yawn. He brought the house down!

Otherwise in Norway we had some great moments. I can remember a squadron BBQ in -15 degrees! The ground crew (what a great bunch we had) also had a choir, and they used to ring families at Colt singing, 'I Just Called to Say I Love You'. On another occasion, while happily paddling a canoe on the Målselv river on a summer exercise I heard whispers of "let's sink the major". Seconds later I was in the water and soaking wet. My retort was "you bastards". But as some of those 'bastards' later made very senior rank I shall not name names.

Exercise Red Erik was the squadron spoof on new pilots at Bardufoss, and the GLO had a part to play, briefing the victim that he had to fly a recce mission against the first SA3 missile site inside the then USSR. The spoof didn't end until he climbed into his jet to fire up his engines.

Life could be serious, and as a 'Pongo' I was impressed by the work rate that could be generated in such a short time. Work seemed to be done by all on the squadron with minimum fuss. The classic at Colt was getting the first tranche ready for Gulf War One, completed in under a week. It was a much more trusting way of life than in the army, and people did their work virtually unsupervised. It was always a pleasure to deal with any branch on the station, and wherever you called there was always a friendly greeting and good assistance. I had the GLO's travelling box rebuilt twice and all it cost me was a jar of coffee each time. It took some time to get used to happy hour, though. Some army mates were quite horrified by it. "Pat, they're all pissed!" was their observation. I told them that if they flew daily at warp snot down in the weeds, having a least one fright per trip, they would probably be the same.

Having touched on the Gulf War I must just say a little more. In Bahrain we worked long hours to ensure that the pilots had the best information and updates that we could get. They were all stars. The ground crew, half the number as on a Tornado squadron, worked miracles. Things I can remember include: Roger Crowder being tasked to engage a Mirage, and seeing it flash by him too fast for him to get near it; Messrs Young and Midwinter having a heart-stopping moment with a ZSU 23-4 AAA unit; Livvo tanking for the first time ever, in a thunderstorm, and successfully completing it; Shutty having to land on a tiny Saudi army airfield having forgotten he was in reheat and running very short of fuel; Mike Rondot bombing with one hand and taking pictures with the other; Nick Collins bombing a petrol station with devastating results; myself having two fabulous lunches when stood down, with Strike Gordon and his four-ship at the Bristol Hotel; and the bar at the top of the hotel where we used to unwind at the end of the day. I also remember Mal Rainier telling the chief of the air staff, in response to the question, "is there anything you need?" that he would like a bubble canopy and twin fins! Then there was the causeway linking Saudi with Bahrain, which the pilots seriously thought about flying under – no one did as far as I know; and finally, AAA holes in two jets. It is a proud thing to me that we lost no one.

Despite that, however, it was the crashes I never got used to in the Jag Force. Colt lost some good guys during my time there. I remember Andy Mannheim having a head-on in Cumbria. I had briefed him for this, his combat-ready check trip. P V Lloyd taxied past me one day, giving me a great wave and a grin; on that mission he crashed into the cliffs at St Abbs Head. John Marsden crashed in the Solway Firth, while Keith Collister died in Saudi warming up for Operation Desert Storm. John Mardon, having recovered from his heart-lung transplant, collided with a light commercial photography aircraft. Good guys and good mates also. All gone, but never forgotten.

Although we lost no one in Gulf War One, the Tornado squadron headquartered fifty metres down the corridor did. All were heart-lurching moments which I can well remember.

RAF funerals were less formal than army ones, yet beautifully executed. Still, it was an hour of sadness each time. The GLO was called on to control the funeral flyby occasionally, and having measured and timed the distance between the cemetery gate and the graveside, I'd call the jets in for their 'missing man' formation flypast. I was not good at being quiet on the radio, and on one occasion a call of "great – absolutely spot on," reputedly echoed round the cemetery and the funeral cortège.

I was loaned to the Harrier Force twice, once in Belize and then on a Berlin four-power exercise at Fassberg, where there were French as well as German air force personnel. My rusty French did not help and they had very little English. Still, it worked somehow. 41 were there too, but I had to task the Harriers because their GLO didn't pitch up. Give me Jaguars anytime.

Belize was a different ball game. As well as the regular work there were all sorts of extra amusements. We went on the range to see the Harriers fire SNEB rockets, on the way back being treated to a fantastic Puma flight at zero feet along a river. And we had a recce right up to the Guatemalan border, enjoying the scenery. The range targets were written-off Land Rovers, moved into position with great difficulty, but by the next morning some were missing as the locals had slipped in and 'liberated' a couple. This apparently happened all the time.

At home 41(F) regularly supported the School of Infantry on a major exercise, flying recce against a tank regiment. They were ace at camouflage and hard to spot. We also flew in support of a firing exercise at Warminster with very good results. We were tasked to fire in support of a televised programme for an army competition, and it was gratifying to see 30mm cannon fire accurately delivered. We had good relations with the RAFLO at Warminster and kept him happy with a host of missions. Some of the boys came to watch the live-fire demonstration from the army's viewpoint, which went well. At the end of it we got on board the bus and diverted via RAF Lyneham, where we hitched a ride on a Herk which dropped us at the end of Colt's runway before carrying on with its own mission.

Having praised the transport force, I have to say that not all trips were trouble free. Of course I'd travelled RAF with the army, so already had a passing acquaintanceship with RAF transport. But now I was getting a closer look. We had some amazing moments travelling to and from Norway, and I learned to understand (almost) the ways of the AT Force. All movements seemed to start in the middle of the night, so we never saw the spine of Norway in daylight. One time a very bored loadmaster told us that they could not get the undercarriage down, and that if they wound it down by hand it would mean an extended stop at Bardufoss with technicians having to come out from the UK to fix it. Instead, they were going to try and shake the wheels down. What a palaver. We were all too tired and cold to take much notice, and tried to sleep as the pilots did shallow dives and pulled up sharply. It did work eventually. On the way home on another occasion we came in to Colt and were told to sit down and buckle up. I thought that I hadn't heard the undercarriage deploy. In we came, the pilot flared – then suddenly opened the throttles and we did another circuit. Yes, he had neglected to lower the undercarriage!

No-one who's ever travelled on a Herk will forget the temperature variations on board. Seemingly there was nowhere in the hold that was comfortable. There were areas where it was far too hot, and equally there were places where it was extremely cold, especially on the feet. At endex one March we reported to our aircraft only to find no loadmaster present. As a result the Herk was loaded by the GLO and his clerk! On another flight returning from north Norway we had to divert to Gardermoen short of fuel. We had been battling headwinds of force eight or nine that had totally shredded the UK. Never a dull moment on RAF AT (and never book a special dinner for the night you're due to arrive home).

I had some fantastic Jaguar flights, both in Norway and in the UK. Mike Rondot gave me my first fast-jet trip and I will never forget it; it was on that regular push, Ex Mallet Blow. On that and subsequent trips I never had to use a 'barf bag', getting the closest to doing so with Andy Morris flying down an S-bend fjord at 450 knots. Luckily, I had digested my breakfast! I flew with Baggers in a squadron flyby on an open day when we flew 'tail-end Charlie' in a big formation. What a fascinating experience.

I was given a farewell trip which I shall never forget, to Bordeaux. We had a picnic in a vineyard at St Émilion and dinner at a restaurant on the coast. The French air force were good hosts and looked after us well. But there was one final hair-raising moment on the way back when a collision looked likely. We survived, but no names, no pack drill.

In summary, I have no regrets about becoming a GLO. I enjoyed every minute I was involved. People were great, very professional and not frightened of hard work. I found that the secret was to do all that the squadron asked of me, with minimum fuss and no moans. All ranks made me welcome – from the station commander to the ground crew.

Some GLOs treated the job as a holiday, while some hated it and did not fit. I made many friends with whom I am still in contact. I am a very proud honorary member of the Gulf War Jaguar Pilots Association, which made a band of brothers out of us all. I did my utmost to put over army tactics and ways, with a little success. It was a sad day when Clancy and I handed in our kit and left our place of work at Colt. I will remember the Jag Force with great affection until my dying day.

CHAPTER 19

OPS, OPS – AND MORE OPS

We've heard that the great majority of the RAF Jaguar's early years were occupied not with combat but with deterrence. Then, out of the blue came the Gulf Conflict, and suddenly the aircraft became a seasoned warbird. Like London buses, troubles never come singly, and soon afterwards the aircraft saw action in the Balkans.

With the ending of the Cold War a substantial reduction in military strength and readiness was anticipated by many. But, although the size of the armed forces was substantially reduced in anticipation of the new world order, the remaining, small Jaguar Force was typical in being almost continually involved in various combat zones over the following years.

One who participated in many of these actions is Bob Judson. For a couple of years he worked for me in the MoD, so it's a particular pleasure for me to watch him reaching high rank. He continues to serve, currently in the PJHQ.

AIR VICE-MARSHAL BOB JUDSON

I have a striking memory of serving on exchange on the RF-4E at German air force base, Bremgarten. In 1989 the news was dominated by the flood of refugees from East to West Germany. Despite this seismic change in pan-German dynamics, Germans were still unprepared for that moment on 9 November. We were in the bar after flying when one of my squadron colleagues came up to me with a truly stunned look on his face: "They are sitting on top of the Berlin Wall – who would ever have believed it?" After so many years of the Cold War, the 'peace dividend' that followed the collapse of the Warsaw Pact was eagerly anticipated.

At that moment none could have predicted that subsequent years would be so totally dominated by operational activity for the British military, especially the RAF. The first Gulf War took place whilst I was still on that exchange tour, and I had the dubious privilege of watching my friends and colleagues head off to Bahrain to do battle with Iraq, whilst I worked with a nation that struggled to come to terms with the possibility of becoming operationally committed outside their own country – not the best memory of my RAF service.

My time would come soon enough though, and in 1992 I headed back to the

Jaguar. I was already a 1,200-hour veteran on the aircraft and was in a confident mood when I arrived at RAF Coltishall. However, I found myself back in a Jaguar Force very different from the one I had left only three years earlier. Blooded by combat operations in Operation Granby, each squadron contained significant experience and the force was already embroiled in the operational activity that had followed almost directly from the Gulf War. My role within this book is to do my best to tell some of that post-Gulf War operational story. What follows are a few of my personal experiences and memories based on the 113 operational missions I flew over northern Iraq and Bosnia-Herzegovina whilst a flight commander on 54(F) Squadron, and subsequently as OC 6 Squadron. Although I subsequently went on to command RAF Coningsby and see the Typhoon into RAF service, in many respects the Jaguar defined me as an RAF pilot, and I have both immense respect and admiration for all those with whom I served. I only hope my account does them justice.

Operational turn-round. The first bomb goes on.

Breath had hardly been drawn at the end of the Gulf War when the Jaguar Force was once more called into action in operations to bring humanitarian relief to the Kurds under the mandate of UNSCR 688. Although the relief effort largely ended in 1991, air policing in the no-fly zone north of the 36th parallel continued under various banners – Operations Provide Comfort; Warden; Safe Haven and Northern Watch – until 2003. Thus, despite a few breaks to allow the Harrier and Tornado forces to take a turn, almost everyone on the Jaguar Force saw action over northern Iraq during that period.

Although Iraqi air operations (including SAM activity) were prohibited under the UN Resolution, Saddam maintained three divisions of military hardware under the NFZ, so the threat was very real. Our role was reconnaissance, but the overall air package (principally provided by the US, UK and France with occasional Turkish support) provided the full spectrum of air power – impressive by any standards.

A cursory glance at a map reveals that our base at Incirlik, near Adana, is far from Iraq. Transit time to the operational area of some fifty minutes meant that all missions required AAR at least once. On initial deployment the tankers had gone to Akrotiri, Cyprus, and for the first couple of months the TOT windows had to be somewhat flexible to cope with difficulties in getting our tankers from Greek airspace into Turkish. An ad hoc timing system had been devised, with the Jaguars being cued to take off by the tankers' call of "Overhead Incirlik". Soon, though, they were based alongside us, and we rapidly developed excellent procedures to get the best out of the available assets.

Engine performance was always problematic, and we were well used to jibes about needing the curvature of the earth to get airborne and only having two engines so that the second one could take you to the scene of the crash if the first one failed! But operations out of Incirlik, just as during the Gulf War, tested the jet's performance to the absolute limit, especially during summer heat. We flew in one of the heaviest and highest-drag fits in the book: two underwing fuel tanks; reconnaissance pod; ECM and chaff pods on the outer wing stations; overwing Sidewinders; fully-loaded guns; and under-fuselage flare dispensers.

Add to that the underpowered engines and the end result made for some interesting take-offs – despite Incirlik's 10,000-foot runway. My personal record was one that saw me stagger airborne just before the departure-end arrestor cable and fly past the TACAN beacon, 400 yards beyond the runway, at a lowly 25 feet above the ground. It subsequently took me nearly 200 miles to reach the cruising altitude of 18,000 feet.

Ironically, USAF pilots often watched us with envious eyes, thinking we were simply showboating and holding the jet low for the best visual impact – we did eventually enlighten them but it was great fun to maintain the illusion for a while.

A typical day would see us launch three pairs of aircraft in sequence to ensure we covered the whole time window for which the package was enforcing the no-fly zone. Air defence (normally F-15s or F-16s) would keep the airspace clear of Iraqi aircraft with support from E-3 AWACS and other surveillance assets. A typical support package comprised aircraft providing airborne jamming, SEAD and on-call ground attack. CSAR, in the form of helicopters to recover downed aircrew and suppression aircraft (normally A-10s) to keep away the enemy before the helicopters arrived, was another critical capability we would not operate without.

Although the missions were not directly offensive in nature, the rules of engagement permitted 'response options' to be executed if the Iraqi air defences activated on any given day. 'Activation' was defined as actual surface-to-air fire (AAA or SAMs) and/or the use of an air defence system's fire control radar – essentially seen as a precursor to an actual engagement. This represented a pretty low bar for us to respond to, but the Iraqis had cleverly placed many of their air defence sites in locations that were difficult to attack without unacceptable collateral damage risks. In response to this, the ground-attack element of the package operated with a set of pre-planned and pre-cleared targets on each mission to cater for not being able to respond directly against the site that had opened fire. It was never really clear how much the top-level Iraqi leadership was involved in orchestrating action against us, but surface-to-air fire was a routine feature of our missions. Although never as intense as the barrage during the Gulf War, it nonetheless concentrated the mind to realise that the small puffy black clouds forming close to your aircraft were not a strange meteorological phenomenon but were altogether more serious.

Our excellent collective ability to pinpoint the threats was a major problem for the Iraqi military and, in an attempt to avoid having all their fire control radars destroyed (simply switching them on invited attack by us within the UN mandate) they opted for using modified SAMs using various forms of optical guidance. Whilst never successful in shooting down a coalition aircraft, these attacks most certainly got our attention; we had no problem motivating pilots to remain proficient at all the relevant anti-SAM manoeuvres.

A typical reconnaissance mission involved six-plus targets within an area the size of Wales. Careful pre-planning was required to ensure that time in the threat area was minimised and that all the support assets were able to be in the right locations throughout the period that we were vulnerable. Whilst much of this coordination was done on the ground, airborne unserviceabilities, weather and a variety of other factors often necessitated a good deal of airborne re-planning, and so time on the tanker often involved more than just AAR. Believe me, flying a Jaguar with no form of autopilot in close proximity to a tanker on a racetrack pattern, in a very tightly controlled piece of turbulent airspace, whilst trying to write down new tasking and subsequently programme the navigation system with all the information as quickly as possible, represented a serious challenge in terms of cockpit management.

So – to the mission itself. After an often crazy take-off we would rendezvous with the tanker. The refuelling towline, in our heavy, high-drag configuration, was beyond the range of an unrefuelled return to Incirlik, so we had either to successfully refuel or divert to another Turkish airfield with no support at all. Our primary alternate (from a very limited set of choices) was Diyarbakir in east-central Turkey – which, for my first few missions, was in the grip of a typhoid epidemic. So not really a destination of choice – which certainly added pressure to get the refuelling done efficiently.

Once complete, with support aircraft in place we were ready to go; at the appointed time we would depart the tanker and drop straight into Iraqi airspace. In the Kurdish-controlled areas we felt relatively safe; we were after all conducting the whole operation to protect the Kurds and they knew it, so we had to hope they weren't going to shoot us down. As we moved into régime-controlled areas though, the atmosphere changed and we were well aware that we were in hostile territory.

Many of the aircraft in the package operated above the effective altitude of most of the Iraqi missiles and AAA. For us, flying reconnaissance, this was not an option, as our camera system had been optimised for low level to stay under the Warsaw Pact radar threat in the Cold War. Thus for the whole of our first period in Iraq we operated at ultra low level.

Although demanding in the extreme, the exhilaration that comes from flying at around 500 miles an hour at 100 feet is hard to describe. The ground rips by at an astonishing rate; every house, vehicle or contour becomes a factor to pay attention to; and bigger hazards such as aerials or power cables have the potential to really spoil one's day. The fun was undeniable; this was, after all, what all of us had trained for years to be able to do and we knew we were good at it. However, there was always an undercurrent of risk and we worked hard to avoid ever becoming complacent. The results reflected our professionalism and, to this day, people in the photo-analysis world still talk about the truly amazing images we brought back of Saddam's hardware.

Having been a died-in-the-wool Germany recce pilot for the previous two tours (one on the Jaguar and then my exchange on the German Phantom), I was in seventh heaven. On every sortie we covered SAM sites, AAA sites, barracks full of tanks, and a mass of other deployed, predominantly Russian-made, military hardware. Whereas the peacetime low flying heights in Germany (minimum 250 feet above the ground) would result in a relatively small image of an armoured vehicle that often required specialist knowledge to identify, the very low operating heights in Iraq meant that our images more closely resembled something you could take with your smartphone in today's world. Tanks almost filled the frame and, if photographing an area target, we often had to ease the height up to ensure that the cameras could cover the whole thing. It never failed to bring a smile to my face and, for me at least, represented the most challenging low flying of my career.

With the targets hopefully in the bag, we would climb back towards the tanker and either repeat the whole process or, if there was no further tasking, head home without further refuelling. Incirlik was always a welcome sight at the end of what was routinely at least a two-hour twenty-minute adrenaline-fuelled trip but, with a cold bottle of water in hand, the debrief process would always occupy us for another hour or two before the working day was done.

Each Coltishall squadron rotated through the operation, with individual pilot and ground crew deployments tending to be between a month and six weeks. This relatively short time away allowed us sufficient time at home to stay current in the myriad other skills we needed beyond the quite narrow type of flying that the Iraq operation demanded. It also made for a fairly decent work-life balance, given that we were also still conducting a wide variety of deployed exercises from Coltishall. The aircraft, being more tolerant of a longer time away, would only be changed when deep servicing was required.

Having deployed to Incirlik in 1991, time had literally flown by for all of us when we rotated out of the operation in 1993 in favour of the Harrier Force. 54(F) Squadron was the last to leave and, in the weeks prior to departure, we invested much time ensuring the best possible transition to the Harrier, including flying mixed-type reconnaissance missions into the area with them so they became familiar with the routine. For our boss, Wing Commander Tim Hewlett, the timing of our departure coincided with his own handover to Wing Commander Tim Kerss and so, much to his frustration, he had to leave before the very end. We had eight aircraft in Incirlik which were to return as two four-ships, transiting accompanied by tankers and with much of the operational equipment aboard. We staggered the departure by a week, with the boss taking the first four, leaving me to complete the handover to the Harriers.

The departure date for our final four was Good Friday, and was memorable for a number of reasons. First, in the finest traditions of the RAF, I thought we should do a suitable flypast to signpost our departure. Having made appropriate arrangements with air traffic control, I duly led the four Jaguars in tight formation past the operating area that had been our home for the past two years. The ground crew loved it, and the USAF at last got to see some real flying rather than the take-off dramas described earlier. However, the commander of British Forces in Incirlik (an air defence group captain at the time) was, apparently, less impressed. He had kindly freed up time in his diary to stand on the top of the hardened briefing facility (the large concrete box that was our operations room). As previous writers have also noted, the Jaguar was indeed extremely comfortable at very low level. From his lofty perch on top of this single-story building, it might have seemed to him that he was looking down on the four aircraft flying down the taxiway!

At the other end of the sortie, six hours and thirty-five minutes later according to my logbook, Tim Hewlett was determined not to miss all the fun, and got airborne from Coltishall to lead us back in for a suitable arrival. After a quick airborne brief, and despite bursting bladders and aching limbs, we followed him back to base for a flypast. He then did a really tight, suitably punchy, break to land – in his lightweight fit! We followed him around the corner – but in full, heavy, draggy, operational configuration. I and my three trusty wingmen found ourselves without much turning performance and with a large crowd on the ground watching us, including the local TV stations. Two choices faced us: do the really sensible thing and overshoot to reposition for another approach; or, blast it round the finals turn in full reheat and contrive to make the arrival look as it should do. You can probably guess which choice we made, and it certainly brought a smile to the boss's face to lead us back in from the end of what, by any measure, had been a hugely impressive period of operations for the whole of the Jaguar Force.

The final memory of the day for me was when I was walking back from the flightline with Tim Hewlett and told him that he should probably expect a one-way phone call from the group captain at Incirlik, given the way we had departed. I have never forgotten how he just looked at me, smiled broadly, and said: "I would have expected nothing less!"

Even before the Jaguar Force left Incirlik, the clouds were thickening over the Balkans. The history of this campaign is long, complex and well recorded elsewhere, so this is not the place for detail. However on 12 April 1993, just six days after I brought those final four Jaguars home from Turkey, a no-fly zone was established over Bosnia-Herzegovina under the auspices of Operation Deny Flight and UNSCR 816. This mandate rapidly expanded in June, under UNSCR 836, to include the provision of close air support on request. The UK's involvement was rapidly to become broader than the Iraq operation, with Tornado F3s conducting no-fly zone enforcement and Jaguars flying reconnaissance and attack missions out of Gioia del Colle in southern Italy. Given that RAF involvement in both southern and northern Iraq no-fly zones was still ongoing, this new commitment to Bosnia meant that our air force was effectively operating on three separate fronts – taxing by any measure.

The Bosnian operation was diverse; we were having to co-ordinate with other assets from bases across Italy, as well as from further afield. Greater capacity meant greater operational opportunity and flexibility, so from the beginning the activity windows were longer, and the small size of Bosnia-Herzegovina itself made for a very dense operating environment.

The Gulf War had forced a rapid and seismic shift in our tactics as the threat had evolved; AAA and optically/thermally-guided missiles rather than radar-guided ones made very low level one of the worst places to be rather than the safest. Particularly in the attack role, this had already resulted in us moving from being a low-level force to one that was more comfortable with high-angle dive bombing.

The threat in Bosnia was different again – we faced a greater prospect of AAA fire and the very real risk of MANPADS, typically shoulder-launched short-range, low-altitude, guided missiles. This meant we certainly couldn't operate at low level, and the prospect of conducting CAS and reconnaissance missions from medium altitude was entirely new. The weapons, the navigation and reconnaissance equipments, were all optimised to do those jobs at low level.

We did in fact have the ability to configure the reconnaissance pod with a mapping camera that permitted imagery from about 5,000 feet, but this was almost the worst of all worlds: not low enough to negate the radar threats, and in the heart of the envelope for AAA systems and MANPADS. Fortunately, as the Jaguar's capability developed, medium-level reconnaissance and precision-bombing capability improved too, but in the early days we were seriously limited by the capability of the equipment.

We weren't the only ones on a steep learning curve. A variety of the nations participating in Deny Flight, both in the air and on the ground, were new to the concept of medium-level CAS, and so some training was called for. Thus it was that on 16 July, I found myself flying to Gioia del Colle as part of a small 6 Squadron-led deployment to take part in Exercise Crater. Flown over Italy, the exercise was designed to provide a training vehicle for the tactical air control parties who were shortly heading to Bosnia with the aim of being able to call in air support to counter Serbian aggression. Media interest was very high, and one of my first memories of that trip was landing in Gioia on the wing of OC 6 Squadron and then walking down the flightline with our helmets still on, dark visors down, to avoid being photographed in a way that could compromise our identities later. A very Top Gun moment!

After a shaky start, we developed ways to get results in the CAS role from medium level, and this would become our stock in trade until the end of the operation. The first steps were very entertaining though. We often found ourselves working with a TACP whose first language was most certainly not English and who was entirely unfamiliar with the air environment. CAS involves supporting friendly troops on the ground and engaging enemy targets in very close proximity to one's own forces. We would be circling overhead with the TACP trying to talk us onto the target visually. The mantra was to work from big to small: get our eyes onto something large, establish a 'unit of measure' so that we would have an idea how far to look for each reference point, and then to be absolutely sure we were both talking about the same point as a target.

It went something like this: we would arrive overhead a city; we would be asked to look at the airport; the runway would be designated as one unit of measure; we would be asked to look four units of measure south of the airport and asked if we could see a small town; assuming we could, we would then be told to look half a unit of measure to the south west for a small wood or a building with a red roof. This is where the fun would begin, for while I'm sure the small wood or the red-roofed building was extremely clear to the TACP on the ground, when flying at some 18-20,000 feet there are quite a lot of woods and red-roofed buildings in the windscreen! In the early days, this would often mean it would take the TACP twenty minutes or more to talk us on to the target. But, as ever, time and technology helped to improve this as our collective experience grew.

My own first experience of Op Deny Flight proper began in November 1993, by which time the Jaguar Force was well established in Gioia and enjoying the best that the Hotel Svevo (our accommodation for the duration) could offer. We flew a mix of reconnaissance and CAS pairs across the day. The distances were shorter than in Iraq, so some missions were unrefuelled, although we often used to tank off a TriStar over the Adriatic to enable longer-duration tasks and those that went to the north of the AOR. For CAS missions we would replace the reconnaissance pod with two 1,000lb unguided, freefall, high-explosive bombs, the remainder of the operational fit remaining the same.

Dramatic aircraft upgrades, described elsewhere, took effect in time, but engine performance remained poor. The runway at Gioia, although of a similar length to Incirlik's, is far from flat, having a pronounced uphill gradient heading south-eastwards. Combining a hill with a heavily-laden, underpowered Jaguar led to predictable results, and on many occasions during the hottest months I watched the airspeed actually decrease in the latter stages of the take-off roll as the aircraft hit the bottom of the hill.

As we settled into the new routine, a new feeling became apparent on many of the CAS sorties – frustration. The passage of UNSCR 836 had been agreed on the basis of a 'dual key' NATO and UN approval chain. This meant, in the early stages of the operation, that before any airstrike could be approved the UN had to give the go ahead from their headquarters in New York. Self evidently, given the real-time nature of the operations and the time difference between Bosnia and New York, this made obtaining clearance to drop nigh on impossible and, tragically, it meant that we often witnessed Serbian artillery shelling Sarajevo and other locations whilst flying overhead in a fully-armed aircraft with everything except the clearance to do something about it. Eventually, the UN reconsidered this position and delegated authority to the secretary general's special representative in Bosnia; however, even then, the release process was time-consuming and convoluted, often meaning that targets could not be struck whilst actually engaged in hostile activity. For me at least, this was a classic example of a mission that was doomed to fail because of the political constraints imposed on its execution.

Perhaps, though, both politicians and military were learning from this new pattern of operation, for the situation did slowly improve and, although I was never one of them, a number of Jaguar pilots did drop both freefall and guided weapons with considerable success. The real tragedy was that by the time we got to that stage, much of the country's infrastructure was in ruins as a result of the Serbian artillery bombardment.

During one of my deployments I had the opportunity to visit Sarajevo, where my former boss Tim Hewlett was by then enjoying his time on the ground as an air advisor in the NATO headquarters. The old expression, a picture is worth a thousand words, could not have been more appropriate, and I will never forget the sight of the ruined city with a devastated population trying to go about their normal daily lives in the midst of ever-present sniper, mortar and artillery fire. A particular memory was the image of the skating rink where Torvill and Dean had won gold in 1984's Winter Olympics; less than ten years later the venue was a broken ruin in the midst of a shattered city – awful to behold.

It was not all downbeat though, and I have terrific memories of both operational successes and the fun we had in the margins of the working day. One particular light moment towards the end of many of our sorties was a standing request to fly over 'Red Crown', the code name given to the US cruiser that provided much of the radar air picture over the southern Adriatic during the Bosnian operation. Beyond this vital role, the ship was confined to a limited area of sea-space with little else to do each day. The majority of the crew must have been bored witless most of the time and were extremely keen to liven up their days. Red Crown flypasts were just such a morale-boosting exercise, and it was always good to finish what were often very frustrating sorties with a low pass over the ship. I have a vivid recollection of being the duty authorising officer (a ground-based supervisory function) for one particular day's flying when the boss, Tim Kerss, was on the final pair. He arrived back from an otherwise uneventful sortie apparently hopping mad and directed me to get all the pilots into the crew room immediately. During the subsequent bollocking, the boss proceeded to explain that, on the way home from his sortie, Red Crown had requested a flypast. Being an obliging chap Tim had complied and, in his words, "did a pretty punchy flypast down the side of the ship". Imagine his surprise, therefore, when Red Crown came on the radio: "Not bad Blackcat, but the previous Jags were much, much lower – they really took the paint off the decks." As the boss, he was obliged to appear furious and to deliver the obligatory rocket. However, behind the charade I suspect he was smiling inside, with pride. Needless to say, though, subsequent Red Crown flypasts were conducted with slightly more circumspection thereafter!

Throughout all the operational years, the normal squadron routine never stopped and we had to cope with normal changes of personnel whose work-up phases were adjusted to fit in with the operational cycle. For brand new pilots fresh from the training system, this was a particular challenge. The complexity of our roles made their initial months far more demanding than I had experienced years earlier when a first tourist. They were always arriving at a squadron that was either on or about to go on operations, which gave us little choice but to help out each other by taking on the work-up progression for a new pilot if his own squadron lacked capacity at any particular point in the year.

A by-product of this arrangement was that new pilots were often unfamiliar with the other pilots on their own squadron, and in our warped minds this often left the door open for great spoofing opportunities. One such event occurred during the heat of the Italian summer in 1994 when a newly minted combat-ready pilot arrived on 54(F) Squadron, having completed his work-up with 6 Squadron back at Coltishall. This chap pitched up at Gioia full of the joys of spring having passed the last major training hurdle that an ab initio RAF pilot faces – his combat-ready check. Little did he know that a baited trap lay in wait for him.

Across much of the time in Gioia we held ground CAS alert as well as flying near-daily sorties. The idea was to generate air support rapidly in the event that a crisis developed. The bureaucratic and convoluted clearance procedure for attack missions meant that this system was rarely used, but it provided an ideal opportunity to set up a top-quality spoof on the poor unsuspecting lad. It went like this: he arrived on the routine VC10 resupply direct from the UK. We told him that, because of a shortage of pilots, he would have to get ready for immediate operations as he would be covering a GCAS window with me starting in four hours. This 'window' was in fact entirely fake, but had been set up with the operations centre in Vicenza, so it appeared completely authentic. Our friend duly spent the next hours frantically getting ready for his stint, reading all the right documents and sorting out his flying kit. The latter was complemented on operations by the addition of a combat survival waistcoat (CSW), which contained a variety of specific survival aids to assist with recovery in the event of having to eject over enemy territory – a vital piece of equipment that we could not fly without.

Prior to the witching hour, I gave a full sortie brief and talked through all the things that he would need to know, but emphasised that he didn't need to worry as we never launched on GCAS anyway. Well, as you've no doubt guessed, this day we were going to launch, and the poor lad was about to experience the ride of his life! About half an hour after we went on state, the call came from Vicenza to scramble, and all hell broke loose. Our ops room was about a five-minute drive from the flightline and, half way there, the victim added a self-induced element of pressure by revealing that he'd forgotten the all-important CSW. I can muster a pretty good 'senior pilot glare' when I need to and, judging by the crushed look on his face, the cumulative effect of the day was now getting to him. Anyway, we proceeded, arranging for the CSW to be driven down separately.

Upon arrival we jumped out of the van and sprinted to the jets. Clearly keen to show the way, I leapt up the ladder and, before you could blink, (largely because all my checks had been done beforehand) I started the engines and was ready to go. The pressure built!

Our engineers were only too keen to play their part in the performance and were fully in on the whole spoof. His jet was never going to be serviceable on that day, as they had arranged for the identification friend or foe equipment (an essential piece of kit that had to be serviceable for us to go and which could only be tested by the ground crew using a special test box) to indicate a 'fail'. Moreover, they had parked the spare aircraft for this particular mission at the opposite end of the apron and up quite a long and relatively steep hill.

But we hardly needed the engineers' input, for our pilot scored yet another own goal. Having got everything started up and ready, he signalled for the IFF test, only to realise immediately that he'd failed to switch on the wretched box during his initial checks! As frustration further built during the four-minute warm-up time, I could almost see him praying it would be OK at the second attempt. Needless to say, the perfectly serviceable box still failed the test, and he was left with no choice but to go for the spare aircraft. On any other day, there would have been a vehicle available to transfer him but, amazingly, today there wasn't one in sight, so the unfortunate chap had to run, with all his flying kit and documents flapping behind him.

Eventually, out of breath and extremely stressed, he arrived at the spare to be greeted by the sight of an engineer's legs sticking out of the cockpit as he worked on something down below the ejection seat. Despite howls of protestation, the engineer could not be budged and so, several minutes later, a completely dejected individual appeared back at my aircraft signalling that he wouldn't be able to go.

We had now missed our designated launch window, so I shut down.

We had him seriously on the hook now and it was about to get much worse as we began the Spanish Inquisition as to why we had failed to get airborne on the first ever activation of GCAS. The commander British Forces (Group Captain Frank Hoare), himself a former Jaguar squadron commander, met us on arrival back at the operations building and demanded an immediate explanation – he was of course also fully in on the whole spoof. The details all came out and the fact that the hapless pilot had forgotten his CSW and failed to switch on the IFF only added to what was, to the uninitiated, a spectacular catalogue of errors. Frank played his part to the full, delivering a massive and public bollocking that even had me quivering, during which he revoked the man's combat-ready status, before storming out of the room to "call the commander-in-chief". I'll leave it to your imagination to picture the scene when Frank returned to the crew room a couple of minutes later with the broadest of smiles, simply saying: "welcome to 54 Squadron!"

In these PC days, such spoofs have tended to fade out. Suffice to say, though, that the victim has never forgotten the event, and to my knowledge he always remembered his CSW and IFF on future operational sorties!

All in all my recollection is that Op Deny Flight really marked the Jaguar's coming of age. The avionics upgrade, described in the next chapter, breathed completely new life into an otherwise ageing airframe and set the scene for both the latter part of our time in Bosnia and also for the Jaguar's second stint in northern Iraq. Without that capability uplift, I believe the Jaguar would have stagnated and become operationally irrelevant when compared to the more advanced capabilities of the Harrier GR7 and the Tornado GR4. With the upgrade, not only did the pilots and ground crew develop a whole new set of experience and skills, but the Jaguar itself earned a justifiable reputation as a seriously combat-proven, highly-capable aircraft, a very far cry from the original advanced trainer concept.

I was away from the front line in staff appointments when the force made a return to northern Iraq, but when I took command of 6 Squadron in July 1999 they were part-deployed on the operation and the routine was much as I remembered it from six years before. Although I wasn't yet combat ready, in August I took the opportunity of a planned aircraft changeover to ferry a jet to Incirlik and visit the guys and girls, and it was striking how familiar everything remained, especially with respect to domestic life at Incirlik. What had changed, in a major way, was the capability of the Jaguar and the nature of the flying we conducted as a result. The aircraft developments that had taken place during our time in Bosnia had revolutionised, amongst other things, the cockpit displays, the navigation equipment and the reconnaissance system.

Gone was the huge, old centreline reconnaissance pod, replaced by a much smaller and very much more capable, slewable, long-range camera that was fully integrated into the aircraft displays such that you could see, with a glance at the moving map, where the camera was looking and the area of ground coverage you were achieving. This was a huge leap in terms of operational capability and completely negated the need for us to operate at low level as we had done in the early days. An oft-used cliché is that 'it's not like it was in our day' and, in the case of the Jaguar, that was certainly true when we returned to northern Iraq. Space precludes me telling more stories here but I would just say that, although we'd lost the fun factor of flying at extremely low level, the flying was as operational as it had ever been and the people were as good, if not better, than they had been at any stage of the Jaguar's history.

Although it was after my time, the Jaguar Force's final act in northern Iraq was scheduled to have been participation in the Iraq Conflict ('Gulf War Two'), operating from Incirlik in 2003. As history records, the Turkish government declined to allow operations from their soil, and so the actual final operational sorties for the Jaguar were on those reconnaissance missions in support of the northern no-fly zone.

Given that, when the Cold War ended in 1989, not many of us thought we were ever going to do any operational flying in our careers, it's amazing how the world turned out in the end.

It was also tremendous to reflect on the ultimate flexibility of the Jaguar Force. For example, whereas the attack mission in the Gulf Conflict was performed by what was primarily a recce squadron, the predominantly recce task in northern Iraq was flown, initially at any rate, by an attack squadron. Yet the outcome was outstanding on both operations. Perhaps best of all though is that, throughout almost twelve years of operational flying starting with the Gulf War, not a single Jaguar was lost on operations. A tremendous statistic which reflects extremely well on all those who flew, maintained and supported the aircraft over such an intense period of its history.

CHAPTER 20

UPGRADING

Unlike many earlier types, the Jaguar entered service with a pretty good proportion of its essential systems functioning and released to service. Nevertheless, during its thirty-odd years of operation the threat evolved and technology advanced at an extraordinary pace. Therefore it's unsurprising that the aircraft underwent upgrades during its life. As always with these things, cost was a dominant issue. Thus, for example, although ECM equipment was desirable from early on, the eventual fitment didn't come until hand-me-down equipment became available following the early reduction in Buccaneer numbers. Similarly, an excellent overwing self-defence air-to-air missile fit was available from the outset as part of the Jaguar international package, but wasn't applied to RAF aircraft until the Gulf Conflict. The bottom line in many cases was that, to obtain funding for upgrades, it was usually necessary to demonstrate that the modification was either an urgent operational requirement or would, in some way, produce economies – in other words be a 'spend to save' measure.

As always with these things, staffs and individuals worked, in their various ways, to produce innovative solutions. An early example was Brüggen's 'home-made' chaff dispenser, which was designed and constructed with the close assistance of the resident 431 MU. It utilised the space designed for the braking parachute (seldom necessary, given the Jag's excellent landing performance) and was activated by the existing linkage and cockpit drag-chute handle. It contained seven small shots of chaff, and whether it would ever have been effective operationally was always open to debate. What was undeniable, however, was that the availability of this 'self-defence' capability enabled another 'excellent' box to be ticked on exercise evaluators' score sheets, thereby contributing to the run of amazing Taceval results obtained by the Jaguar Force in Germany.

An even more cleverly-managed – and certainly more effective – example was the GR3 upgrade, a project with which, as an assistant director in MoD, I had slight association during my last tour in the RAF. Indeed, I cadged the final jet flight of my RAF career in the Boscombe Down T-bird which was fitted out as the trials aircraft for new engines, HMS and TERPROM. The chap who did most of the work on that and related innovative schemes was Wing Commander Pete Birch who, in making something of a career as the project officer, was intimately involved in driving them through. We'll now turn over to him the further discussion of Jaguar developments.

WING COMMANDER PETE BIRCH (RETD)

It was a November Sunday and 54(F) Squadron were deploying to Denmark for yet another exercise. Newly combat ready, I was number three in a formation being led by God (the Sqn QWI). We were delayed a little by unserviceability, but left the UK late afternoon in glorious sunshine and blue skies. As we progressed north eastwards a layer of cloud appeared beneath us, and as we approached Tirstrup the sun was setting. We began our descent for the planned formation landing. "Close, go" came the command, and I confidently moved in on my leader. We then descended into cloud – it was dark, very dark – but I was OK. I could formate quite happily for landing. Helpfully, Tirstrup ATC updated us on the weather: heavy rain, strong crosswinds and low cloud. Realising that this was outside limits for formation landing, the leader split off his two fledglings for individual approaches. I broke away but could barely see my instruments in the gloom. Scrabbling around, I eventually got a few cockpit lights turned on, and ten or fifteen minutes later landed safely. Breathing a sigh of relief I clambered rather sheepishly from the cockpit, vowing to read the aircrew manual again – more carefully.

Later, over a beer, I discussed my experience with the other JPs, several of whom had had similar problems. Clearly, night flying wasn't our speciality. Looking for a defence, we tallied up the switches and rheostats which controlled the cockpit lights; we reckoned there were over forty.

Some years later I was RAF Coltishall's Staneval. Among other things I was responsible for running the night-vision goggle cadre, a small group of experienced pilots charged with developing Jaguar night, low-level flying using NVGs. These NVGs amplify light at the red and infra-red end of the spectrum. Green light, at the other end, was not amplified; thus there was no problem with the HUD's green writing. Very low levels of light are sufficient to create an image which gives sufficient visual cues to fly.

As an example of how sensitive the tubes are, I recall coasting out from north Norfolk and seeing aircraft lights, as well as a lightning flash. London military radar confirmed that the aircraft were two F3s just east of Dundee, and that one of them was returning to Leuchars after a lightning strike. Those aircraft were 230nm away!

The original lighting system in the Jaguar was based almost exclusively on red lights, designed not to ruin night vision. This was bad news for NVGs; although low levels of red light could be tolerated, warning lights would cause the goggles to flare and effectively 'blind' the pilot. Moreover the reflections on the inside of the canopy reduced the gain of the goggles, impairing the picture quality.

Thus in the early days you could always spot an NVG-qualified Jaguar pilot by the strips of black bodge tape on his helmet. Should a particular light in the cockpit be bothering him, a strip was torn from the helmet and stuck on the offending light or instrument. As a JP I had often wondered why every so often I'd found tape covering random areas of the cockpit.

So now we were working on a solution, and BAe were asked to propose a modification. Concurrently, a company called Oxley Avionics, leaders in NVG filters, was also approached, and I was working with engineers and industry to help specify a system. By chance I had found my niche, and could begin to address some of the issues with the Jaguar. We sat down together and tried to understand the problem from everyone's perspective, including financial limitations. From the outset it was clear that we didn't need to design a Rolls-Royce and that a cost-effective solution had to be found; accordingly significant compromises would be required.

The cost difference between the BAe proposal and the Oxley solution was dramatic. Only the Oxley was affordable, so it was adopted. The first idea was to control all the cockpit lights with one simple switch with three settings: on/off/NVG. The 'NVG' setting gave bright green lighting, while the 'on' setting gave much lower green lighting for normal night flying. The 'off' position also was important because, surprisingly, some of the original rheostats didn't have one, relying solely on 'fully dim' when lights weren't required. This had had consequences when the Jaguar was parked outside in the rain, when water would unceremoniously be dumped on the circuit-breaker panel on canopy opening. Over the years water would find its way into the panel's copper tracks until, in time, small crystals would grow between them. Eventually, and inevitably, provoking the common tannoy broadcast:

"Emergency state 2: Jaguar, returning with smoke and fumes in the cockpit."

The crystals would have shorted out the copper tracks and burned the circuit board, producing acrid white smoke.

So the NVG modification introduced green lighting and also a new, waterproof cover for the panel. Combined with the 'off' switch, it eliminated shorting.

Elsewhere, NVG-friendly reddish-orange filters were designed for the CWP and various other warning indicators. Testing of the various components was completed in a HAS at Boscombe Down which had been modified to simulate various moon and starlight conditions.

The first NVG flight in the modified aircraft was a delight; the lighting controls were simple and the instruments could easily be read without flaring the goggles. But perhaps the most impressive part was the overall NVG image. Without the stray red light from canopy reflections the goggles performed spectacularly.

Once Oxley had produced a modification kit, a scheme was devised so that service engineers could embody the mod during routine servicing. The days of bodge tape on the helmet and acrid smoke in the cockpit were over!

The Jaguar support authority introduced the NVG upgrade as a service engineered modification. In the past this procedure had been used by the RAF as a quick way to introduce only small improvements. Large modifications had always been undertaken by the aircraft's design authority – in this case BAe. However the team had now proven that upgrades could be achieved far faster and more cost-effectively by introducing genuine competition into the process and by taking a more active involvement in design, procurement and implementation. In the MoD, the Jaguar air staff were happy with the process: upgrades had become affordable.

And from small acorns big oak trees grew.

By 1994 the Jaguar Force was already deployed to Italy supporting UN operations in Bosnia. After a visit by the chief of the air staff to the Jag base at Gioia del Colle and to 5ATAF at Vicenza, it was felt that the RAF lacked the ability to designate for and deliver PGMs, therefore diminishing the value of the UK's effort to the UN. The Tornado Force, with their TIALD pods, were unavailable, being occupied over southern Iraq. So an urgent operational requirement was generated for the Jag. The beauty of this course was that it would by-pass the usual MoD programming and funding constraints.

As it happened the defence research agency had been working on a technology demonstrator to improve the operation of the TIALD laser designating pod – using two-seat Jaguar XX833. This had been extensively modified with development avionics and the 1553 databus. Most of the avionics comprised equipment to be used in the Tornado mid-life update programme, but some elements were speculatively loaned by avionic manufacturers.

The first meeting of our team, now comprising the RAF engineering authority, DERA, the Jaguar air staff and Coltishall Staneval, was at Farnborough. The UOR demanded aggressive timescales: the project aimed to deliver twelve operational aircraft capable of self or co-operative designation within a year. In order to meet the timescales it was decided to take the DERA technology demonstrator's design in its entirety.

I should add here that there was much speculation about whether a single-seat pilot could operate the aircraft and designate. There certainly was a significant lobby from the Tornado Force expressing the opinion that it couldn't be done safely.

Undoubtedly there were many hurdles to leap. The original 5:1 scaled HUD was not capable of drawing any more symbology and therefore a new HUD was required. XX833 used a Marconi 1:1 HUD which had plenty of expansion capacity. The TPs had developed a highly-innovative symbology which was markedly different from the existing Jaguar pattern. I was adamant that managing the Jaguar Force with one squadron running a completely different HUD symbology was not practical, but this observation was not popular as it threatened timescales.

To provide a self-designation capability, the TIALD pod would have to be carried on the port inboard pylon and therefore the databus would need to be provided to both the inboard and centreline pylons. This was described as 'relatively straightforward' so the obvious question was why not route it to all seven pylons? Whilst not essential for the UOR it would provide for future developments. Eventually it was agreed that all pylons would get the databus.

RAF Coltishall's hierarchy agreed my stance on retaining standard HUD symbology. It was also considered that, to provide an initial operational capability, the involvement of current front-line pilots would be essential. So I acquired a team of five, including a QWI from each squadron. This team would fly with the test pilots on all development sorties and would be fully engaged with the programme as the project developed.

Once we had settled on the HUD display – and, incidentally, decided on the need to add basic flight instrumentation to the head-down TIALD display to reduce pilot disorientation during target designation – we moved to reducing pilot workload. During the target-acquisition phase it was imperative that TIALD pointed as accurately as possible to the pre-planned position of the target, so this required maximum navigation accuracy. The DERA development Jaguar had the standard IN, but also a GPS receiver. This GPS was one of the first for use in an aircraft, although would soon need to be replaced by a new receiver which could use encrypted military data. Test flying of the production receiver proved highly successful. The navigation accuracy was improved but also, should GPS lock be lost (generally because the receiver's aerial was masked by manoeuvre), it would be regained almost immediately, further improving the overall solution.

If an LGB is released at too great a range it will not have enough energy to reach the target. As the release point gets closer to the target the probability of a successful attack increases. Too close represents the 'cliff edge': the bomb's seeker head will not see the reflected laser energy from the designator and the bomb will fly over the top of the target without guiding. For each attack these ranges were calculated from a document known colloquially as the 'LGB bible'. To simplify an attack and to reduce pilot workload, could we dynamically calculate and display the LGB release envelope?

The mathematician who had produced the software model for the LGB bible was tracked down and a meeting arranged. The discussion progressed well; with improving computing speed it would be possible. Then came the crunch: "Can you have the software ready to fly in six weeks?" After a few moments of utter astonishment an affirmative answer came.

The algorithms were supplied to the DERA software team and we were able to start work on displaying the release envelope. The solution proved simple: two marks were shown around the outer circle of the head-down artificial horizon on the TIALD display, one representing the start of the envelope and the other the cliff edge. An ideal release point was displayed as well as a range marker unwinding around the circle. All the pilot had to do was to acquire and track the target, fire the laser, release the weapon at the ideal position and maintain designation until impact. Simplicity itself!

While development flying was progressing, work began in a hangar at Boscombe Down on three single-seat Jags to develop the modification. The first aircraft was for DERA engineers and was used to design the modification. The second was modified by personnel from DERA and RAF engineers from RAF St Athan. The third was modified solely by the St Athan team. To look in the cockpits at the early stages was mind boggling. The old equipment had been removed and there were wires everywhere ready to receive a multi-purpose colour display, digital map generator, new HUD and a new stick top and hand controller. How could these aircraft ever fly again?

But they did, and they worked.

Most of the development flying for the UOR was dedicated to improving the integration of TIALD with the aircraft's systems, improving the navigational accuracy of the aircraft and ensuring that the controls and displays were intuitive and simple to use. Vast improvements were made during development, and the system became very straightforward. By the time the first single-seater was cleared for front-line ops the small cadre of pilots were already very familiar with the equipment, so a short work-up of three sorties was sufficient to declare the initial operational capability.

Once the three aircraft had been completed, the modification production line moved to the MU at RAF St Athan where the remaining seven single-seat and two T2s were upgraded to the same standard. The value of St Athan to the upgrade cannot be understated; this small group of engineers radically changed the operational capability of a front-line aircraft.

Indeed, the engineering effort then, and throughout the upgrade, was remarkable: the roles of the Jaguar Support Authority and the Jag AEDIT were pivotal to the project. It was also fortunate that, in Air Commodore Alistair Lang, we had an engineer and leader with the vision and audacity to try something different. Without Alistair's leadership (and top cover) none of these upgrades would have happened.

The first operational sortie was flown over Bosnia with two TIALD-equipped Jags in the self-designating fit in mid 1995. On this mission the aircraft were held on the tanker because there was a group of French special forces under attack just south of Sarajevo. However, after holding for about forty-five minutes on the tanker the aircraft were stood down. So no combat on Jaguar TIALD's sortie one. But the aircraft continued to operate over Bosnia for around a month before, ironically, the Jag Force was replaced by Harriers. So after all that effort, the RAF still did not have a precision weapon delivery capability in the Bosnian theatre!

In due course though, as things became more unstable, two Jaguars were deployed back to Gioia to designate for the Harriers. The combination of Jaguar and Harrier working together proved successful; in particular, the Harrier's laser spot tracker meant that both aircraft could see what was being designated. The capability was used in earnest several times. On one memorable sortie the Harrier pilot talked the Jaguar pilot on to a target and they collectively prosecuted a successful attack. Over a period of weeks, joint operations achieved a success rate of over 90% – a remarkable improvement on the 50% achieved in delivery of PGMs during Gulf War One.

For a pilot to use TIALD he needed to gain familiarity with TIALD functions and HOTAS controls. If we had a simple simulator to gain familiarity before the first flight we could improve the training course. As it happened, I had been acting as an advisor to a computer game company, Digital Image Design, who were developing a flight simulator game called EF2000 based on the Eurofighter. This company produced a state-of-the-art PC-based graphic engine for their games. It was decided that, for a very small fee, DID would produce the simulator. Accordingly, they would then be able to state in their advertising efforts for their game that they produced a simulator for the RAF.

This equipment was ideal for teaching the first introduction to TIALD. It saved at least an hour of flying for each student, saving more than its unit cost each time it was used. The simulator was so successful that it was decided to procure one for each Jaguar squadron as well as the OCU. A meeting was arranged between DID and a specialist contract civil servant from Logistics Command. This progressed well initially, until the name of the system was mentioned: TIALD Simulator. At this point the civil servant announced that he couldn't contract for simulators; he only did training aids! In order to avoid a wasted journey it was suggested that we changed the name. "How about the TIALD Interactive Training System?" "Oh, that would be fine." So the TIALD sim became the TITS! In due course versions were produced for both Tornado and Harrier.

The simulator gained some unusual publicity including in *Wired* magazine, the technology supplement of *The Times*, and on BBC Breakfast TV. All concentrated on the fact that computer games technology was for the first time being used by the military for training.

But the point really was that commercial electronics and software could be used in the military environment, and this aspect was repeated in the TIALD recording system. For debrief on the Jag, a commercial video player was adopted alongside the HUD video player, rather than investing in an expensive debrief suite. This proved a perfectly adequate and cost-effective solution, and we stuck to our limited budget.

With the successful completion of the UOR, the project team began to work on a fleet-wide upgrade which became known as Jaguar 96. This would improve Jag capability by incorporating the lower-cost elements of the UOR to the whole fleet. So the new HUD, GPS, stick top and hand controller would go in, together with installation of the databus to the seven pylons. But at the same time we identified TERPROM as a system worth including in the upgrade.

DERA had already been investigating TERPROM. Used in cruise missiles, this compared its digital terrain elevation database with readings from the vehicle's radar altimeter to calculate a navigational solution. The output from the Jaguar's INS and GPS would be combined with TERPROM to generate a 'system position', which would be weighted towards the element of the system that was performing best.

The potential operational benefits excited the upgrade team. The improvements to basic navigation were obvious, but TERPROM would also provide the ability to calculate a passive range to a target. This could be used to calculate an accurate impact point without firing the laser ranger. The same applied to TIALD, with initial tracking position and stability both improved. A new, off-boresight ranging capability could be used in conjunction with other avionics to store the lat, long and height of a point of interest.

Funding this enhancement would be a problem, but the upgrade team saw a way; the system would enhance flight safety. Because TERPROM knew the aircraft's location from system position, and it also knew the elevation of the terrain ahead, it could calculate whether there was a risk of 'controlled flight into the terrain'. TERPROM could be programmed with parameters such as pilot reaction time and available g to produce a 'pull-up' warning if necessary.

So we got the equipment, and its safety aspect did work well. Following the system's introduction there were no Jaguar CFIT incidents, while I am personally aware of two pilots admitting to being alerted and possibly saved by 'pull-up' warnings. Thus it is likely that Jaguar TERPROM did pay for itself. Such systems are commonplace today, but the Jaguar was first. The Jaguar 96 upgrade entered service in 1997, with the upgraded aircraft being designated GR3.

Notwithstanding this leap in capability, technology was advancing at an even faster rate. Nowhere was this more apparent than in displays, where the performance of the UOR MPCD was already badly eclipsed by the quality and reliability of liquid crystal displays now extensively available in laptop computers. So this aspect now formed the centrepiece for what would become the Jag 97 upgrade, with use of COTS technology providing substantial savings. Tenders were invited, aggressive timescales were imposed, and companies were encouraged to demonstrate actual equipment rather than paper submissions. Very quickly the competition was concluded: a 6 x 8 inch LCD display had won, boasting MTBFs greater than the life of the aircraft and costing less than quarter of the price of the original 5 x 5 inch display.

When installed, the LCD dominated the instrument panel. It was very large and clear, was not affected by bright sunlight, and gave us plenty of room for development.

DERA had been researching helmet-mounted sights on XX833 for some time, while Jaguar Force experience in medium-level FAC in the Bosnia theatre had highlighted the need to improve target acquisition. The new integrated avionics suite of the proposed Jaguar 97 project would enable off-boresight target cueing using the new, highly-accurate navigation system.

Putting these elements together, a requirement was written and an evaluation team established. Helmet sights from the UK, the USA, Israel and France were considered. Very quickly it became apparent that there were issues with the clearance of the more advanced solutions, many of which were a long way from operational service.

The helmet display chosen was an LED sight projected onto the visor in front of the pilot's right eye. This was relatively simple, utilising four cueing arrows which would effectively lead the pilot's eyes in a decreasing spiral towards the target. It was possible that increasing the number of arrows would speed acquisition, but there was disagreement among the group about changing the display. To settle the debate a simple trial was run on a simulator at Farnborough. Coltishall pilots flew the simulator, and targets were injected into the visual with cueing provided by various means, time taken to acquire the target being measured. The evidence led the team to decide on a new display incorporating eight cueing arrows, the best compromise with limited financial resources.

So now the HMS could be used to cue targets. Many of the sorties in Bosnia involved being talked on to a target by a FAC on the ground. This may sound simple but it was often very difficult. "You see the wood? South by one kilometre there's a red-roofed barn. East of it by five hundred metres is a tree. Your target's under the tree."

We were now operating from medium level, and as you've already heard, from 20,000 feet you can see a lot of woods, trees and red-roofed barns. Although you were given the coordinates of the target you could previously only be cued onto if it was in the field of view of the HUD, which meant diving towards the target. With the HMS this all changed: the pilot's eyes could be taken to the target off-boresight, which greatly simplified medium-level FAC.

Not only could external information now cue the pilot, but the reverse was true; if the pilot saw a target he could, by pointing the HMS at it, cue aircraft systems. A point of interest on the ground could have, working in conjunction with TERPROM, its latitude, longitude and height recorded.

This capability was also particularly useful for AAMs. Because the databus had been wired to all seven Jaguar pylons the avionics could now talk to any device on each pylon. This included the Sidewinder AAM. In combination with the HMS a pilot could now control the Sidewinder's seeker head by looking at a target. The missile's seeker would slew to the target; once uncaged and locked on, the HMS would then display where the missile was tracking. If the target lay under this point and was in range the missile could be fired with a good probability of success.

This greatly aided the Jaguar, whose lack of manoeuvrability in a dogfight had hitherto hindered its chances. How much better would it perform, therefore, if fitted with the new ASRAAM? The team's eyes glinted in anticipation of the Jaguar becoming the first RAF aircraft capable of utilising the full digital potential of the new missile, using the HMS. Indeed the software to control the missile was already available and was part of the Jag 97 loads. To progress the project we needed to clear the carriage and release of the missile from the aircraft's overwing pylons. This was of course potentially costly, and indeed proved a show-stopper. We tried everything, including making it a spend-to-save measure, arguing that if the Jaguar could achieve the capability for £x, why was it going to cost at least £10x for the Harrier and even more for the F3? Unfortunately all our arguments failed; perhaps making the relatively un-sexy Jaguar the lead aircraft for the expensive new missile was a step too far for the MoD ...

Space precludes more than a passing mention of other developments. For example the digital replacement reconnaissance pod (goodbye to wet film!) benefited hugely by its integration with the databus and TERPROM. From then on, missing a recce target was a rarity.

Electronic flight reference cards and approach plates were introduced, together with a 'diversion' function which greatly simplified the pilot's workload when the weather went down or the aircraft malfunctioned. Incidentally, it's worth noting that these features had already been specified for the Typhoon; the plan was for software to draw the pages, with the data to generate the picture having to be cleared each time a new plate was introduced. We considered this over-complex and way beyond the resources of the Jaguar programme. It turned out that TIFF images of the material were already produced for the printers, and it was a relatively simple job for us to take this output for the MPCD. The Typhoon subsequently followed this lead.

And the introduction of covert external formation lights, in the form of IR LEDs, more or less brings us back to where I started – NVG ops.

To round off this gallop through the Jaguar upgrade story I'll just touch on a couple of other elements which illustrate how significant improvements were achieved with economy hitherto undreamed of.

First, there was mission planning for the new Jaguar avionics. A number of systems were investigated from around the world, the most likely contenders being the Tornado system TAMPA, the proposed Harrier planner HAMPA, the USAF's system AFMSS, and the modular mission support system (MMSS) produced by Orbital Sciences Corporation. Most of these were based on powerful UNIX computers, militarised, painted green and presented in ruggedised containers. The exception was the MMSS, which was PC-based.

In competition the MMSS came out as the winner. PCs at the time had started using Pentium processors, with power increasing rapidly. The team felt that laptops would soon have enough memory and processor power to run the system, while Moore's Law stated that available hardware would double in power each year. This turned out to be correct, although we did not predict that the use of imagery would become freely available from Google Earth!

The MMSS became the Jaguar mission planner, and it was absolutely stunning. Satellite imagery could produce a very realistic view of the target area at the proposed attack altitude, while the pilot could watch a fly-through simulation of an attack run. Threats could also be entered, and recommended terrain masking displayed. Magic!

The aircraft's map display showed a track-line and dynamic minute marks, calculated from the aircraft's actual ground speed. If a route had been uploaded from the mission planner it would be displayed overlayed over the digital map. The system drew a small oval, known as the 'egg', on the route showing where the aircraft was planned to be. So to fly on track on time the present position marker and the egg had to correspond. Hence if the aircraft was not at the planned position and time it became common to say that one had 'lost the egg'.

The Jaguar mission planner quickly built a solid reputation and was later adopted by the Tornado and Harrier Forces as well as by ground Special Forces.

Second, while the Jaguar was policing the northern Iraq no-fly zone, a specific problem was reported: the Sky Guardian RWR was identifying a particular American aircraft as a SAM. The signature of the two radars was very similar, and Sky Guardian was unable to differentiate them. However the Jaguar's ECM pod wasn't reacting to the American radar, and this got me thinking.

It turned out that Sky Guardian analysed elements 1 & 2 of the three elements in the signal to identify it. The ECM pod also analysed the signal, but looking at elements 2 & 3. So if the information gleaned by the two equipments could be blended we would not only be able to differentiate between the SAM and the American airborne radar but also greatly improve the overall effectiveness of the Jaguar system.

Both the RWR and the ECM pod would have to 'talk' to the databus. We visited both manufacturers, and the team that produced the pod were enthusiastic. They clearly understood the potential gains and felt that by including a 1553 interface in the pod, further development of their system could follow. A very low price was agreed for a technology demonstrator.

The RWR was a different story; the manufacturer was adamant that a major modification would be required at significant cost. However I had seen the same RWR recently in an Omani Hawk and its data was being displayed in the HUD. I was convinced that a serial interface already existed in the standard Sky Guardian which could in turn be used to make the output available to the databus. Back at Coltishall a corporal electronic expert was given the task of finding it. Half an hour later I received a call: "Got it!" All that was required was two wires.

Thus the Databus EW system (DEWS) was born, another highly cost-effective improvement utilising the 1553 databus and the massive additional computing power provided by the Jaguar 97 upgrade.

The reader will readily see that lack of fleet standardisation could have become a problem with this constant updating. This wasn't a new problem. I recall spending many hours in officers' mess bars listening to war stories about the Hunter. There was a famous page in a flight safety magazine years ago which pictured eleven Hunter cockpits – each with a differently located turn and slip indicator. This to illustrate an accident in which the pilot failed to recover from a spin – because he couldn't locate the one, vital, instrument for spin recovery.

The Jaguar cockpit had already become a mess from previous mods, so with the fleet-wide Jaguar 97 upgrade (designating the aircraft GR3A) we had an ideal opportunity to produce a standard cockpit. Experts were called upon as required; on one memorable occasion the late Dr Roger Green, who was chief scientist (psychology) at the DERA Centre for the Human Sciences and was also chairman of the Air Safety Working Party of the European Transport Safety Council, joined the meeting. His wealth of experience was based partly on analysis of accidents.

He jumped at the chance of helping us with the Jaguar cockpit, saying that he had never been asked to help improve a design. Previously he had always picked up the pieces!

With so many software-driven systems in the loop, software standard needed an equally strong grip. As one simple example, when FRCs and maps were amended it was vital that the electronic displays were upgraded in harmony. The aircraft's system had a self-checking capability, ensuring that both the data and software loads in the aircraft were up to date and compatible. To ensure this was all kept under control a new post was created at Coltishall to manage the data and mapping for the aircraft and JMP. As well as producing the Jaguar's compatibility matrix, this post supplied data for many other RAF types as well as for the Special Forces.

Following significant publicity in the technical press, and indeed from the BBC's Today programme, interest was generated from around the world. The obvious potential customer was Oman. A delegation from DESO, DERA, BAe and the RAF visited the country to outline the upgrade and its capabilities. The RAFO was keen to follow the RAF and contracted for the Jaguar 97 upgrade to be applied to their aircraft. The work was done in Oman by British and Omani engineers. Part of this contract was to continue to fund our Jaguar software development team, cost-effectiveness continuing to be our watchword.

So what began as a small upgrade to make Jaguar cockpits NVG compatible ended by being a fleet-wide modification which radically improved the aircraft in terms of operational capability but also addressed areas of flight safety, simulation, training and mission planning. And, most importantly, the Jaguar upgrades were hailed as a model for smart procurement. What a shame the aircraft was axed so soon after gaining its extraordinary new capabilities. Still, it influenced the development of, among others, the Typhoon, as well as revolutionising procurement and generating overseas sales for British industry.

In relating the story it's hard to pick out any one key element. But perhaps the handful of people at Boscombe Down who developed and tested the software should be mentioned. Their speed and focus were remarkable; on one occasion a software upgrade took only two weeks from definition to operational service, including development testing and clearance. A quite remarkable achievement.

To repeat the words used on the Today programme, the Jaguar upgrade was: 'On time, under budget and above specification. It was an RAF success.'

CHAPTER 21

SINGLE-SEAT – IF ONLY FOR A MOMENT

From about the ten-year point in the Jaguar's service history, the Germany-based squadrons began to be replaced by the Tornado. Whether this had been the original intention remains a moot point; the fact remains, though, that with the Tornado effectively replacing the Vulcan too, the entire size and shape of the RAF changed. And at that point many young, perfectly usable Jaguar airframes found themselves consigned to storage at, inter alia, RAF Shawbury.

Many Jaguar pilots were, naturally, posted to the new, two-seat, jet. Of course, switching from single-seat to multi-crew or the reverse wasn't a new idea, as we've seen from the many Phantom pilots who had earlier transitioned successfully to the Jaguar. But the nature of our ever-shrinking RAF meant that, from the mid-1980s until well past the millennium, Tornado pilots tended to remain type-cast.

One who 'escaped', if we may put it so, was Nick Cogley. I didn't know him during my RAF service, but nowadays he is a near neighbour. And at one point we anticipated flying together in an airliner cockpit, for I was a training captain in the airline which had offered him a job when he'd opted to leave the RAF. But plans made are plans which may be changed; events, specifically the recession, persuaded him to stay with the RAF and Tornados, so we never did share a flight deck.

Nevertheless his unusual 'crossover' to Jags is sufficient of a curiosity to make it notable. Not least because he is able to bring a fresh eye to what were arguably the Jaguar's finest years – if, regrettably, the final ones.

FLIGHT LIEUTENANT NICK COGLEY

My first flying tour was on the Tornado GR1, at RAF Brüggen. The fast-jet training system at that time had been, it seemed to me, set up primarily to develop single-seat pilots, and I'd initially found it far from easy to bring another crew member into the loop. Flying with navigators who outranked me was also something of a minefield. Although as the pilot I was the captain, the senior and more experienced rear-seat brethren were often the formation supervisors.

There are many apocryphal stories about extra fuel being more useful than a navigator – not least because fuel doesn't 'nag' in your headset! Of course I wouldn't admit to such thinking but, although I did adjust and came to enjoy the Tornado, I retained a hankering for single-seat. As a young air cadet I'd attended a summer camp at RAF Coltishall in 1986. From the top of the air traffic control tower I'd watched the pilots walking out to the Jaguars parked on the line. Even now, I was determined to join them as one of the lucky few, however long it would take.

My best chance of success was to complete an instructional tour at RAF Valley and then pursue the aim. The usual career path following instructing would have involved a short refresher course and a return to the GR1, but as I reached the end of my QFI tour I seized the opportunity and asked the station commander if he would support my request for a single-seat crossover. I had put considerable effort into my instructional tour and knew that this would help my chances, but I tried not to be too optimistic, as only a few pilots had managed to secure such a change of aircraft type.

The following day, the pilot posting officer was visiting RAF Valley. I happened to pass him in the corridor before my planned meeting with him, and he said: "Mate, it looks like you are going Jags, we will chat about the detail in our meeting!" It turned out that the station commander had personally contacted him regarding my posting and endorsed my request. It was actually going to happen – and I would finally make it back to Coltishall as a pilot, eighteen years after my visit as a cadet.

I arrived on the Jag OCU with a renewed sense of enthusiasm. The squadron warrant officer introduced himself to me in the crew room, and we were in the middle of an enjoyable conversation when one of the younger student pilots asked him quite innocently if he had ever considered a crossover himself to become a commissioned officer. The riposte was superb as the WO frowned through his bi-focal glasses: "Young man, it has taken me over twenty years to get to the top of my shit pile, why on earth would I want to start again at the bottom of yours?!"

The Jaguar exuded an air of mystique for many pilots who harboured a desire to fly it. It had a reputation for biting you hard if you mishandled it which, as I would find out, also made it a challenge to fly well. The reality of flying a single-seat jet would prove to be just as good as the thought of it, but was still a few weeks away as there was ground school, simulator and two-seat trainer work to be done.

So on the day of my first solo in the Jaguar, I could hardly wait to walk out to the jet. It wasn't like I was an inexperienced pilot, having already completed two tours – but it was still the sortie I had been looking forward to for my entire career. As I strapped myself in and started up, the noise from the engine intakes directly behind my head was a reminder that I was completely on my own. It was a different feeling to flying in a Hawk or Tucano with the rear seat strapped up. This jet was designed with only one seat, and it was quite simply a wonderful feeling being trusted to fly it solo for the first time.

Surprisingly, however, it also proved to be an incredibly similar experience to flying the Tornado. The cockpit was ergonomically similar, with switches all over the place and the feeling that it had been designed by an engineer and not a pilot. My new role was also much the same as my two-seat role, and the only immediately noticeable difference was the overwhelming silence due to the lack of airborne crew company. In some areas, the Jaguar was superior to the Tornado.

The upgraded Jaguar GR3 had a superb navigation solution which was so accurate you had to try very hard to miss your planned target. In fact, it was so good that, in order to make OCU sorties more difficult, we were sometimes made to disable most of the navigation kit upgrades so that the aircraft's present position degraded sufficiently to force the operator into having to intervene. The digital map and overlay were equally first-rate, with clarity and simplicity incorporated into the design. Take, for example, the emergency function on the multi-function display. If you suffered an in-flight emergency such as an engine fire, you could look down at the MFD and press the 'Emerg' soft key, followed by the corresponding 'Fire' key. The immediate actions were instantly displayed on screen, and once you had completed them satisfactorily the next button press would display the nearest suitable diversions, approach aids, distance and bearing to each airfield. Selecting the desired airfield soft key entered the position directly into the navigation system.

Of course the lack of TFR and FLIR limited the Jaguar's ability to operate at night in poor weather at low level. But, even though the Tornado GR4 upgrade has subsequently enabled that aircraft to leap-frog its predecessor in many respects, the Jaguar's avionic simplicity, as exemplified by that emergency sequence, has not necessarily been bettered in the Tornado. I shall return to Tornado matters, but for now resume my story having successfully completed the Jaguar OCU and then moved on to 6 Squadron, 'The Flying Can-Openers'.

Although the writing was on the wall for the Jaguar fleet when the jet was withdrawn from Op Northern Watch in Turkey, we all still hoped that it would have a future role. Even if we believed deep down that the aircraft was essentially doomed, we wouldn't admit it. It was still a great time to join, and we were going to enjoy the final years. The removal of the enduring operational deployment provided us with the opportunity to pick up all of the 'fun' detachments that the other fast-jet fleets were too busy to service. So my tour included overseas exercises in Romania, Poland, Jordan, Oman and the USA.

Nellis Air Force Base is just about the best location in the world to carry out a flying exercise, as every pilot involved from every nation that has been lucky enough to have taken part in Red Flag would agree. There are downsides; the planning cycle is tortuous and the de-briefs are uncomfortably long. However, this is more than offset by the quality of the training and the Las Vegas nightlife. The Red Flag communal planning rooms are exceptionally well set out for COMAO planning but the individual squadron planning areas are not as spacious. Cramped is probably a fairer description, which can make for a difficult and often tense working environment when the pressure is on.

That Red Flag exercise was the last large-scale detachment launched from RAF

Coltishall. Two teams were selected for the exercise; day and night. I was on the night team and the training would include opposed large force employment of up to fifty aircraft against a simulated Russian air threat, live weapon releases and low-level NVG flying. The desert was very dark, as the moon cycle was not favourable, and this made low flying on NVGs very demanding. In fact it was impossible for the first week, when we elected to employ the aircraft at medium level until moon conditions improved.

The timeline for Red Flag is demanding at almost every stage, including the time available from the out-brief to take-off. You get a two-minute window to taxi in order to take off in sequence; if you miss your taxi slot you are sent to the back of the take-off train, and that might result in you not making the push time. If you can't make the push then you don't fly.

On one of the night missions the Jaguar 'can do' attitude and the tight timeline resulted in the delivery of a medium-level live weapon into the Nevada desert that wouldn't go 'bang' however hard it struck the ground. The way it happened was this. A live weapon requires an appropriate fuse setting which, without going into detail, was normally submitted to the armourers in good time. The pilot would then check paperwork when he walked to the aircraft. On this particular night, for whatever reason the weapons chits were not present. Clearly, because of the tight timeline the crews needed to get to the jets immediately to make their taxi and take-off time and subsequently the range slot to deliver the weapons.

Now, one of the safety features with this particular fuse was that an incorrect setting would mean that it would not function on impact. As sod's law would have it, on this one occasion when time pressures and other factors had prevented cross checking, the fuse had indeed been incorrectly set. Consequently, the live weapon buried itself deep in the desert without detonating and a unit inquiry ensued. Looking back, I believe that this incident and the resulting inquiry proved a timely reminder call to all Jaguar pilots and ground crew to maintain their focus until the out-of-service date passed safely.

But there were many other incidents during the twilight years of the Jaguar – most of which we can now find amusing looking back. Air combat was often more a test of your eyesight than your handling ability. The Jag's turning circle was not much smaller than that of the average airliner, and one of my colleagues decided that the best tactic to employ to maintain 'tally' was to avoid looking in at the aircraft instruments for the duration of the flight. Unfortunately, the day he tried this tactic the external underwing tanks decided not to feed any fuel, and his first indication of the weakness of his strategy was deafening 'clangers' accompanied by a red fuel caption. He was off the coast of Norfolk, out of fuel and out of any realistic options except ejection. But he elected to jettison the external tanks and make a desperate try for Coltishall. It was an almost impossible ask and there was a real chance that both engines would flame out as he powered up on finals. But miraculously, with the fuel gauges reading zero, he flared over the threshold and shut down clear of the active runway. There was little more than 40kg of fuel remaining in the tanks.

On another occasion, during a simulated evasion sortie, one of the pilots managed briefly to shut down both engines. Our normal technique of chilling the engines at idle to negate an IR missile threat was unwittingly taken a little too far this time. This unfortunate situation was further compounded by the aircraft only being at 250 feet when it happened. Again, disaster was narrowly averted; he managed to relight an engine just before the Jaguar ran out of flying speed.

When the station commander finally announced that RAF Coltishall was closing and the Jaguar was soon to be nothing more than scrap metal and memories, it wasn't a surprise but it was still a huge disappointment. Affection for the aircraft was inextricably bound up with affection for RAF Coltishall. With the end approaching for both, in November 2005 a highlight was a visit by Queen Elizabeth to the station. I was lucky enough to be selected to fly in the nine-ship diamond flypast, and this included the privilege of lunch and a brief conversation with Her Majesty. At the Loyal Toast, Mr Vice stood as usual and delivered the normal salutation of "Ladies and Gentlemen, the Queen", which was followed by the national anthem. We toasted Her Majesty and she smiled, raised her glass from her seated position at the top of the table and quietly said "cheers". I think she shared – or at least sensed – our affection for the station.

It seemed to us pointless to move the remaining fleet of Jaguars to RAF Coningsby for the relatively short planned period of eighteen months. Despite the savings from closing Coltishall a little earlier, it simply couldn't be cost effective to move everything. And, as it turned out, the actual time remaining for the aircraft would be even shorter than was expected. However, the move was completed in April 2006 and we found ourselves settling quickly in to our new surroundings.

Detachments continued. Our first from Coningsby was to Thumrait in Oman. There, a porta-cabin city had been constructed which was 'functional' but uninspiring. Imagine our delight on the Friday when the ablutions blocks overflowed, making the accommodation uninhabitable. Two free nights in the rather excellent Hilton Hotel in Salalah were a nice surprise. Certainly better than the night we found the met man lying naked and distinctly worse for wear in that very same ablutions block.

The flying there was pretty good, with the squadron enjoying a huge variety of training including live weapons drops and operational low flying. My personal favourite was firing CRV7 rockets in the range at night with the Special Forces controlling the action. The rockets resembled something from Star Wars when fired individually and viewed through NVGs; simply awesome fun. I was equally pleased when I released a laser-guided bomb and guided it safely to the target ensuring a friendly de-brief from the squadron QWI. This was made even better because the boss went dry on his first pass, guaranteeing that I could banter him hard about his poor technique!

A further detachment to Amman, Jordan continued the Jaguar 'Farewell World

Tour', and provided the squadron with another valuable training opportunity. Along with visits to Petra and the Dead Sea, one of the more interesting evenings was a traditional dinner courtesy of the Jordanian station commander. Two of our female officers were invited to share the top table with our boss, and the food was delivered to the table shrouded in a towel. The towel was removed to cheers from the Jordanian officers, and the ladies were invited to 'tuck in' – to a whole goat's head surrounded by a moat of rice! It was like a scene from Indiana Jones, with the eyes and tongue proving a particular favourite with one of the older Jordanian officers next to me. There was no vegetarian alternative – but in any case the ladies bore up bravely.

As the months at RAF Coningsby passed by, 6 Squadron slowly started to reduce in size. The boss was working extremely hard to secure as many Typhoon OCU slots as possible, and many of the younger pilots were serving an enforced short first tour due to the impending out-of-service date. Some of my colleagues were being informed of their future postings, and this gave them a renewed sense of purpose as their futures became clearer. The actual disbandment date was such a well-kept secret that we continued to plan for events that would never actually take place. I suspect the Jaguar was no longer seen as operationally deployable in its final year, which was a real shame because, as an operational squadron, we were at the peak of our ability.

I was perhaps even more sad than anybody else. It had taken me over ten years to make it to an operational Jaguar squadron and I wasn't too keen on giving it up. Sure, the jet was ridiculously underpowered, even though it had at long last received engines uprated to Mark 106 standard. Of course I wasn't the first Jag pilot to discover, on first taking off with 1,000lb bombs on board that, as one selected the gear up, the aircraft actually started to slow down as the gear doors extended into the airflow. But that had certainly been a shock for one used to the Tornado's brute strength. But for some unfathomable reason it was and still remains the best aircraft I've had the pleasure to fly by a country mile.

So I left 6 Squadron with a profound sense of sadness. The Jaguar fleet had left RAF Coltishall and had been reduced in size to one squadron in less than two years. It would soon be consigned to RAF history.

I returned to the Tornado, but this has proved an enlightening and enjoyable experience. The new weapons and software upgrades have transformed what was a Cold War aircraft into a potent, modern weapons platform that has excelled in its new theatres of operation. Also, if I was being honest, the Tornado has rightly been the platform of choice for the crucial roles that have characterised the needs of the Afghanistan conflict and the unexpected requirement for intervention in Libya.

There is no doubt that operating as a part of a crew in both of these operations has renewed my belief in the power of effective teamwork. Having said that, the Tornado's replacement is to be a single seater, so we can only hope that the promised further avionic advances prove operationally effective. Whatever the future holds, though, I will always remain proud of having been part of the Jaguar story.

EPILOGUE

IAN HALL

Jaguar careers came in all shapes and sizes. Nick Cogley's pattern was unusual, but there were others with equally odd – if completely different – experiences. The prize for Jaguar longevity must, in all likelihood, go to Terry Lloyd. In his capacity as the simulator project officer in MoD(OR) he flew the aircraft at Warton before the first airframe was delivered to the RAF. Thirty-three years later, as a retired officer, he was still instructing on Coltishall's Jaguar simulator long after the final squadron had left for Coningsby, the powers-that-be having continued tradition by having the Jag sim wrongly located. To be fair, it would have made no sense to have moved it to Coningsby for just one squadron and for such a short time. In between times, while on a tour at the RAF Abingdon maintenance unit, he had air-tested just about every Jaguar the RAF had ever owned. He'd flown in Oman both on secondment and, after leaving the RAF, on contract. He'd rejoined the service – and then left again, before coming full circle to that last Jag simulator job.

The longest-serving Jag Mate? That would be Terry Lloyd.

On the other hand there was the curiosity of Graham Wright's long career, during which he not only flew only the one type, but also never served at any other flying station but Coltishall. His five tours spanned the range from junior pilot to station commander and, as he said when he closed the station for flying ops in 2006 (incidentally as an air commodore, Coltishall's only ever commander of that rank), no-one could have doubted his loyalty to the jet or to the base.

Those are examples of the disparate types who flew the jet. There were of course hundreds of Jaguar Boys, many and various, and here we've heard the stories of barely a couple of dozen. One thing they all had in common, though, was an affection for the aircraft. And, to a man, they all remember with fondness, and more than a little sadness, those friends and colleagues who fell along the way.

GLOSSARY OF TERMS

AAA — Anti-Aircraft Artillery
AAM — Air-to-Air Missile
AAR — Air-to-Air Refuelling
ACT — Air Combat Training
12th AF — 12th Air Force – part of USAF/TAC
AEDIT — (The Jaguar) AEDIT – Aircraft Investigation and Development Team
AFB — (USAF) Air Force Base
AGL — Above Ground Level
alpha — Angle-of-Attack, measured in degrees. Primary Jaguar flight parameter
AMF(L) — Allied Command Europe Mobile Force (Land)
amsl — Above Mean Sea Level
ANG — (US) Air National Guard
AOC — Air Officer Commanding (of an RAF Group)
AOR — Area of Responsibility
APC — Armament Practice Camp
ASF — Aircraft Servicing Flight
ASRAAM — Advanced Short-Range Air-to-Air Missile
5ATAF — 5th Allied Tactical Air Force (Italy)
ATC — Air Traffic Control
AT Force — Air Transport Force
AVTUR — Aviation Turbine Fuel
AWACS — Airborne Warning and Control System
BAC — British Aircraft Corporation
BAe — British Aerospace plc
Balbo — A large formation of aircraft (after an Italian air leader)
BDA — Battle Damage Assessment
bean counter — (slang) accounter, supply accounter
Bernoulli — Italian scientist who worked with fluid dynamics – Bernoulli's principle applies to lift generated by a wing. 'Short of Bernoullis' (slang) = lacking lift
Bingo — Fuel quantity call – required to fly to refuelling point (either on the ground or an airborne tanker)
Blue — Weather reporting term – better than 8km and 2,500ft. Slang for perfect weather

Bogey — Aircraft identified as hostile
Bounce — Attacking manoeuvre on another aircraft (often for training)
Bowser — Fuel tanker
CAP — Combat Air Patrol
CAS — Close Air Support
CBU — Cluster Bomb Unit
CFIT — Controlled Flight into Terrain
CinC — Commander in Chief (of an RAF Command)
COC — Combat Operations Centre
COMAO — Combined Air Operations Conventional (attack), non-nuclear
COTS — Commercial Off-the-Shelf Technology
Crab — RN slang for RAF person
CSAR — Combat Search and Rescue (SAR in hostile territory)
CSOAF — Commander SOAF
CSW — Combat Survival Waistcoat
CTTO — Central Trials and Tactics Organisation
CWI — Continuous-Wave Illumination (of radars of that characteristic)
CWP — Central Warning Panel
DACT — Dissimilar Air Combat Training
Deci — Italian Air Force Base Decimomannu – NATO facility in Sardinia
DERA — Defence Experimental Research Establishment
DESO — Defence Export Services Organisation
DetCo — Detachment Commander
DR — Dead Reckoning
ECM — Electronic Countermeasures
Endex — The end of the exercise
EO — Electro-optical
EW — Electronic Warfare
EWO — Electronic Warfare Officer
Exec — Deputy Squadron Commander
F3 — Tornado F3 (air-defence variant)
FAC — Forward Air Control(ler)
FAF — French Air Force
FIN 1064 — Ferranti Inertial Navigation (System) 1064
Fish-heads — (slang) Sailors
FLIR — Forward-Looking Infra-Red

187

FR	Fighter Reconnaissance	MoD	(UK) Ministry of Defence
FRA	First-Run Attack (in air-to-ground weapon training)	MoD(OR)	MoD (Operational Requirements)
FRCs	Flight Reference Cards	MoD(PE)	MoD (Procurement Executive)
Gash	(RN) Stores and equipment not accounted for and retained – alternatively 'rubbish' or 'spare'	MPs	Military Police
		MPCD	Multi-purpose Colour Display
		MQ	Married Quarter
GCA	Ground Controlled Approach (radar talk-down by voice)	MRCA	Multi-Role Combat Aircraft (eventually Tornado)
GCAS	Ground (standby) Close Air Support	MTBF	Mean Time Between Failure
		MTOW	Maximum Take-off Weight
GLO	Ground Liaison Officer	MU	Maintenance Unit (RAF central maintenance depot)
Goon suit	Immersion suit (waterproof flying suit)	NAS	(US) Naval Air Station
		NAVWASS	Navigation and Weapon Aiming Sub-System
GPS	Global Positioning System		
HAS	Hardened Aircraft Shelter	NBC	Nuclear, Biological and Chemical
HE	High Explosive	NDB	Non-Directional Beacon
HMS	Helmet-Mounted Sight	NFZ	No-Fly Zone
HOTAS	Hands on Throttle and Stick	nm	Nautical Mile
HUD	Head-Up Display	NVG	Night-Vision Goggles
IFF/SIF	Identification Friend or Foe equipment/Selective Identification Feature (radar transponder)	OC	Officer Commanding (of a unit)
		OCU	Operational Conversion Unit
		OHP	Overhead Projector (visual aid device common in 1970s)
ILS	Instrument Landing System		
IN	Inertial Navigation (equipment)	OLF	Operational Low Flying (RAF – flying below 250ft agl)
IP	Initial Point – of an attack run		
IR	Infra-Red	Patch	(slang) married quarters
JCT	Jaguar Conversion Team	PBF	Protected Briefing Facility (hardened building)
Jebel	Hill, mountain (Arabic)		
JEngO	Junior Engineering Officer	Pickle	Manual release of a weapon (pickle button)
JMP	Jaguar Mission Planner		
JP	Junior Pilot	PI	Photographic Interpreter
Kipper fleet	(slang) RAF maritime patrol aircraft	PGM	Precision-Guided Munitions
		PJHQ	Primary Joint Headquarters
Kit	(slang) Jaguar nav/attack system	Pongo	(slang) Army person
Knot(kt)	Nautical mile per hour	PMC	President of the (officers') Mess Committee
Laydown	Level attack delivered from low altitude		
		PMD	Pilot Map Display
LCD	Liquid Crystal Display	PTR	Part-throttle reheat
LED	Light Emitting Diode	Q	(colloq) QRA
Letraset	Self-adhesive lettering kit used for visual aids	QFI	Qualified Flying Instructor
		QNH	Atmospheric pressure (of a region or an airfield) with reference to sea level
LGB	Laser-Guided Bomb		
LLTV	Low-Light TV		
LOROP	Long-Range Oblique Photography	QRA	Quick Reaction Alert
LOX	Liquid Oxygen	QWI	Qualified Weapons Instructor
MANPADS	Man-Portable Air-Defence System (typically, shoulder-launched missile)	Radalt	Radar Altimeter
		RAE	Royal Aircraft Establishment
		RAFG	RAF Germany (the Command)
Maxeval	Maximum evaluation – the last practice before Taceval	RAFLO	RAF Liaison Officer
		RAFO	Royal Air Force of Oman (formerly SOAF)
MFD	Multi-Function Display		
Mineval	Mini evaluation – station generated exercise	Recce Puke	(slang) Reconnaissance pilot
		Red	Weather term – cloud base lower

than 200ft, visibility very poor. Unflyable conditions (peacetime)

Rheindahlen HQ RAFG (as well as HQ 2ATAF, HQ BAOR and HQ Northern Army Group)

RIC Reconnaissance Intelligence Centre

RNAS Royal Naval Air Station

R&R Rest and Recuperation

RSO (Weapons) Range Safety Officer

RWR Radar Warning Receiver

SACEUR (NATO) Supreme Allied Commander, Europe

SAM Surface-to-Air Missile

SAR Search and Rescue

SASO Senior Air Staff Officer

Schuler Inertial platform rotation/position correction characteristic loop

SEAD Suppression of Enemy Air Defences

SEngO Senior Engineering Officer

SEPECAT The joint company formed by BAC and Bréguet to produce the Jaguar Société Européenne de Production de l'Avion Ecole de Combat et d'Appui Tactique)

SFC Specific Fuel Consumption

SOAF Sultan of Oman's Air Force (later RAFO)

SOC Sector Operations Centre (air defence)

SquIntO Squadron Intelligence Officer

SSM Surface-to-Surface Missile

Strike (Role) Nuclear Attack (in earlier days 'strike' was the RAF term for conventional ground attack – as in 'Strike Wing Aden')

Staneval Standardisation and Evaluation (commonly, aircrew forming a part of a unit-level audit system. Staneval [W] = Staneval [weapons], Staneval [F] = Staneval [pure flying])

SUCAP Surface Combat Air Patrol (anti-shipping)

T-bird Two-seat variant (in Jaguar, T2, T2a, T4)

Tally Visual contact

TAC (USAF) Tactical Air Command

TACAN Tactical Air Navigation equipment

TACP Tactical Air Control Party

Taceval Tactical evaluation (NATO operational readiness audit system)

TERPROM Terrain Profile Matching – self-contained navigation system

TFR Terrain-Following Radar

TIALD Thermal Imaging and Laser Designation (pod)

TOT Time on Target

TOW Take-off Weight

TP Test Pilot

Triple-A AAA

TWU Tactical Weapons Unit (RAF training unit)

ULL Ultra Low-Level flying (later known as OLF)

UNSCR UN Security Council Resolution

UOR Urgent Operational Requirement

USMC US Marine Corps

VOR (Beacon) VHF Omni-range

Wadi (Arabic) Valley, often dried-up

WO Warrant Officer

WMD Weapons of Mass Destruction

Wild Weasel (USAF) Aircraft armed with anti-radiation missiles

WIWOL (RAF slang) 'When I was on Lightnings'… (WIWOLs = ex-Lightning pilots)

WSO Weapons System Officer (RAF tactical aircraft – second crew member, formerly navigator)

WST (Nuclear) Weapons Standardisation Training

INDEX